S c.2
4-85

DISCARDED

355 War   S   c.2

War in peace, v.8

Sellersburg Library
430 N. Indiana Avenue
Sellersburg, IN 47172

DISCARDED

D1205673

War In Peace

Volume 8

War In Peace

The Marshall Cavendish Illustrated Encyclopedia of Postwar Conflict.

Editor-in-Chief
Ashley Brown

Editorial Board
Brig-Gen. James Collins Jr (USA Retd.)
Vice-Admiral Sir Louis Le Bailly KBE CB
Ian V Hogg; David Floyd
Professor Laurence Martin
Air-Vice Marshal SWB Menaul CB CBE DFC AFC

MARSHALL CAVENDISH
NEW YORK, LONDON, TORONTO

Reference Edition Published 1985

Published by Marshall Cavendish Corporation
147 West Merrick Road
Freeport, Long Island
N.Y. 11520

Printed and Bound in Italy by L.E.G.O. S.p.a. Vicenza.

All rights reserved. No part of this book may be reproduced or
utilized in any form or by any means electronic or mechanical,
including photocopying, recording, or by an information storage and
retrieval system, without permission from the copyright holders.

$\copyright$ Marshall Cavendish Limited 1985
$\copyright$ Orbis Publishing 1983, 1984

British Library Cataloguing in Publication Data

Brown, Ashley
    War in peace : the Marshall Cavendish
    illustrated encyclopaedia of post-war conflict.
    1. History, Modern—1945-   2. War—History
    —20th century
    I. Title   II. Dartford, Mark
    909.82   D842

    ISBN 0-86307-293-3
        0 86307 301 8   vol. 8

Library of Congress Cataloging in Publication Data

Main entry under title:

War in peace.

    Includes bibliographies and index.
    1. Military history, Modern—20th century.   2. Military
art and science—History—20th century.   3. World politics—1945-
I. Marshall Cavendish Corporation.
U42.W373 1984   355'.009'04   84-19386
ISBN 0-86307-293-3
        0 86307 301 8   vol. 8

Editorial Staff

Editor	Ashley Brown
Editorial Director	Brian Innes
Editorial Manager	Clare Byatt
Editorial Editors	Sam Elder
	Adrian Gilbert
Sub Editors	Sue Leonard
	Simon Innes
Artwork Editor	Jonathan Reed
Artwork Buyer	Jean Morley
Picture Editor	Carina Dvorak
Picture Consultant	Robert Hunt
Design	EDC

Reference Edition Staff

Editor	Mark Dartford
Designer	Graham Beehag
Consultant	Robert Paulley
Indexers	F & K Gill
Creation	DPM Services

Editorial Board

Brigadier-General James L Collins Jr (USA Rtd) received his MA at the US Military Academy, Va, and was a postgraduate at both the Naval War College and the Armed Forces Staff College. Commissioned into the US Army as 2nd Lieutenant in 1939, General Collins has held a variety of distinguished posts, including Chief of Military History, US Department of the Army, Director of the Defense Language Institute and Commander of the Military History Center, Washington DC. He served with Military Assistance Command in Vietnam, and commanded V Corps Artillery in Germany. He was Director of the US Commission for Military History, American Institute and is a member of the Historical Association, and the US Army Association. His published works include, inter alia, *The Development and Training of the South Vietnamese Army 1950−1972* (1975) and *Allied Participation in Vietnam* (1975).

David Floyd was educated at Oxford, and began his career with the British RAF mission in Moscow during World War II. After the war he served in the diplomatic service in Romania and Yugoslavia, following which he joined the staff of the London *Daily Telegraph*. For more than 30 years he was the *Telegraph*'s correspondent on Eastern European and Communist bloc affairs. He now works as a freelance journalist and translator, and is one of the most respected British commentators on the politics of the Soviet Union.

Ian V Hogg served for 27 years in the Royal Artillery, and retired in 1972 with the rank of Master Gunner. He has since devoted his time to writing and research, and is a well-known expert on all aspects of gunnery, firearms and the history of fortifications. His many published works include *A History of Artillery, Military Smallarms of the 20th Century, Coastal Defences of England and Wales* and *Pistols of the World*.

Vice Admiral Sir Louis Le Bailly KBE OBE CB is Director-General of Intelligence at the Ministry of Defence in London. He was educated at the Royal Navy College, Dartmouth and served during World War II with the RNEC, and on *HMS Hood*. His distinguished postings include Naval Attache to Washington DC, and Commander of the British Navy Staff. He is a member of the Institute for the Study of Conflict, and Deputy-Director of Marine Engineering.

Air Vice Marshal SWB Menaul is Defence Consultant to the Institute for the Study of Conflict and the Institute for Foreign Policy Analysis at Cambridge, Mass. He was educated at the RAF College, Cranwell and served with Bomber Command from 1936−1940. During the latter part of the war he was an instructor, and also served with the famous Pathfinder squadron. He has held various senior posts in the UK and abroad, including Commander of British Atomic Trials Task Forces, Commandant Joint Staff College, and Director-General of the Royal United Services Institute. His recent published works include *Soviet War Machine* (1980) and *Countdown: British Strategic nuclear forces* (1980).

Dr John Pimlott was educated at Leicester University, studying History and the British Army. Since 1973 he has been a civilian lecturer in the Department of War Studies and International Affairs at the Royal Military Academy, Sandhurst, where his teaching specialisations include the Middle East and post-1945 British Defence Policy. He has written a number of books, including *B-29 Superfortress* (1980), *The Battle of the Bulge* (1981), *World War II in photographs* (1984), *The Middle East Conflicts* (1983) and *Vietnam: The History and the Tactics* (1982).

Contributors

David Blue served with the CIA in various countries of Southeast Asia, including Laos, and is a writer on and a student of small wars.

Gordon Brook-Shepherd spent 15 years in Vienna, first as lieutenant-colonel on the staff of the British High Commission and then as a foreign correspondent for the *Daily Telegraph*. A graduate in history from Cambridge, he is currently Chief Assistant Editor of the *Sunday Telegraph*.

Jeffrey J. Clarke is an expert on recent military history, particularly the Vietnam War, and has written for the American Center of Military History.

Major-General Richard Clutterbuck OBE has been Senior Lecturer in politics at Exeter University since his retirement from the army in 1972. His works include *Protest and the Urban Guerrilla*, *Guerrillas and Terrorists* and *Kidnap and Ransom*.

Alexander S. Cochran Jr is a historian whose area of research is modern Indochinese affairs with particular reference to the war in Vietnam since 1945. He is at present working in the Southeast Asia Branch of the Center of Military History, Department of the Army.

Colonel Peter M. Dunn is a serving officer in the USAF. His doctoral thesis is on the history of Indochina during the mid-1940s.

John B. Dwyer served both with the infantry and with armoured units in Vietnam. He was editor and publisher of the Vietnam veteran's newsletter *Perimeter* and has been a writer and correspondent for *National Vietnam Veteran's Review* for the past few years. His particular interest are Special Forces and Special Operations.

Brenda Ralph Lewis has specialised in political and military history since 1964. She s a regular contributor to military and historical magazines in both Britain and the United States.

Hugh Lunghi served in Moscow in the British Military Mission and the British Embassy for six years during and after World War II. He was interpreter for the British Chiefs of Staff at the Teheran, Yalta and Potsdam conferences, and also interpreted for Churchill and Anthony Eden. He subsequently worked in the BBC External Services and is a former editor of *Index on Censorship*.

Charles Messenger retired from the army in 1980 to become a fulltime military writer after 21 years service in the Royal Tank Regiment. Over the past 10 years he has written several books on 20th century warfare, as well as contributing articles to a number of defence and historical journals. He is currently a Research Associate at the Royal United Services Institute for Defence Studies in London.

Billy C. Mossman is a well-known American writer and historian. He is currently working on a volume on the Korean War for the US Army Center of Military History.

Bryan Perrett served in the Royal Armoured Corps from 1952 to 1971. He contributes regularly to a number of established military journals and acted as Defence Correspondent to the *Liverpool Echo* during the Falklands War. His recent books include *Weapons of the Falklands Conflict* and *A History of Blitzkrieg*.

Chapman Pincher is one of England's leading authorities on international espionage and counter-intelligence. He is the author of political novels and books on spying, the most recent of which is *Their Trade is Treachery*, which deals with the penetration of Britain's secret services by the Russian secret police.

Yehoshua Porath is a noted scholar at the Hebrew University in Jerusalem. He has made a special study of the Palestinian problem and is the author of two books on the subject, the most recent of which is *The Palestinian Arab National Movement 1929—39*, which was published in Britain in 1977.

Contributors

Antony Preston is Naval Editor of the military magazine *Defence* and author of numerous publications including *Battleships, Aircraft Carriers* and *Submarines.*

Brigadier-General Edwin H. Simmons, US Marine Corps, Retired, is the Director of Marine Corps History and Museums. At the time of the Inchon operation and the Chosin Reservoir campaign, he, as a major, commanded Weapons Company, 3rd Battalion, 1st Marines. Widely published, he is the author of *The United States Marines.*

Ronald Spector is an expert on Vietnam and has recently completed a book on that subject for the Center of Military History in the United States.

Andres Suarez served in the Cuban ministry of education from 1948–1951, took part in the Cuban revolution, and served in the ministry of housing from 1959. From 1965, he has been Professor of Latin American Studies at the University of Florida. Other publications include *Cuba and the Sino–Soviet Rift.*

Sir Robert Thompson KBE, CMG, DSO, MC is a world authority on guerrilla warfare, on which he has written extensively. He was directly involved in the Emergency in Malaya in the 1950s and rose to become permanent Secretary for Defence. From 1961 to 1965 he headed the British Advisory Mission to Vietnam and since then he has advised several governments, including the United States, on counter-insurgency operations Sir Robert Thompson is a Council member of the Institute for the Study of Conflict, London. His books include *Defeating Communist Insurgency and Revolutionary War in World Strategy, 1945–69.*

Patrick Turnbull commanded 'D' Force, Burma during World War II. His 29 published works include a history of the Foreign Legion.

Contents of Volume

The Irish question

British government policy in Northern Ireland,1967-72

For almost half a century, from the partition of Ireland in 1921 to 1968 when the present troubles began, the British government's attitude towards Northern Ireland was one of thankful neglect. Under the Government of Ireland Act, 1920, a subordinate parliament was established at Belfast which had considerable control over local matters. It was responsible for social legislation, such as health and education, and also law and order. Although Section 75 of the 1920 Act specifically preserved the sovereign supremacy of the Westminster parliament over Northern Ireland, successive Unionist governments were effectively allowed to be their own masters. In Westminster the convention grew up that Northern Ireland was simply not discussed.

When James Callaghan became home secretary in December 1967 he found that Northern Ireland affairs, for which he was technically responsible, were dealt with in the 'General Department' of the Home Office, along with British Summer Time, London taxi cabs, liquor licensing and the protection of animals and birds. All this changed in the late summer of 1968. It is fair to say, nevertheless, that British policy towards Northern Ireland – at least in the early stages – was characterised by ignorance and an understandable reluctance to become too closely involved.

In the 1960s, however, there had been increasing concern with the problems of the province among some left-wing Labour MPs. In the 1966 general election Gerry Fitt was elected as Republican Labour MP for West Belfast and he worked hard, with considerable success, to develop British Labour interest in the Northern Ireland situation. Fitt was the only non-Unionist out of Northern Ireland's 12 West-minster MPs. The other 11 were all members of the Ulster Unionist Party which for over 70 years had been closely associated with the British Conservative Party.

The British Prime Minister Harold Wilson himself favoured change in Northern Ireland. After the first violence in October 1968 he summoned the Northern Ireland Prime Minister Captain Terence O'Neill to London and insisted on a package of reforms. The London government was depending on O'Neill to put his own house in order, but the Ulsterman failed fully to push through all the reforms. After his resignation, and as disorder built up during the summer of 1969, it became increasingly clear that London would have to take some sort of direct action. For one thing the Royal Ulster Constabulary (RUC) were stretched almost to breaking point. For another, the international impact being made by dramatic newspaper and television pictures of rioting in the province laid the British government open to charges of inaction or indifference. The crucial questions concerned possible military aid to the civil power: who would decide to use the army and who would direct its actions? As it happened, troops had already been deployed to guard water and electricity installations after Protestant paramilitary bombings in the spring, but the possible use of troops to quell riots was a much more sensitive issue.

Whatever the niceties, in August 1969 the hard logic of violent events in Northern Ireland began to dictate British policy. After extensive rioting had broken out in Londonderry and spread to Belfast and other centres, Harold Wilson agreed to send the army in. The British government also began to take a more vigorous line with the Ulster politicians.

Above: British troops taking cover behind two FV1609 Humber Pig APCs as they are subjected to a hail of stones and bottles thrown by rioting youths on Sunday, 30 January 1972 – 'Bloody Sunday' – the day on which 13 Catholic civilians were shot dead by the security forces.

The last three prime ministers of Northern Ireland before direct rule: Captain Terence O'Neill (far left) whose reforming policies proved too pro-Catholic for his Protestant colleagues; his successor Major James Chichester-Clark (centre left); and Brian Faulkner (left) whose success in persuading the British to introduce internment led to the fall of Stormont.

Below: The aftermath of a bomb blast in an Ulster street. A casualty, wracked with pain, is lifted onto a stretcher by civilians and paras. Note the use of a scarf, tied into a loop knot, to support and contain a fractured leg, a standard military first aid technique.

On 19 August Captain O'Neill's successor, Major James Chichester-Clark, went to London to agree immediate policy with Wilson and Callaghan. Joint working parties of both governments were formed to monitor the progress of reform. Two senior civil servants were posted to Belfast as representatives of the British government. The General Officer Commanding Northern Ireland, Lieutenant-General Sir Ian Freeland, was put in overall charge of security. A commission under Lord Hunt was set up to examine both the RUC and the B Specials. In October its report led to the disarming of the police and the disbandment of the Specials. Unionist unease at these measures was soothed by the 'Downing Street Declaration' which confirmed that the province 'should not cease to be a part of the United Kingdom without the consent of the people of Northern Ireland'. Effectively this meant that while Protestants remained in the majority the Union was secure.

Towards the end of August James Callaghan visited Northern Ireland. He was greeted by the Catholic community like a conquering hero. He emphasised that the British government supported the full introduction of civil rights reforms. In security policy General Freeland was allowed to adopt a relatively conciliatory approach. During September the barricades in Londonderry and Belfast were 'talked down'. Apart from intermittent rioting, there was a period of comparative calm until the early summer of 1970. During these months Wilson and Callaghan maintained a relatively low-key policy, hoping to satisfy the Catholics with the agreed reforms, while

Force levels 1969-72

January 1969	3000 (normal garrison)
October 1969	8000
January 1970	7300
July 1970	11,243
January 1971	7742
August 1971	12,300
January 1972	14,218
July 1972	21,288

Deaths in Ulster 1969-72

	1969	1970	1971	1972
Army	0	0	43	103
RUC	1	2	11	17
UDR	0	0	5	25
Civilians	12	23	114	322
Total	13	25	173	467

limiting further reform in order to avoid finally alienating the Protestants.

Although both parties at Westminster broadly supported this policy, after the Conservative victory in the June 1970 general election there was a stiffening on the security side. In response to renewed disorder, including the growing use of firearms, the new home secretary, Reginald Maudling, let the army move into the Catholic ghettos to 'root out' the men of violence. During a 34-hour curfew of the Belfast Lower Falls area in early July, military raids and searches uncovered over 200 weapons and 21,000 rounds of ammunition. But the army's actions stirred up great antagonism and indirectly stimulated recruitment for the Provisional IRA which had emerged at the beginning of the year.

Throughout 1970 and the first half of 1971 the British government stuck to its policy of letting the Unionist politicians in Belfast take primary charge of the local situation. But in the face of increased street violence, the start of a full-scale terrorist campaign, with direct attacks on army and police, and the indiscriminate bombing of civilian targets, Unionists began to call for the introduction of yet tougher security measures, and in particular internment without trial. Chichester-Clark pleaded with London for additional troops and internment. When in March 1971 he was offered no more than a few extra soldiers he resigned and was replaced by the astute and articulate Brian Faulkner.

Introducing internment
Faulkner began by offering moderate Catholic politicians a limited share in government. Had his plans been successful, it would have fully justified the continued British policy of political non-intervention, but a fresh wave of violence in June and July rapidly overtook his preliminary talks. Faulkner too needed something to satisfy his hardline backbench supporters – internment. On 5 August he went to London to press for the measure. Although the army General Officer Commanding since February, General Sir Harry Tuzo, did not favour it, the RUC chief, Graham Shillington, did. Disturbed by the continuing spiral of violence, the British politicians could offer no alternative policy, apart from the 'ultimate' option of direct rule. Reluctant to go so far, they were still anxious to do something to restore the morale and authority of the Unionists, to whom in any case they were politically quite close. In the end Faulkner won the day and on 9 August the government introduced internment.

Internment was an unmitigated disaster. The operation was based on defective intelligence, and was carried out without any cooperation from the Dublin government; as a consequence many of the people initially arrested were not directly involved in terrorist activities. The policy provoked very deep resentment in the Catholic community. It did not lead to a cessation of violence, as had been hoped, but stimulated both political and practical support for republican terrorism. In 1971 before internment there were 13 security force and 17 civilian deaths; for the remainder of the year the figures were 46 and 97.

The future of the Stormont administration was sealed by the failure of internment. The basic British policy which had been followed since 1968 – that of pressing for reforms while effectively keeping Northern Ireland at arm's length, leaving day-to-day admi-

nistration to the province's government – had done nothing to quell the rising level of violence. 1972 was even worse than 1971. The year began very badly. On 30 January – 'Bloody Sunday' – 13 civilians were shot dead by the army in Londonderry during a riot following an illegal march. An official inquiry by the Lord Chief Justice of England, Lord Widgery, found that none of the dead appeared to have been shot whilst handling a firearm or bomb.

The incident had an immediate and catastrophic impact. The Catholic community finally and irrevocably withdrew their consent from the Unionist regime. The Conservative government in London resolved that they themselves should take over control of security. It was more than Brian Faulkner could tolerate. In March 1972 his government resigned, Stormont was prorogued and the British government took over direct rule of Northern Ireland. William Whitelaw was appointed the first-ever Secretary of State for Northern Ireland. **Keith Jeffery**

Above: Covered by two soldiers watching for snipers, troops fire rubber bullets (spare rounds in ammo box, foreground) at riotous elements in Londonderry in February 1972. In the aftermath of 'Bloody Sunday' violence increased dramatically until by March 1972 the British government was forced to introduce direct rule and to take immediate responsibility for running the province.

Men of violence

The rise of the Provisional IRA

Below: The unmistakable face of terrorism – a masked member of the Provisional IRA, with a Thompson M1928 sub-machine gun.

Protestant propagandists were quick to represent the disturbances of August 1969 as a Catholic insurrection led by the Irish Republican Army (IRA), but in fact the events found the IRA unprepared and largely disarmed. Under the leadership of Cathal Goulding from 1963, the organisation had moved away from its traditional commitment to the unification of Ireland by violence – the 'physical force' tradition – and had adopted a Marxist policy in which both Catholic and Protestant workers were seen as an exploited class opposed to 'British imperialism'. The concentration on social and economic issues was accompanied by virtual demilitarisation. But their traditional role in Ulster was a very different one – the defence of Catholic areas against Protestant mobs. This was a role that in the summer of 1969 they were quite unable to fulfil. Many Catholics felt outraged that there was no protection when it was needed: on the walls of the Catholic enclaves of Belfast appeared the slogan 'IRA – I Ran Away'. Only in the Lower Falls had the IRA been able to deploy three Thompson sub-machine guns.

In the aftermath of the August disturbances and the appearance of the British Army on the streets, dissension was rife within the IRA in Northern Ireland. Hardliners in Belfast called for the replacement of the Dublin leadership of Cathal Goulding and an end to Marxist policies; they also opposed the Belfast leaders who, as members of citizens' defence organisations, were engaged in negotiations with the British Army to reduce tension and bring down the barricades. In December 1969 the IRA army council confirmed its 'constitutionalist' policy by recognising the Dublin, Stormont and Westminster parliaments. In protest, a member of the Dublin IRA leadership, Sean MacStiofain (John Stephenson), and others declared the foundation of a 'Provisional Army Council'; the breakaway group soon became known as the Provisional IRA, Goulding's organisation being called the 'Official' IRA. Sinn Fein, the IRA's political wing, also split soon afterwards.

MacStiofain was a deeply religious Gaelic enthusiast who had served in the RAF and learned his Irish in jail after raiding Felstead School for arms in 1953. The leaders of provisional Sinn Fein, Rory O'Bradaigh (Rory Brady) and Daithi O'Conail (David O'Connell), were also veterans of the 1950s IRA campaign. The men who emerged to prominence in the North, however, such as Billy McKee, Joe Cahill and Seamus Twomey, were representatives of the 1940s era who had seen little point in the 1950s campaign, but felt that now in the new climate of Northern Ireland politics there was an opportunity to strike out for the Holy Grail of Republicans of all eras – the 'full national demand' as it is known – British withdrawal from Ireland.

Initially, however, the Provisionals had to set about producing some 'defenders' for the Catholic districts. In January 1970 the 'Provos' probably numbered some 30 individuals in Belfast, about one-quarter the size of the Official IRA organisation. But although they had to start virtually from scratch, conditions for recruitment were improving all the time. The British troops had initially been hailed as saviours by the Catholics when the Westminster government sent them in, but there was no long-term political strategy formulated beyond containment of the situation, with the result that the British Army was left to try to apply a military solution in a highly volatile situation. Inevitably, given the abrasiveness of a relationship between civilians and an army on the streets, the Catholics came to regard the troops more as hostile intruders than as peacemakers.

The Provisionals were organised into three brigades – one each for Belfast, Londonderry and the Border area. The Belfast Brigade comprised three battalions under the overall chief of staff, Billy McKee. Arms and money were in short supply during the first half of 1970, but enough sub-machine guns, rifles and pistols had been obtained either by theft or from over the border to equip the Provisionals for their first significant action. On the night of 27 June 1970, as rioting raged in Belfast, there were gun battles in the Ardoyne and in the Short Strand district. St Matthew's Catholic Church in the Short Strand was attacked by armed Protestants and defended by Provisionals including Chief of Staff Billy McKee and Third Battalion commander Billy Kelly. McKee was badly wounded in the prolonged gunfight, but the church was successfully defended. A week later, from 3-5 July, came the British Army curfew and house-to-house search in the Catholic Lower Falls district. The use of CS gas and the ransacking of houses won the Provisional IRA a tidal wave of recruitment.

Boy scout bombers

In the wake of the curfew, by early 1971 IRA sources estimated that the 'army' had approximately 1000 volunteers in Belfast alone. Recruits were mainly young men and women, often in their teens or younger – the IRA has a Fianna, or boy scout, wing which acts as couriers and often as a quite effective intelligence network, as does the IRA's female wing, Cuman na mBan. Unemployment and injustice had filled young Catholics with a sense of resentment and bitterness which made the pool of potential new recruits almost inexhaustible. In these early days it was nothing for 10 or 12 volunteers to go out on a job, such as a bombing, which could easily have been carried out by a single individual.

Later on in the struggle this factor was also to help the IRA in an inverted sort of way because the excessive use of manpower inevitably made for large-scale arrests, which built up the prison population so that it came to have a disproportionately powerful effect on the Catholic population when the hunger strikes began. Almost every family had someone – a relation, friend or neighbour – in jail.

Arms and money began to come in from America where a septuagenarian survivor of the Anglo-Irish war of earlier in the century, Michael Flannery from County Tipperary, and some like-minded associates founded the Irish Northern Aid Association; however, distance and surveillance meant the Provisionals got their guns in a trickle rather than a flood.

After a quiet period during which the flood of new recruits were given basic training – usually ten days in the Republic or in the Northern Ireland border areas – and organised, from early 1971 the Provisionals moved increasingly onto the offensive (the Official IRA soon effectively went out of existence as a

Above: Joe Cahill, who became chief of staff of the Provisional IRA in Belfast in March 1971. Left: Sean MacStiofain (centre) and Seamus Twomey (right). MacStiofain had for many years been a leading member of the old IRA before he led the Provisionals' breakaway; Twomey was responsible for ordering the worst Provisional IRA bomb outrages in Belfast during 1972.

Below: Troops, firemen and civilians tear at wreckage as they desperately attempt to free victims trapped by rubble after an IRA bomb attack in Belfast which killed three people.

Left: A soldier of the Royal Green Jackets is helped into the back of an APC after being wounded in a nail bomb attack. The nail bomb was a crude but effective weapon and was used openly against troops on the streets. The rules of conduct permitted troops to fire on nail bombers though the difficulty of identifying such weapons before they exploded meant that such a response by the British Army was rare.

Right: The price of fraternisation with British troops – this teenage girl has had her head shaved before being tarred and feathered by the woman's section of the Provisional IRA, the Cuman na mBan.

military organisation and eventually became the Workers Party which by 1983 had two members in the Southern Irish parliament). The Provisionals engaged in sniping attacks on soldiers and the RUC, sometimes attempting to bomb police barracks, but the main thrust of their campaign was to destroy the Northern economy, for which Britain would have to pay, and to overthrow Stormont. The technique employed was the bombing of civilian targets.

First, old buildings near the centre of cities were destroyed to create an impression. Then business premises with valuable and inflammable stock – cars, carpets, paint, electrical goods – were attacked, usually with bombs of around 5kg (11lbs) carried in duffel bags. With increasing technological skill, the Provisionals then began going inside larger premises to plant bigger bombs. The *Daily Mirror's* new million-pound plant at Suffolk, Belfast, was the first target for such attacks on 17 July 1971. By the end of 1971 the Provisionals had begun using car bombs.

In an attempt to curb the bombing, supplies of gelignite were controlled north and south of the border. The Provisionals replied by devising bombs made out of a range of readily-available chemicals. Bombs were made out of potassium nitrate, sugar and diesel oil; from fertilisers, industrial cleaning agents and weed-killer; even tooth-cleaning powder, car battery acid, washing soda and epsom salts were used. Methods of delivering devices were also varied – ranging from cars and lorries to dustbins (rolled downhill) and children's prams. Even though the bombs frequently claimed IRA lives through premature detonation constant research and a high level of recruitment eventually brought the Provisionals to remote-controlled devices.

The growing level of Provisional IRA activity – in July 1971 there were 20 explosions in one 12-hour period alone – inevitably provoked a positive effort by the security forces to restore control. In March 1971 Billy McKee was arrested, Joe Cahill taking over as chief of staff in Belfast, but as long as the high rate of recruitment was maintained, deaths and arrests could not seriously affect the Provisionals' operational

capacity. The crucial factor was the continuing support of a sufficient proportion of the Catholic population. The Provisional campaign took a heavy toll of civilians, including bomb victims – often women and children – passers-by caught in cross-fire, and victims of sectarian murders; this unquestionably caused widespread revulsion and shook 'Provo' support even in the Catholic enclaves.

But the authorities' reaction continued to alienate Catholics. The introduction of internment in August 1971 was intended to curb the rising terrorist violence, but it largely missed the IRA. The outrage felt by Catholics at the arrest of many innocent people was compounded when stories began to appear of the mistreatment of suspects in custody. Throughout the last five months of 1971 violence in Northern Ireland was sustained at new heights. Riots, bombing and sniping racked the cities. In country districts, ambushes and the use of landmines spread. Thirty-five people were killed and 100 major bombing incidents recorded in August alone. Between September and November in border areas the army was fired on 243 times. The total civilian and security force death toll in Northern Ireland in 1971 was 173, compared with 25 deaths the previous year.

By the second half of 1971 policing in many Catholic areas had become impossible, and in some parts of the Bogside and the Falls Road even the army could only penetrate in force. The Provisionals did their best to establish a sort of 'extraterritorial' status for these districts, with barricades manned by IRA men to control entrance and exit, and the police and the courts replaced by IRA substitutes. IRA punishments, both against common criminals and against those suspected of informing or associating with the British, were severe: women had their heads shaved and were tarred-and-feathered; many men were subjected to a 'kneecapping'. Although this rough justice offended many Catholics, fear of the Protestants and the British Army dictated solidarity and acquiescence in IRA intimidation.

In December 1971, despairing of stopping the Provisionals altogether, British Home Secretary

Reginald Maudling enunciated the doctrine of limiting their actions to 'an acceptable level of violence'. But after the 30 January 1972 'Bloody Sunday' incident even this aim seemed unrealistic. Catholics were used to the shock of the accidental killing of civilians by British Army fire, but the shooting of 13 apparently unarmed people in full view of TV cameras outraged every section of Irish Nationalist sentiment. IRA recruitment increased sharply; the two high points of the decade for the Provisionals were at hand.

The first occurred on 24 March when the end of Stormont and the commencement of direct rule from Britain was announced. A principal aim of Republican policy for over 50 years was thus attained, but the further demand for British withdrawal remained. Some optimists within the Provisionals began to feel that even the final goal was in sight when on 7 July, while a truce was in force in Northern Ireland, a top-level IRA delegation was flown to London by the RAF to talk to William Whitelaw, the new secretary of state for Northern Ireland. The delegation consisted of Sean MacStiofain, Daithi O'Conail, Gerry Adams, Martin MacGuinness, Seamus Twomey, Ivor Bell and a lawyer Myles Shevlin. It was the first time the IRA had negotiated with the British since the Anglo-Irish Treaty talks of 1921. However, the talks came to nothing and the tide of events began to turn against the Provisionals shortly thereafter.

The truce ended two days later and on 'Bloody Friday', 21 July 1972, Provisional IRA bombs killed nine people and injured 130 in 19 attacks within a mile radius of Belfast city centre. 'Operation Motorman' which ended the 'No-Go' areas of Belfast and Derry on 31 July was the army's response. In the four months before Motorman there had been 500 explosions and 5940 shooting incidents. In the four months after, the figures fell to 393 explosions and 2833 shootings.

Along with the Northern crackdown, the Southern authorities also acted, arresting Sean MacStiofain and Rory O'Bradaigh and on 1 December introducing a measure which allowed a person to be imprisoned on the word of a police superintendent who believed him to be a member of the IRA. As a result several important IRA men were picked up and the year ended with the IRA seemingly about to be crushed. This was a view which was to be proved fallacious.

Tim Pat Coogan

Below: IRA gunmen man a checkpoint at the entrance of a No-Go area of Londonderry. The British policy of non-intervention in these areas ended on 31 July 1972 with Operation Motorman which virtually halved the number of bombing and shooting incidents taking place in Belfast and Londonderry.

Brutality or ill-treatment?

Disorientation techniques and deep interrogation

When the British Army first went onto the streets of Northern Ireland, it was as a peacekeeping force to separate two warring communities. But by August 1971 and the introduction of internment, the army's role had expanded into a counter-insurgency operation against the Provisional IRA. Since 1945 the army had gained considerable experience of counter-insurgency in such far-flung locations as Malaya, Cyprus and Aden, but the sensitivity of a campaign within the United Kingdom itself posed special problems – techniques that might pass muster in an outpost of Empire could be branded unacceptably brutal so near to home.

The key to successful counter-insurgency remained the same everywhere, however: it was intelligence. If the security forces could build up a clear picture of the enemy's operational and organisational structure, identifying individuals involved at all levels, they would be able to break the insurrectionary movement. In 1971 the first serious effort was begun to tackle the intelligence gap in Northern Ireland, especially through the expansion and training of the RUC Special Branch, but the unwillingness of the Catholic population to provide information obstructed intelligence gathering.

When internment was instituted, the army and police knew they lacked the level of intelligence to make the operation truly effective, but they seized on internment as a golden opportunity to get the information they needed from the best possible source – the Nationalist Catholics themselves. The security forces were obviously well aware that suspects picked up in the internment sweep would not willingly inform, but the use of crude physical torture in the manner of a South American military regime was ruled out. Consequently, they sought to apply interrogation techniques which would be effective while stopping short of certain very ill-defined limits.

In most cases the result was rough treatment which continued, although perhaps more systematically, procedures that had already become common in security force operations. The most basic was wall-standing, used by the army when searching groups of people on the street. The suspect was forced to stand with his legs apart and his arms raised above head level leaning against the wall; the feet were placed about one metre (three feet) from the wall, so that the weight of the body was carried on the toes and the hands. This position left the suspect vulnerable and immobilised, making him easy to control. But wall-standing also had the effect, if kept up for periods of over an hour, of creating oxygen fatigue, muscular cramping, weakness and unconsciousness. Hooding suspects was another technique with a legitimate

purpose: it made suspects easier to control and stopped visual contact with other suspects. This too was to prove to have another use in interrogation.

At most of the interrogation centres in which RUC Special Branch men processed those picked up under internment, a combination of prolonged wall-standing and occasional violence were more or less standard practice, according to the European Court of Human Rights report. Extreme physical exercises were also imposed to a point where they became painful to the older or weaker suspects. Many of those treated in this way proved to be completely innocent of involvement in terrorism.

Sensory deprivation

These were not original methods, but 14 suspects were singled out for something that was quite new – interrogation in depth through 'sensory deprivation' or 'disorientation'. The Nato intelligence services had been interested in sensory deprivation since the late 1960s, not only because of its counter-insurgency potential but also because of its possible effect on their own men if used by the Russians. In April 1971 the RUC Special Branch were instructed in the new techniques at an English intelligence centre, and between 11 and 16 August they tried them out on 11 carefully selected suspects picked up in the first internment sweep; another three men had been subjected to disorientation by the end of October.

The deep interrogation technique had five main elements: prolonged wall-standing for periods of 20-30 hours; hooding for hours at a time; exposure to continuous monotonous noise, described as a high-pitched throb like an air compressor; deprivation of sleep; and deprivation of food. The combined effect of these five elements was to induce hallucination and a state of total mental confusion. According to some reports, men interrogated after prolonged sensory deprivation found it hard to remember their own names. According to the security forces, however, a large amount of vital intelligence was obtained.

When descriptions of this treatment began to appear in the press, there was an immediate political response. On 31 August the British government appointed a committee of inquiry under Sir Edmund Compton, which was followed by a second inquiry under Lord Parker of Waddington the following year. Both reports cleared the security forces of brutality but agreed there had been 'physical ill-treatment'. Doubts were not stilled, however, and on 2 March 1972 the British government announced that deep interrogation would no longer be used and tightened up controls over interrogation generally. Five years later the government gave a solemn undertaking that such techniques would never be reintroduced.

The Republic of Ireland government was not satisfied with the British response and pursued the matter in the European Court of Human Rights, accusing Britain of torture. The judgement, delivered in 1978, rejected the Irish case, while accepting that 'inhuman and degrading treatments' had been meted out. The 14 subjects of the sensory deprivation experiment all took civil action for damages in the courts, and received payments of up to £25,000.

The British counter-insurgency effort soon developed in more promising directions, with the computerisation of masses of detailed information gathered on the streets and an increasing flow of tip-offs from Catholics disillusioned with the Provisionals. Finally, the supergrass system – offering amnesties and new identities to imprisoned terrorists ready to inform – proved a far more effective means of securing intelligence 'out of the horse's mouth'.

Brian Markworthy

Left: A suspect, hiding his face from the cameras, is loaded into the back of a vehicle by Military Police. Left below: The forbidding Castlereagh interrogation centre. Below: British troops surround a group of suspects and make them adopt 'the stance'. Wall-standing in this position provides security for guards but can prove extremely painful if maintained for extended periods.

Left: Death in the streets of Londonderry during the confused events of Sunday, 30 January 1972. The attempt by paratroopers to cut off rioters near the Rossville flats ended in the tragedy of 13 dead.

Below: A British soldier watches as the Woodburn hotel in Belfast blazes fiercely after an IRA bombing attack in November 1971. The introduction of internment in August of that year had been the signal for a rapid deterioration of public order in Northern Ireland; the aftermath of the arrest of hundreds of Catholics was partly a wave of civil disobedience (non-payment of rates, for example) but also a massive increase in acts of violence. Thirty people were killed in political violence in the seven months before internment, but 143 died in the five months after.

Bloo

Internment and its aftermath

Despite the start of the Provisional IRA bombing campaign in 1970, there had still been little direct conflict between the 'Provos' and the British Army by the beginning of 1971. In January it was still possible for the local army commander to negotiate with Provisionals in the Ballymurphy district of Belfast with a view to preventing outbreaks of rioting. But a new and deadly phase of the Northern Ireland conflict was about to begin.

On 3-4 February 1971 the army cordoned and searched the Catholic Clonard and Ardoyne districts of Belfast, stating that these areas harboured members of the Provisional IRA. During the days of violent disturbances that followed, the Provisionals adopted a policy of shooting to kill British soldiers; the day after the first soldier was killed by an IRA sniper on 6 February, the Northern Ireland prime minister, Major Chichester-Clark, declared that 'Northern Ireland is at war with the IRA Provisionals'. On 10 March, in tragic confirmation of the new aspect of the Provisionals' campaign, three young Scottish soldiers were lured onto a country road outside Belfast and shot in the back of the head.

Over 10,000 British troops were in Northern Ireland, but during the months that followed they proved incapable of stemming the rising tide of bombing and sniping, or of preventing serious outbreaks of rioting by Catholics and Protestants alike. The new Stormont prime minister, Brian Faulkner, engaged in a political initiative to involve Catholic politicians in government, but incidents on the street fouled all hopes of conciliation. In Londonderry in early July, after four days of rioting in the Catholic Bogside, British soldiers shot two civilians dead in separate incidents; local inhabitants were convinced that the two men had not been involved in the disturbances, and the deaths became the occasion for Catholic politicians to withdraw from Stormont.

Many Unionists had long advocated internment as an answer to the violence. It was allowed for under the Northern Ireland Special Powers Act and had been used, both north and south of the border, to stop the IRA campaign of the 1950s. It permitted the government to hold people in custody indefinitely without trial and without any specific charge being made. The British government and the army were reluctant to use

Below: The Magilligan Camp in County Londonderry, the target of the march of 22 January 1972 that was the prelude to the events of 'Bloody Sunday'. Over 300 internees were held in the camp, which was used to house the overflow from the main camp at Long Kesh.

ly Sunday

Death in Derry

Simon Winchester, a reporter with the *Guardian* newspaper, was present in Belfast on 30 January 1972, the day that was to become known as 'Bloody Sunday'. In his book *In Holy Terror* he vividly describes the events of that afternoon in which he was an involuntary participant:

'But suddenly a scream went up. "The soldiers, the soldiers!" someone yelled ahead. I looked around to my left. A line of armoured Pigs was speeding towards us: two 3-ton lorries were roaring up; soldiers were jumping out and rushing at us. I did immediately what everyone else on the ground did: I ran forward, as hard and as fast as I could.

'But then the firing started – ten or a dozen heavy, hard bangs, that two years of street experience taught me were rifle shots, and they seemed to be coming from behind. I dropped flat, tasting the dirty asphalt of the Rossville Flats forecourt, muddying my corduroys as I fell into a glass-strewn puddle. The noise stopped for a second: I was up and on again, heart pounding with fear, breath coming in strained gasps. I got to a line of bunkers under the wall of a block of the seven-storey flats. I stopped and looked around, aware of a huge and panicky crowd all around me. In the courtyard the armoured cars were slowing and turning as more and more soldiers – paratroopers, I could be sure from their camouflage jackets

and their rounded helmets – jumped out and took up firing positions. And in the middle of the courtyard lay a man ... he was badly hurt: a wound in his leg was bleeding heavily ...

'Then I rushed on again and into the crowded stairwell of the flats, sheltering for a few precious moments while the firing went on and on. From here I could discern both the hard rifle fire of the army SLRs and what I thought might have been the sharper cracks of .22s and the low steady thudding of a sub-machine gun. But there was a helicopter chugging overhead as well, and gas guns were still discharging in the background, and men and women screamed and glass crashed and voices were raised in hysterical panic, so it was difficult to be very sure. But gunfire was raging out in the open, and people, it seemed clear, were being hurt.

'I ran on and out of the stairwell, feeling by now terribly alone and vulnerable as I crossed open space. Paratroopers were crouched around the far side of Rossville Street and by another new block of flats at Glenfada Park: beside me, on the west side of the flats, lay two bodies – one a young boy, dressed in jeans, the other an older man in a brown coat. At first I had thought they were sheltering from a rain of rifle fire: I had dropped down, and a hundred others grouped around a red phone box had dropped as well. But when the firing stopped again we all got up: the two on the ground lay still. They were dead.'

internment and doubtful of its effectiveness, but in April 1971 a working party of military intelligence officers and the Royal Ulster Constabulary (RUC) Special Branch was set up to prepare a list of possible internees. The level of intelligence was poor: very little was known about the Provisionals, who were of course the main source of terrorist acts, so the majority of those on the list of 500 which finally emerged were older-style Republicans, 'Official' IRA men, or simply radical opponents of Stormont who had participated in the civil rights movement.

After two especially provocative incidents in mid July – the rescue of a wounded Provisional from a hospital in Belfast by IRA men carrying sub-machine guns, and a massive explosion which demolished a new *Daily Mirror* printing plant – it was agreed to introduce internment. Preliminary raids were carried out across the province on 23 July and again a week later in a desperate attempt to improve intelligence before the operation proper. Documents seized did

prove useful, but inevitably this unusual activity by the army and police alerted many IRA men that internment was in the offing. The internment sweep was timed for 10 August, but on 7 August an innocent Catholic, Harry Thornton, was shot by a soldier on the Springfield Road when his van backfired outside an RUC post; the subsequent rioting was so severe that Operation Demetrius, as the internment sweep was called, was brought forward by 24 hours.

At 0415 hours on 9 August 1971 the army moved into Catholic areas throughout Northern Ireland to arrest 450 individuals. Local inhabitants did their best to warn of the army's approach, beating dustbin lids in a ceaseless cacophony. Soon, the army was facing much worse than a barrage of noise; indeed, the Catholic reaction was far worse than any of the authorities had expected. Fighting between Catholic snipers and rioters and the army, and between Catholics and Protestants, caused chaos. Within 48 hours 23 people were dead, whole streets had been burned out, and some 7000 Catholics had taken temporary refuge in camps south of the border.

The Protestant response

On 9 August 342 people were arrested and taken to holding centres where their cases were examined; by mid-December the number had risen to 1576. Of these 642 had been sent on to the internment camp at Long Kesh, the others being released. The small proportion of arrested suspects actually interned shows how poor intelligence was and how random were many of the pick-ups – a fact exploited to the full by the Provisionals, who on a number of occasions actually fed the army with false tip-offs so that they would arrest people known by the local community to be harmless, crippled or in some other way especially liable to excite sympathy. For the first time, armed Provisionals openly patrolled parts of the Catholic enclaves, and the scale of bombings and shootings rose sharply. In October the authorities were forced to begin re-arming the RUC, and Protestant extremists set about organising paramilitary forces to counter the IRA. In December Protestants resorted to bombing, when Loyalist extremists bombed a pub on North Queen Street, Belfast, killing 15 people.

In the wake of internment, a large proportion of the Catholic population refused to pay rent, rates or gas

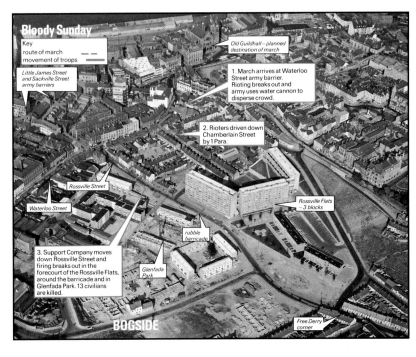

Bloody Sunday

Key
route of march — — —
movement of troops

Little James Street and Sackville Street army barriers

Old Guildhall – planned destination of march

1. March arrives at Waterloo Street army barrier. Rioting breaks out and army uses water cannon to disperse crowd.

2. Rioters driven down Chamberlain Street by 1 Para.

Rossville Street

Waterloo Street

Rossville Flats – 3 blocks

rubble barricade

3. Support Company moves down Rossville Street and firing breaks out in the forecourt of the Rossville Flats, around the barricade and in Glenfada Park. 13 civilians are killed.

Glenfada Park

Free Derry corner

BOGSIDE

and electricity bills in a massive act of civil disobedience. Most Catholics withdrew from participation in local government, and the alliance of forces that had formed the civil rights movement in 1968-69 mobilised against internment. Faced with constant hatred and harassment, the attitude of many British soldiers serving in Northern Ireland had also toughened. The renewal of the tactic of civil rights marches in a surrounding atmosphere of urban terrorism and a toughened army stance led to the tragedy of 'Bloody Sunday' in January 1972.

The prelude to 'Bloody Sunday' came on 22 January when 3000 marchers set out along Magilligan Strand near Londonderry to protest at the new internment camp opened in the district to relieve pressure on Long Kesh. All marches in the province had been banned since August, and the march along the beach was stopped by a barbed-wire barrier manned by men of 1st Battalion, The Parachute Regiment and 2nd Battalion, the Royal Green Jackets. As some demonstrators tried to go round the barrier, the soldiers responded with rubber bullets, CS gas and batons.

Opposite above: The civil rights march in Londonderry which preceded the outbreak of violence on 30 January 1972. The marchers were protesting against internment, and the intention was to march from the Creggan Estate through the Bogside to the Old Guildhall. Below: Men huddle under cover as the shooting starts after the main body of marchers had turned aside from an army roadblock and made for 'Free Derry' corner.

Most Catholic leaders present regarded the army action as excessively fierce; it certainly redoubled the determination of the marchers to carry through another demonstration the following weekend – a civil rights march from the Creggan Estate in Londonderry through the Bogside to the Old Guildhall. The march was to be addressed by veteran socialist Lord Fenner Brockway, as well as by Catholic MPs Bernadette Devlin and Ivan Cooper.

As the 6000 marchers assembled on Sunday, 30 January, trouble was expected, and the world's press had come to Londonderry to witness the protest. Some Protestant extremists had threatened to attack the marchers and the army had decided that the march would not be allowed to reach its objective. The army plan was to divert the march so that it would remain within Catholic areas; furthermore, an 'arrest group' was prepared behind the army barricades, with the mission of snatching as many rioters as possible. The arrest group comprised three units of 1 Para.

Up to a point, events went as predicted. The march set out in a quite relaxed mood, with many young children and women pushing prams in its ranks. Once the leaders of the march had understood that they would not be allowed to follow their planned route to the Old Guildhall, they redirected the demonstration to Free Derry corner. As the main body of the march turned aside from the army barriers, however, some 200 youths attacked the troops with stones and bottles. The army waited until the rioters and the peaceful demonstrators were separated and then set in motion their plan to catch the stone-throwers. At 1610 hours C Company of 1 Para advanced on foot through the barricade in pursuit of the rioters; other units took up positions on the flanks of the rioters, while Support Company drove forward in their Pigs and dismounted behind the missile-throwers to trap them. It was at this point, as the Paras deployed from their vehicles on open ground near the Rossville Flats, that the serious shooting began.

About what followed little can be established with certainty. It is undisputed that within 20 minutes, 13 Catholic civilians had been shot dead or mortally wounded, and 12 others had gunshot wounds. All deaths and injuries were inflicted by the Paras, who fired a total of 107 rounds. The army consistently claimed that soldiers had opened fire in response to fire received, shooting at identified targets, even if it was partially conceded that some soldiers may have

shown inadequate control when firing. To most Catholics on the other hand, the Paras appeared to have committed simple murder, deliberately shooting down unarmed demonstrators. The Widgery Tribunal set up to investigate the events concluded that the soldiers had only fired because they had been fired on, but also stated that 'none of the deceased or wounded is proved to have been shot whilst handling a firearm or bomb.' It is now generally accepted that the Paras did come under fire at some point – to use a riot as an opportunity to shoot at soldiers in the open was a standard IRA tactic – but it is also almost unquestionable that some of the soldiers involved were guilty of, at the very least, a grave lack of discipline.

Indiscriminate bombing

'Bloody Sunday' was a severe shock to Irish Catholics in the North and to the Irish south of the border. On 1 February the British embassy in Dublin was attacked with firebombs. The Official IRA was stimulated into a burst of terrorist activity: on 22 February they exploded a car bomb in the Aldershot barracks of the Parachute Regiment, killing five kitchen staff, a gardener and a chaplain – this was the first IRA bomb attack in England since the 1930s. The Provisionals stepped up their campaign in Northern Ireland, pursuing a declared policy of killing as many British soldiers as possible. Their bombing attacks increased to about four a day, and were ever more indiscriminate. On 4 March a bomb in the Abercorn restaurant in Belfast killed two people and injured 136; on 20 March a bomb in Donegall Street, Belfast, killed six people and injured 147.

The seemingly uncontrollable deterioration of the security situation provoked a political crisis which led the British government to introduce direct rule on 28 March. This was accompanied by a series of measures designed to win back Catholic allegiance. Internment was scaled-down – a tacit admission that the policy had been mistaken – and prosecutions resulting from the winter's illegal civil rights marches were dropped. In an about-face, the army was now asked to keep a low profile in relation to the Catholics, effectively conceding control of parts of Belfast and Londonderry to the Provisionals. But direct rule brought no immediate relief for the overstrained army or harassed civilians. The bombing and shooting went on unabated, and there seemed no end to the Northern Ireland nightmare. **Brian Markworthy**

Above: Paratroopers lead away Catholics during the events of the afternoon of 30 January 1972. The sequence of events after the main march had been diverted from its original route was the crucial issue in later interpretations of the episode. Firing started as the army deployed to cut off a group of rioters, and the paratroopers involved were unequivocal in their assertion that they had been fired upon and were aiming at identified gunmen or bomb throwers. The tribunal set up to investigate the affair was ambivalent in its conclusions, finding that 'none of the deceased or wounded is proved to have been shot while handling a firearm or bomb'.

Key Weapons
MODERN SMGs
part 2

Previous page: A young street fighter in El Salvador is interviewed by a reporter while holding an Uzi sub-machine gun. Although the gun's magazine holds an allocation of up to 40 rounds this Salvadorean has taped-on a second magazine for increased firepower. Left: Beside equipping both regular and insurgent forces the Uzi has proved a highly popular police weapon. Here a US presidential guard prepares to use his Uzi during the assassination attempt against President Reagan on 30 March 1981.

The Czech CZ23 was a most influential sub-machine gun and its hollow bolt design was widely copied. One of the first – and certainly the most famous – copies was the Israeli Uzi. During the 1948 Arab-Israeli War the Israeli Army was poorly provided with sub-machine guns (most of what they had were old British Stens) and Israeli troops felt the lack of them in the close-quarter fighting encountered in the campaign. Shortly after the war had ended Major Uziel Gal set to work to examine existing sub-machine guns and design one for Israeli production. Working swiftly Gal produced a weapon – the Uzi – which entered service in 1951.

The most striking aspect of the Uzi was its small size and compact appearance, compared to most designs which preceded it, this being due to the adoption of the telescoping bolt and the magazine in the pistol grip. The Uzi bolt is square in section and

hollowed out at its front end so that it wraps around the barrel, allowing the barrel to be set well back into the body. Construction is largely of steel pressings and heat-resistant plastics, and the tolerances are sufficiently liberal to allow the gun to go on working in combat conditions where dust and sand are prevalent. A press-in piece at the rear of the pistol grip acts as an effective safety device, only allowing the bolt to move forward if the weapon is being firmly held, so avoiding accidents if the weapon is dropped or allowed to fall on its butt.

Originally, the Uzi had a wooden stock but this was soon replaced by a folding steel one, and in 1960 the gun was further modified by the fitment of a larger bolt-retracting handle and an improved fire-selector catch. The Uzi has been widely admired for its compactness and reliability and it is licence-built in Belgium by FN who market the weapon in Europe, a

Uzi sub-machine gun

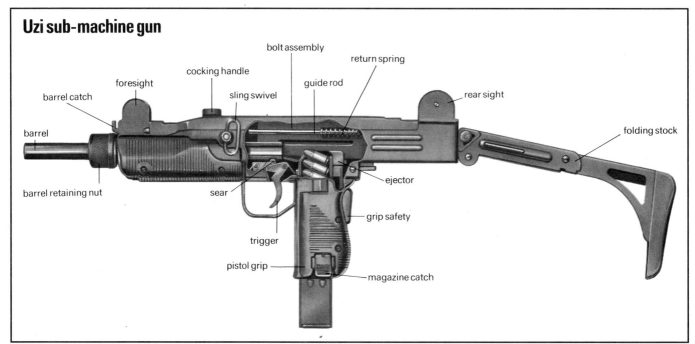

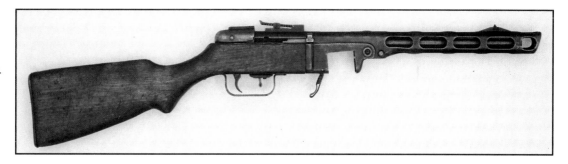

Although the Soviet Union has concentrated on the AK assault rifle, its World War II sub-machine guns are still in use today. Right: The PPSh-41, without magazine. Below right: The Type 50 is the Chinese copy of the PPSh-41 and comes with a 35-round box magazine (above), while the Chinese copy of the PPS-43 is the Type 54 (below).

Italy has been an important manufacturer of sub-machine guns and even its older designs have had a long postwar career, notably the M38/49, depicted (below) with a member of the MPLA in the Angolan capital of Luanda during the independence celebrations of 1975. A newer type is the Model 12 which arms a number of states including Brazil's anti-terrorist police units (below right).

major customer being the West German Army where the Uzi is termed the MP-2. Outside Europe the Uzi has been exported to Iran, Venezuela and Thailand.

In Italy the Beretta Company had been making sub-machine guns since the end of World War I and during the 1930s they developed the Modello 38, a well-made and popular gun that eventually became the standard postwar sub-machine gun of the Italian Army under the designation M38/49. Designed to fire 9mm Parabellum ammunition the M38/49 was fitted with two triggers, the forward one firing single shots and the rear one full automatic fire. There are two sub-variants: the Model 4 fitted with a conventional manual safety catch and the Model 5 with an automatic catch.

During the 1950s Beretta began experimenting with a successor to the M38/49 and subsequently developed the Model 12. The Model 12 is completely built from metal pressings: the pistol grip, magazine

Above and above right: The Czech Skorpion sub-machine gun, with its small 7.65mm ammunition (centre) compared with standard 9mm (top) and a .303in rifle round. Below: The pistol-like Polish PM-63 with forward grip folded back. Below centre: The German MP40 of World War II fame. Bottom: The two modern West German Walther designs, the MP-L (left) and the short-barrelled MP-K (right).

housing, front grip and gun body are welded together to make one solid unit. Inside the body is the telescoped bolt, with about six inches of its length surrounding the barrel. There is a grip safety on the forward edge of the pistol grip which locks the bolt except when it is squeezed in by grasping the grip in the firing position. The Model 12 has been adopted by special units in the Italian Army and by a number of other armies, notably in the Middle East and Africa, and it has been licensed for manufacture in Brazil and Indonesia.

The Soviet Union, perhaps the greatest user of sub-machine guns during World War II, adopted the AK-47 assault rifle after the war as an all-purpose firearm and consequently had only limited interest in sub-machine gun development. Despite the AK-47, the vast number of sub-machine guns produced by the Soviet Union during the war ensured that they remained in use throughout the Warsaw Pact while others were exported to client nations. The most famous Soviet sub-machine gun was the PPSh-41 which was used throughout the war and became something of a symbol of the Red Army. Like many wartime designs the PPSh-41 utilised sheet metal pressing and extensive riveting and simple welding, although a bulky wooden stock gave it an old-fashioned pre-war look. A very reliable weapon, it worked by the standard blowback system and featured a 71-round drum magazine. Some five million PPSh-41 sub-machine guns were manufactured and post-1945 a large number of these were exported to the communists in China. After the communist takeover in 1949 the Chinese began manufacturing the PPSh themselves, calling it the Type 50. Even more rudimentary in construction than the Soviet original, the Type 50 was nevertheless an effective weapon, used extensively in Korea and later by the Viet Minh in Indochina.

Another sub-machine gun of Soviet origin used in Asia was the PPS-43. Developed from the PPS-42 – a weapon brought into being during the siege of Leningrad – it was an even simpler sub-machine gun than the PPSh-41, constructed entirely from metal except for the plastic pistol grip. The metal shoulder stock could be folded over along the top of the receiver, making the PPS-43 a relatively compact weapon. Large numbers were sent to China after 1949, and in 1953 the Chinese instigated a mass-production programme for this weapon. Designated the Type 43 it has been widely used by China and her allies, including the North Vietnamese during the war against the Americans.

Apart from the Soviet Union the other important arms manufacturer in the Warsaw Pact is Czechoslovakia, which has developed a number of interesting sub-machine gun designs. After the famous CZ23 series, the major design has been the Vz61 Skorpion. The Skorpion operates on the usual blowback system utilising a solid bolt, but despite its conventional

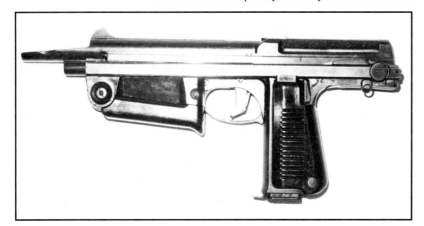

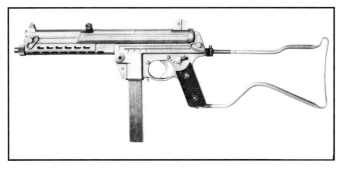

operation it is a highly unusual weapon. Instead of the 9mm or even the Soviet 7.62mm round the Skorpion was chambered for the 7.65mm automatic pistol cartridge, which is not generally considered a combat round and had never before been used in sub-machine guns. This led to a reduction in size, so that the Skorpion, with its wire butt folded, was no more than 27cm (10.6 inches) long. It is so small that it can be comfortably fired in one hand, like a pistol, if necessary. Indeed, the object behind it was to provide tank crews with a weapon they could wear in a holster and carry on their person but which had automatic fire power that could be used in the event of having to bail out from a wrecked tank in battle.

In theory the lightweight Skorpion – with a light bolt – would have had a very high rate of fire, but the designer foresaw this and fitted a very ingenious 'rate reducer'. Inside the pistol grip is a tube containing a weight and a spring. As the bolt recoils it strikes the weight and drives it down the tube, against the spring. The bolt is then held at the rear of the body, while the weight travels down and is thrown back by the spring; when it reappears at the top of the tube it trips a release and the bolt goes forward to fire the next shot. The delay thus induced is a mere fraction of a second, but it is sufficient to bring the rate of fire down to an acceptable 600 rounds per minute.

The Skorpion has since been made in larger sizes to take the 9mm short and 9mm Parabellum cartridges, but these are rarely seen. The original 7.65mm model is, however, a popular weapon with terrorists due to its small size making it easy to conceal.

Another small weapon, which, like the Skorpion is frequently classed as a 'machine pistol' rather than a sub-machine gun, is the Polish PM-63. Its design is really that of a large automatic pistol since it uses a moving slide instead of an internal bolt. The gun consists of a frame with pistol grip, into which goes a magazine and a fixed barrel. The slide surrounds the barrel, extends forward under the muzzle to act as a primitive compensator to stop the muzzle rising when firing automatic, and forms the breech block at the rear.

Once the weapon is cocked, the slide remains in the rear position, and it is released by pressing the trigger. It then runs forward, propelled by a spring, rams a cartridge into the breech and fires it. There is no form of breech lock and the slide is simply blown back, ejecting the empty case, compressing the return spring so as to be ready to reload and fire again. Left in this manner one would expect a high rate of fire, as with the Skorpion, but once again a rate reducer is utilised. The PM-63 is chambered for the Soviet 9mm Makarov cartridge, rather more powerful than the 7.65mm of the Skorpion but much less effective than the 9mm Parabellum.

The German MP40 sub-machine gun was a highly influential weapon; its use in the early campaigns of World War II demonstrated to the world the advantages of the sub-machine gun and led to a rush of attempts to develop easy-to-manufacture sub-machine guns, including the British Sten and the US M3. The MP40 was a development from the MP38 and the MP38/40, and its folding metal stock and the extensive use made of metal pressings set the precedent for future designs.

Since World War II the German arms manufacturers, Walther and Heckler and Koch have both produced their own sub-machine guns. The Walther

Heckler and Koch have brought out a wide range of sub-machine guns, all based around the MP5. Above: The original MP5 (here an export model) was initially designated the HK54 and was derived from the G3 rifle. Right: The MP5A1 is fitted with a sliding metal stock.

Above: The MP5A2 is distinguished from the standard MP5 by a new forward hand grip, a rotating rear sight and a modified front sight. Right: The MP5A3 is identical to the MP5A2 except that it is fitted with a sliding metal stock.

Above: The MP5 SD is a specially silenced model which can be fitted with the standard stock, with a sliding metal stock or with none at all. Right: The most unusual weapon in the MP5 range is the MP5K, used by anti-terrorist squads, which features a forward-mounted hand grip.

Above: The Ingram Model 10 (top) and Model 11 sub-machine guns have been privately designed as lightweight, easy to conceal weapons suitable for counter-terrorist operations. Apart from the barrel the whole weapon is made from metal pressings; even the bolt is manufactured from sheet metal and then filled with lead. Both models can be fitted with the sound suppressors illustrated.

MP-L/MP-K has a rather unusual shape since the barrel is below the tubular gun body. This is because the body serves to contain a large cylindrical section of the bolt, below which is a small appendage which actually loads and fires the cartridge. This allows much of the mass of the bolt to overhang the barrel at the moment of firing, a variation of the overhung bolt technique. The Walther is produced in two versions, the standard MP-L and the short-barrelled MP-K, and like most modern sub-machine guns has a folding stock. The Walther is widely used by European police forces and by some smaller armies.

The Heckler and Koch MP5 is unusual in that it is a delayed-blowback gun firing from a locked breech. The bolt is similar in some respects to the Walther design, with a large mass projecting over the barrel for compactness, but it is locked by two rollers engaging in recesses in the body, and these must be withdrawn from the recesses before the breech block can move backwards. The delay is extremely short, but this arrangement makes this weapon much more accurate than the vast majority of sub-machine guns.

A number of MP5 variants have been produced: the MP5A2 with a fixed stock; the MP5A3 with sliding metal stock; the MP5 SD silenced-version; the MP5K, a specially-developed counter-insurgency model which dispenses with a stock and has a shortened barrel with a second handgrip mounted forward of the magazine. The MP5 is favoured by, among others, the British SAS, and it is in military service with the West German, Swiss and Dutch armies as well as many police and security forces.

In spite of the success of the Thompson and M3 sub-machine guns, the United States military has shown little interest in the sub-machine gun since 1945. The only design to make much impact in America has been a private venture, promoted by designer Gordon Ingram. Following military service during World War II he returned to civil life intent upon making a sub-machine gun for police and military use. After several designs he developed the Model 10 which consisted of a square body made of steel pressings, an overhung bolt and a magazine in the pistol grip. The Model 10 featured a telescoping wire butt and when folded the gun was no more than 27cm (10.6in) long. The gun has a provision for a screwed bush around the barrel to allow a sound suppressor to be fitted. Ingram developed his gun in various calibres – the Model 10 which takes .45in and 9mm Parabellum ammunition, the Model 11 taking .38in – and it has been sold around the world, frequently being used by paramilitary and anti-terrorist units.

Ever since the end of World War II it has been predicted that the sub-machine gun will lose its military application, to be completely replaced by the assault rifle. This seems unlikely, but even if the military do abandon the sub-machine gun it still has a long career ahead of it as a weapon of guerrilla and counter-insurgency forces.

Sub-machine guns

Type	Country	Calibre	Weight	Cyclic rate of fire	Muzzle velocity	Magazine
Uzi	Israel	9mm	4.1kg (8.9lb) (loaded, 25 rounds)	600rpm	400mps (1312fps)	25/32/40-round box
M38/49	Italy	9mm	4.6kg (10.2lb) (loaded, 20 rounds)	500rpm	381mps (1250fps)	20/40-round box
Model 12	Italy	9mm	3kg (6.6lb) (empty)	550rpm	381mps (1250fps)	20/30/40-round box
PPSh-41	Soviet Union	7.62mm	5.3kg (11.7lb) (loaded, drum magazine)	900rpm	490mps (1600fps)	35-round box 71-round drum
PPS-43	Soviet Union	7.62mm	3.62kg (8lb) (loaded)	700rpm	490mps (1600fps)	35-round box
Vz-61	Czechoslovakia	7.65mm	1.55kg (3.4lb) (loaded, 20 rounds)	750rpm	294mps (970fps)	10/20-round box
PM-63	Poland	9mm	1.8kg (4lb) (loaded, 25 rounds)	600rpm	320mps 1050fps)	15/25/40-round box
MP-K	West Germany	9mm	3.43kg (6.6lb) (loaded)	550rpm	356mps (1168fps)	32-round box
MP5A3	West Germany	9mm	3.41kg (7.6lb) (loaded)	800rpm	400mps (1312fps)	15/30-round box
MP40	Germany	9mm	4.7kg (10.4lb) (loaded)	500rpm	381mps (1250fps)	32-round box
Ingram Model 10	USA	.45in	3.82kg (8.4lb) (loaded)	1100rpm	280mps (920fps)	30-round box

Born in battle
How Bangladesh gained independence

The state of Pakistan that came into being after the partition of the Indian sub-continent at independence in 1947 was divided into two parts that were separated by over 1600km (1000 miles) of Indian territory. The common link between East and West Pakistan was Islam, the religion of the majority of the people. But in every other way East and West Pakistan were quite different from each other – in language, race, culture and economic structure.

Political power was concentrated in the West; it was the site of the capital and its people had a near monopoly of appointments in the higher levels of the civil service and armed forces. But the majority of Pakistan's population was in the East – some 75 million out of the 140 million total in 1970 – crowded into the delta formed by the Brahmaputra, Ganga and Meghna Rivers. The East also produced much of Pakistan's wealth, accounting for 75 per cent of the country's foreign earnings with its agricultural exports like jute and tea. In return, it received less than 30 per cent of Pakistan's total imports and investment. The rulers of Pakistan in the West milked the East like a colony, and over the years this discrimination became intolerable.

During the presidency of Field Marshal Ayub Khan from 1958 to 1969, Sheikh Mujibur Rahman emerged as the leading political figure in East Pakistan at the head of the Awami League organisation. His advocacy of a federal structure for Pakistan, in which the two halves of the country would have had a large measure of autonomy under a weakened central government, led to his imprisonment by the military regime in 1968. But mounting discontent in the West as well as the East led to the fall of Ayub Khan's regime in March 1969; his successor, General Yahya Khan (the commander-in-chief of the army), promised free elections and released Sheikh Mujib, but secretly hoped to maintain the military in control.

The elections of 17 December 1970 were a disaster for the military regime. Sheikh Mujib's Awami League virtually swept the board in East Pakistan, as did Zulfiqur Ali Bhutto's Pakistan People's Party in the West. Because of the way seats were distributed in the national parliament, this result meant that Sheikh Mujib had a decisive majority in Pakistan as a whole. Encouraged by Bhutto, General Yahya Khan temporised in an attempt to induce Sheikh Mujib to moderate his proposals for autonomy, and finally on 1 March 1971 announced the indefinite postponement of the opening of parliament. The following day Sheikh Mujib called a general strike, and East Pakistan was in a virtual state of insurrection against the government in the West.

Having reinforced his garrison in East Pakistan with three extra divisions from the West, on 25 March Yahya Khan ordered Lieutenant-General Tikka Khan, the martial law administrator in the East (all of Pakistan was under martial law), to clamp down on the Awami League and its numerous supporters and sympathisers. Within days Sheikh Mujib and other

Despite his imprisonment in 1968 for advocating a federal structure for the two states of Pakistan, Sheikh Mujibur Rahman (above, flanked by bodyguards) was released in early 1969 after the fall of Ayub Khan's regime. His political party, the Awami League, quickly gained a strong following and swept the board in the elections of December 1970. This success was unacceptable to the military government of General Yahya Khan, and the opening of parliament was postponed. In response, Sheikh Mujib proclaimed a general strike, and within days the crisis that led to the creation of Bangladesh was under way.

Awami League leaders had been arrested, while most of the East Bengal Regiment – a part of the Pakistani Army – and the paramilitary East Pakistan Rifles had been shipped to internment in the West. Within a month armed resistance was largely overcome.

It is conceivable that the situation might have been stabilised had it not been for the brutal policy pursued by the army under Tikka Khan. The aim was to intimidate the population into submission, with especial attention paid to groups considered rife with disaffection – notably the educated elite and the Hindu minority. Hindus made up over 10 per cent of East Pakistan's population, sharing a common language and culture with the Muslim Bengalis despite the religious difference; they were soon fleeing to neighbouring India in their millions. But no section of the population was completely spared in a campaign of rape and murder whose victims may have numbered hundreds of thousands. As popular resistance to the army grew into guerrilla warfare in the summer of 1971, the reign of terror intensified, and the number of refugees who had fled to India swelled to a total of over 10 million.

The remaining Awami League leaders had declared the independence of East Pakistan as the state of Bangladesh as soon as the army crackdown began, and they set up a government-in-exile in India, but at first there was little they could do to make their declaration a reality. The crucial factor in the situation was the attitude of the Indian government under its prime minister, Indira Gandhi. Initially, India was cautious in its response, although sympathetic towards the Awami League, but the massive growth of the refugee population posed a problem which could not be ignored. By the summer of 1971 opinion in the Indian government had swung towards backing for an independent Bangladesh, which the Indian leaders were also aware would deal a crippling blow to their traditional enemy, Pakistan. Still, the Indians did not wish to commit their armed forces, and instead settled for supporting the Bangladesh army-in-exile, the Mukti Bahini, while preparing contingency plans for an invasion of East Pakistan.

Yahya Khan knew that a defence of East Pakistan against India was impossible, but he counted on diplomatic manoeuvring backed up by the threat of military action in the West to prevent an Indian attack. Pakistan expected diplomatic support from China and

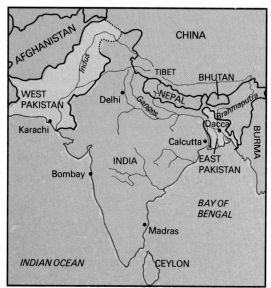

While Zulfiqur Ali Bhutto took over from General Yahya Khan (above) as Pakistan's new president after the abortive military campaign, Bangladesh celebrated independence and the return of its leader Sheikh Mujib (left).

The birth of the new state of Bangladesh was accompanied by the most horrible atrocities. The Pakistani Army had embarked on an orgy of killing during the period from March 1971, killing hundreds of thousands in a systematic reign of terror (below, victims of some of the last of these massacres), but in its turn, the Awami League exacted vengeance after the Indian victory in December. Left: Biharis accused of collaborating with Yahya Khan's regime plead for their lives shortly before being bayonetted to death.

cooperation with India. From that point onwards, the Russians gave India full diplomatic support, guaranteeing that Pakistan would not be able to use the United Nations to stop any armed intervention by India – such efforts would be blocked by the Soviet veto in the Security Council.

By November 1971 India and Pakistan were clearly on the brink of war. Indian support for attacks across the border by the Mukti Bahini had developed into tank and air battles between Indian and Pakistani forces. In the end it was Yahya Khan who decided to precipitate events, launching a pre-emptive air strike in the West on 3 December which was the signal for open war. The strategies of India and Pakistan were a mirror image of one another: Pakistan sought to carry out a successful offensive in the West while winning time with a holding action in the East; India set out to contain the Pakistani offensive in the West and to achieve rapid success in the East before the imposition of a diplomatic solution by outside powers.

Surrender in the East

Within a week it was clear that the Pakistani gamble had failed. In the West the Pakistani offensive had petered out, and in the East the Indian advance was swift against demoralised troops, outnumbered and surrounded by a hostile population. The Pakistanis appear to have lacked confidence in their own strategy, failing to commit the better part of their airforce and armoured formations to the Western battlefield. As military defeat loomed, Pakistan desperately sought a diplomatic initiative to block an Indian victory. Since the Soviet Union prevented effective UN intervention, the United States attempted to intimidate India by sending a naval task force from the Seventh Fleet, including the aircraft carrier USS *Enterprise*, to the Bay of Bengal, but the force sailed away again without taking any action. On 16 December the Pakistani Army in the East was forced to surrender, and the following day Yahya Khan reluctantly accepted a ceasefire in the West.

In 14 days, India had achieved a fundamental change in the balance of power in South Asia. Indian armed forces had routed the Pakistanis, long considered superior fighting men, and dismembered the Pakistani state. The new state of Bangladesh was quickly declared and in January 1972 Sheikh Mujib returned from imprisonment to become its first leader. In Pakistan, Yahya Khan was deposed and arrested, his place being taken by the Pakistan People's Party leader, Bhutto.

If these immediate consequences of the war were predictable enough, the longer-term outcome was perhaps less so. Under President Bhutto, relations between Pakistan and India improved considerably, damping down the smouldering hostility which had lasted ever since independence. In the East, relations between Bangladesh and India went through a total reversal. Sheikh Mujib and the Awami League were very closely associated with India, and under their rule the new state seemed almost subject to Indian control. But the immense economic problems which plagued Bangladesh proved well beyond the regime's ability to cope, and in August 1975 Sheikh Mujib and his family were killed in a military coup. Subsequent Bangladeshi governments have been hostile to India, establishing close links with China and even, up to a point, with the former enemy of the independence struggle, Pakistan. **R.G. Grant**

the United States, whereas India had links with the Soviet Union, but none of the great powers wanted a war to break out in the sub-continent. The United States had stopped major arms supplies to Pakistan at the end of the 1965 Indo-Pakistan War, although Pakistan still enjoyed the backing of the US administration. China expressed support for Pakistan, but had no wish to get involved. Initially the Soviet Union also encouraged India to follow a policy of restraint, since it was in the process of improving relations with Pakistan, but in the summer of 1971 events unconnected with India and Pakistan transformed the scene.

In July 1971 President Richard Nixon's national security advisor, Henry Kissinger, visited Peking; this was a development viewed from Moscow with the deepest disquiet. The Soviet leaders were anxious to find a support for their own position in Asia against a perceived joint US-Chinese threat, and in August they negotiated a treaty of peace, friendship and

Holding the line

Pakistan repulsed in the West

As early as September 1971 Pakistan's President Yahya Khan had accepted that only a military offensive in the West might hold India's hand in the East. Yet the political crisis in the East had had a profound effect on the readiness of the armed forces in the West. Three divisions had been despatched to the East and although the Pakistani II Corps had been hastily activated to form a strategic reserve, its infantry were still in the process of receiving Chinese equipment and were only half-trained. Even though in the winter snow blocked the Himalayan passes, limiting the possibility of a Chinese intervention, by December, the pressure from within President Yahya's own circle for military action had become irresistible.

A well-coordinated attack on a crucial sector might have succeeded, but instead Pakistan decided to launch a series of separate assaults which largely followed the pattern of the 1965 war. On the other side, India's military leaders adopted a defensive policy of containing attacks, improving positions, and trying to remove threatening Pakistani salients.

On the evening of 3 December the Pakistan Air Force struck against Indian airbases; on the same night the Pakistani Army launched a ground offensive in Kashmir and the Punjab, which were defended by India's Western Command under Lieutenant-General K.P. Candeth. In Kashmir Pakistani forces simultaneously moved against Punch and Chhamb. An infantry brigade of the 112th Azad Kashmir Division advanced on Punch from Kahuta while commando groups infiltrated behind Indian lines, but the Indian XV Corps withstood the assault. A second drive against Punch was launched on 9 December, but Indian air superiority meant that An-12 transport aircraft and Vampires were able to bomb the Pakistani forces with impunity, and by 11 December the Indian Western Command had seized the initiative, embarking on a series of raids to take enemy observation posts in the mountains.

The major Pakistani assault came further south, however, in front of Chhamb. Two infantry brigades of the 23rd Azad Kashmir Division and a tank regiment, supported by artillery and aerial bombardment, struck into the exposed Indian salient west of the Munawar Tawi River on 3 December. It took six days to capture Chhamb, and although the Pakistanis then established a bridgehead west of the river, they were driven back to the east bank by a division of Lieutenant-General Sartaj Singh's XV Corps after three days' fierce fighting. By this time Pakistan had committed a force of division strength, but suffered heavy losses: Indian estimates give Pakistani losses on the Chhamb front as 36 tanks and 1350 men, as against their own loss of 17 tanks and 440 men. To the south of Chhamb, the Indians had seized the Akhnur Dagger in a night attack on 6 December; it was strategically important since it lay dangerously close to a major road into Kashmir running through Akhnur.

Indeed, night attacks proved a key feature of Indian operations in the West. Western Command's biggest

offensive operation, a pincer movement by elements of five divisions of General K. K. Singh's I Corps on the Shakargarh salient began at night. But the defenders, a brigade of General Tikka Khan's I Corps, occupied well-prepared positions and fought tenaciously, supported by elements of all four of the corps' divisions. On 15 December an armoured brigade of Indian Centurions launched an attack but was matched by two regiments of Pattons from Pakistan's 6th Armoured Division, so that by the time of the ceasefire on 17 December the defenders still held most of the salient west of the railway line.

Around the Amritsar salient the three divisions of the Indian XI Corps under General W.C. Rawlley had little difficulty in containing attacks by the two divisions of Pakistan's IV Corps. The Indian bridgehead over the Sutlej River near Firozpur was driven in on the first night of the war but in two night attacks beginning on 5 December the Indians first took the Sehjra salient, to eliminate a potential threat to Khem Karan, and then drove the Pakistanis from their bridgehead over the Ravi at the Dera Baba Nanak bridge, each attack delivered from an unexpected direction to take the defenders by surprise.

Duelling in the south

In the extreme south the Pakistani 18th Infantry Division fought an unequal dual with India's Southern Command which had two divisions and enjoyed total air superiority. On the Rajasthan front, a strong Pakistani force comprising an infantry brigade, a regiment of Type 59s and a squadron of Shermans advanced across the desert, entering India near Longewala on 5 December, but once the force had been detected it was exposed to air attacks. Caught in the desert without air cover, the Pakistanis lost an estimated 37 tanks before they withdrew.

The Indian counter-attack was far more successful. A brigade of the 11th Infantry Division took Islamgarh while the division's 85th Brigade advanced down the disused Barmer-Hyderabad railway until held by Pakistan's 55th Brigade outside Naya Chor. The soft desert sand around Naya Chor restricted the movement of Indian forces and they never succeeded in dislodging the Pakistanis. Further south, however, in the Rann of Kutch, Indian Border Security Forces, reinforced by a battalion each of infantry and commandos, made substantial advances. The ground gained, although politically valuable, was militarily worthless, but the advances did force the Pakistanis to commit part of their strategic reserve by despatching their 33rd Division to cover Hyderabad.

A striking feature of the 1971 war was the naval conflict which began on 3 December with the sinking of the Pakistani submarine *Ghazi* off India's main naval base of Vizakhapatnam. In the absence of the carrier *Vikrant*, stationed in the Bay of Bengal, Vice-Admiral S.N. Kohli, India's Western naval commander, used his newly-acquired force of eight Soviet-made Osa-class missile boats to launch two

The Indian Army of 1971 was still dependent upon Britain for much of its weaponry. The Vijayanta tank (right, in action) was a special design by Vickers, while the 25-pounder (below) was a standard artillery piece. The Pakistani Army (bottom, Pakistani troops man an anti-aircraft gun) also reflected a British influence – particularly in their helmets and personal equipment.

devastating attacks on Karachi, on 4 and 8 December. Using Styx surface-to-surface missiles, his force sank the destroyer *Khaibar*, the minesweeper *Muhafiz* and two merchant ships, damaged another minesweeper and half a dozen other ships, and struck Karachi's oil storage facilities. One of the Daphne-class Pakistani submarines had revenge for the second raid, however, by sinking an Indian frigate. Nevertheless, on the sea as in the air, the Indians were never seriously challenged during the war.

When the ceasefire came on 17 December, the Indians had clearly established their superiority in the West, improving their strategic position by small gains and holding the Pakistani offensive. Although the decisive action of the war took place in the East, the Western campaign resulted in heavier combat casualties and losses of equipment: the majority of the 8000 Pakistani troops killed were in the West, as were about half the 3283 Indian dead, and most of Pakistan's 220 and India's 73 tank losses. Without the overwhelming strategic advantage it had enjoyed in the East, India had still proved its military superiority over Pakistan.   **E.R. Hooton**

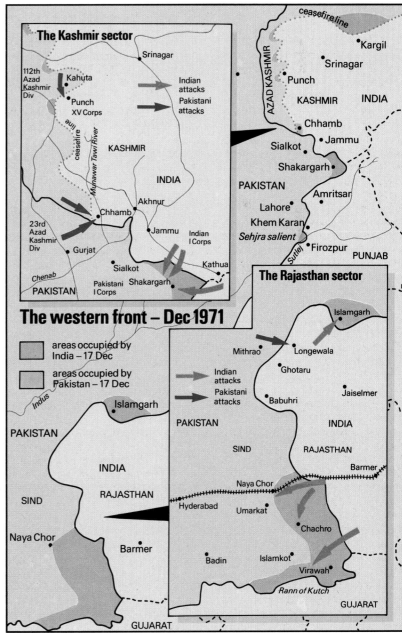

The Kashmir sector

Srinagar

112th Azad Kashmir Div

Kahuta

Punch XV Corps

Indian attacks

Pakistani attacks

Munawar Tawi River

ceasefire line

KASHMIR

INDIA

Akhnur

Chhamb

23rd Azad Kashmir Div

Gurjat

Jammu

Indian I Corps

Chenab

Sialkot

Kathua

PAKISTAN

Pakistani I Corps

Shakargarh

ceasefire line

Kargil

Srinagar

AZAD KASHMIR

Punch

KASHMIR

INDIA

Chhamb

Sialkot

Jammu

Shakargarh

PAKISTAN

Lahore

Amritsar

Khem Karan

Sehjra salient

Sutlej

Firozpur

PUNJAB

The western front – Dec 1971

areas occupied by India – 17 Dec

areas occupied by Pakistan – 17 Dec

Indus

Islamgarh

PAKISTAN

SIND

INDIA

RAJASTHAN

Naya Chor

Barmer

The Rajasthan sector

Islamgarh

Mithrao

Longewala

Ghotaru

Indian attacks

Pakistani attacks

Babuhri

Jaiselmer

PAKISTAN

SIND

INDIA

RAJASTHAN

Barmer

Naya Chor

Hyderabad

Umarkat

Chachro

Badin

Islamkot

Virawah

Rann of Kutch

GUJARAT

GUJARAT

Air superiority
The IAF rules the skies

Below: A Chinese-built Pakistani F-6 (a copy of the Soviet MiG 19) lands after a mission over the battle zone. The PAF received a sufficient number of these aircraft from China in the late 1960s to equip three squadrons.

Although the air battles of the 14-day war between India and Pakistan in December 1971 were in no sense decisive, the opposing air forces were heavily engaged throughout the conflict in support of the ground forces. The variety of the aircraft involved in the fighting was astonishing, with warplanes from the Soviet Union, China, the United States, Britain and France represented in the two air forces. From the outset the advantage lay with the larger and better-equipped Indian Air Force (IAF), which was the second strongest air arm in Asia after that of China. Its 45 frontline squadrons outnumbered those of the Pakistan Air Force (PAF) by three to one.

The most modern IAF aircraft were either Soviet-supplied or locally-manufactured. They included the agile Mach 2 MiG-21 air superiority fighter, the Sukhoi Su-7BM fighter-bomber and the In-dian-designed HAL HF-24 Marut attack aircraft. The British-designed Gnat lightweight fighter equipped eight squadrons, but had been superseded by the MiG-21 as the IAF's standard air superiority fighter. British Hunters and Canberras were used in the ground attack and interdiction roles. As well as strengthening and modernising its aircraft inventory in the aftermath of the 1965 war with Pakistan, the IAF had also improved the standards of its aircrew training. Pakistan's pressing need after 1965 was for modern combat aircraft, because its traditional source of supply, the United States, had been cut off. As a member of the Cento and Seato pacts, Pakistan had received F-86 Sabre air-superiority fighters, a single squadron of F-104A Starfighter interceptors and two squadrons of B-57B interdiction-bombers before American supplies ceased. In the late 1960s Pakistan added to these two squadrons of French Mach 2 Mirage III interceptors and sufficient Chinese-built Shenyang F-6s (MiG 19s) to equip three squadrons.

Before major hostilities began, a number of small-scale aerial skirmishes were fought over both the Western and Eastern fronts. On 22 November PAF Sabres from East Pakistan clashed with IAF Gnats and two Sabres were shot down. The war proper opened on 3 December with an attempt by the PAF to execute pre-emptive air strikes against Indian airfields in the West. The attacks began at dusk on a Friday – the Muslim sabbath – in a bid to catch the IAF at its least ready, but they failed to achieve any real success. The IAF, anticipating a possible attempt by

the PAF to imitate Israel's tactics in the 1967 Six-Day War, had dispersed many of its aircraft to auxiliary airfields and the defences of the permanent bases were well prepared, with the aircraft housed in concrete shelters. The rapid fall of night after the first PAF strike made it difficult for them to sustain their initial effort, even though there was a full moon. Only some 30 per cent of the PAF's air strength was committed to the attack – a half-heartedness that was to characterise the entire Pakistani aerial campaign. IAF Gnats mounted combat air patrols over the main airfields and once even proved capable of intercepting the PAF's Mirage IIIs. Hunter and Su-7BM fighter-bombers retaliated with attacks against Pakistani air bases and troop concentrations; the IAF mounted over 500 sorties during the first 24 hours of the war.

The White Tigers

The Indian strategy was to mount a defensive holding operation in the West, while East Pakistan was overrun by the Indian Army. The IAF flew some 4000 combat sorties in the West and half this number against East Pakistan where air opposition was considerably lighter. Indeed, the entire air defence force of East Pakistan comprised a single squadron of the PAF, No 14 Squadron equipped with elderly F-86 Sabres. This unit could do little in the face of overwhelming Indian air superiority and by the fifth day of the fighting air opposition had virtually ceased. Thereafter the IAF carried out close air support sorties for its advancing ground forces and ceaselessly harried the retreating Pakistani Army. On 9 December alone over 200 sorties were flown by the IAF over East Pakistan. Indian air superiority was also exploited to carry out airborne and heliborne raiding operations behind enemy lines.

Indian naval aviation also played its part in the offensive in the East. The Indian Navy's only aircraft carrier, the INS *Vikrant* (the modernised light fleet carrier HMS *Hercules*) operated off East Pakistan in the Bay of Bengal. Her main striking force comprised the 18 Hawker Sea Hawk fighter-bombers of No 300 Squadron ('The White Tigers') and four Breguet Alizé turboprop anti-submarine warfare aircraft. The Sea Hawks carried out bomb and rocket attacks on airfields and shipping targets at Cox's Bazaar and Chittagong, while the Alizés' main role was the night-time mining of shipping channels and harbours.

In the West the emphasis was on interdiction missions, which were aimed at destroying PAF aircraft on their airfields, disrupting communications to delay troop movements, destroying stocks of fuel and ammunition and preventing the concentration of Pakistani ground forces. The IAF Hunters, Su-7s and B-57Bs were heavily committed to these attacks. On 13 December, for example, interdiction targets included a petrochemical complex at Khairpur, ammunition trains, troop concentrations and a radar site. Many of the IAF's air strike missions were directed by a Tu-126 airborne warning and control system (AWACS) aircraft on loan from the Soviet Union. Operating at 6000m (20,000 feet) well inside Indian territory, the Tu-126's radar could track night interdiction sorties for 160km (100 miles) into West Pakistan. The Tu-126 not only assisted in the strike aircrafts' navigation, but also warned them of the reactions of PAF interceptors. As well as the regular interdiction and attack aircraft, the IAF employed converted An-12 transports as *ad hoc* night bombers, dropping explosive loads attached to cargo pallets. By day the Su-7 was the most active Indian fighter-bomber and these aircraft flew some 1500 sorties.

The PAF concentrated on the counter-air missions, carrying out numerous strikes on Indian airfields and intercepting IAF attack aircraft on many occasions. Close air support sorties were flown by F-86 Sabres and F-6s towards the end of the war, but the struggle to master the numerically superior IAF absorbed most of the PAF's effort. The IAF's fast and agile MiG-21s generally proved far superior to the older PAF fighters, including the F-104A Starfighter. However, the PAF's precious Mirage IIIs were carefully husbanded and never met the MiG-21 in combat. The IAF claimed the destruction of 94 PAF aircraft, including six Mirages and nine Starfighters, for the loss of 54 of their own warplanes. The PAF admit to the loss of only 26 aircraft (none of them Mirages and only two Starfighters) for the destruction of 104 IAF aircraft. Whatever the truth of these claims, it is clear that even if the IAF sustained the heavier losses, it retained the initiative in the air throughout the 14-day war and forced the much smaller PAF to fight a largely ineffective campaign. **Anthony Robinson**

Below: A Hawker Sea Hawk takes off from the deck of INS *Vikrant* for a raid on Chittagong. The *Vikrant* was a modernised British light fleet carrier (originally HMS *Hercules*) and gave added punch to Indian air operations over East Pakistan. The PAF proved incapable of matching the IAF in the East – the Pakistanis deployed only one squadron of F-86 Sabres as their air defence force in this sector.

The lightning campaign
India's victory in the East

Despite the lengthy build-up to the crisis in East Pakistan, the Awami League had made no preparations for armed resistance against the forces of West Pakistan, so only the regular formations of the East Bengal Regiment (EBR) and the paramilitary East Pakistan Rifles (EPR), aided by sections of the police, were able to put up serious opposition after the 25 March 1971 clampdown. They were no match, however, for Pakistan's standing garrison of one and a half divisions, augmented by three divisions from the West. Those elements of the EBR and EPR which escaped the initial Pakistani strike against them suffered severe casualties in a number of conventional clashes before being forced to retreat across the Indian border; by mid-April all of East Pakistan, except some tiny border enclaves, was under West Pakistani control.

Unwilling to commit its own forces to an attack on East Pakistan, the Indian government decided to help the provisional government of Bangladesh arm and train a military force to retake the territory. A retired officer, Colonel M.A.G. Osmani, was made com-

mander-in-chief of the force, originally called the Mukti Fauj, but later renamed the Mukti Bahini. The EBR and EPR became the nucleus of a regular army, the Nyomito Bahini, while most of the refugees who flocked to join the force were given basic training as guerrilla freedom fighters, the Gono Bahini. Groups of guerrillas also sprang up inside East Pakistan; many of them were linked to the Mukti Bahini organisation, although others remained independent, often being politically to the left of the Awami League.

It was during the monsoon period from June to September that guerrilla activity, both by units infiltrated from India and by local groups, began to have an impact. Communications in East Pakistan were extremely vulnerable to commando-style raids, since the destruction of a relatively small number of bridges or other crucial points left no alternative routes for conventional armed forces to follow. Guerrillas moved freely across the monsoon flood waters in light craft while the Pakistani forces could barely venture outside the main towns. Attacks on railways, power

Above: An Indian T55 moves along the Jessore Road. Below: The Pakistani Army Commander in the East, Lieutenant-General A.A.K. Niazi. Right top: Pakistani troops set up a mortar emplacement and dig in.

plants and shipping – vessels were sunk in Chittagong harbour using limpet mines – disrupted the export of the tea and jute crop, a vital source of income for the Pakistani government.

The end of the monsoon and the subsidence of the water level in October presented the Pakistanis with an opportunity to initiate a counter-insurgency campaign, but it also offered the Mukti Bahini a chance to initiate conventional attacks across the border. Lieutenant-General A.A.K. Niazi, who replaced Lieutenant-General Tikka Khan as commander in East Pakistan on 3 September, stationed most of his army in forward positions to counter this external threat – the Pakistanis were especially concerned to prevent the Mukti Bahini seizing a substantial border area and declaring it a 'liberated zone'. The paramilitary Razakars, recruited from the Bihari minority which was hostile to the idea of an independent Bangladesh, were left to carry out counter-insurgency operations in the interior, a task they performed with extreme brutality.

Activity on the border soon drew the Indian and Pakistani Armies into direct conflict, which escalated from artillery exchanges in October to major clashes involving tanks and aircraft in late November. At Boyra on 21 November there was a tank battle in which some 13 Pakistani Chaffee light tanks were lost; at the same time, an air battle saw two Pakistani Sabres shot down. By the end of the month the Mukti Bahini had seized an area near Jessore, with the support of Indian artillery. The Indian Army was still restricted to operating in the immediate border area, but the Pakistani attack in the West on 3 December freed them from restraint.

The Indians prepare

Planning for an Indian offensive in the East had begun in May; the Indian Army chief of staff, General S.H.F.J. Manekshaw, decided on a set-piece battle to be conducted by Eastern Command under Lieutenant-General J.S. Aurora. There was never the slightest doubt that, given time, India could take East Pakistan, but the nature of the terrain posed formidable problems. Many of the rivers that veined the delta were unbridged, and the water table was so high that even in the dry season vehicle movement was restricted, with most of the major roads and railways built on banks. Inevitably any attacks would run the risk of being forced into narrow channels and even limited fortifications would be capable of inflicting unacceptable losses. Fortunately for India, the terrain also hamstrung the defenders who were split into four unsupported sectors by the major rivers, the Ganga (Padma), Jamuna (Brahmaputra) and Meghna, offering the opportunity to defeat the enemy piecemeal if the attacks were made quickly and with sufficient weight.

Aurora assigned two divisions (4th Mountain and 9th Infantry) with 50th Parachute and 3rd Armoured Brigades to strike from the Calcutta area at the Pakistani garrisons west of Dacca around Jessore and Jhenida; II Corps was created to control these forces in October. XXXIII Corps was positioned north of II Corps with 20th Mountain Division, 71st Mountain Brigade, two armoured regiments and an engineer brigade; its task was to destroy the garrison northwest of Dacca around Bogra. IV Corps under Lieutenant-General Sagat Singh was to strike from the east with the 8th, 23rd and 57th Mountain Divisions, the two

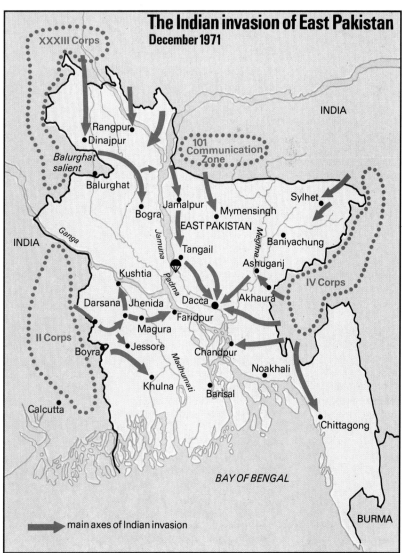

The Indian invasion of East Pakistan
December 1971

main axes of Indian invasion

battalions of Kilo Force, two armoured squadrons and seven battalions of the Mukti Bahini. The sector north of Dacca, between the Jamuna and Meghna Rivers, offered the only possibility of a direct advance on the city with no major river crossings, but only a light force was assigned to it – Major-General Gurba Singh Gill's 101 Communications Zone with 95th Mountain Brigade. The assembling of these forces in the summer proved a relatively straightforward affair but creating the necessary logistic infrastructure during the monsoon was a formidable task; civilian vehicles with their drivers had to be used to transport the 64,000 tonnes of supplies that were needed, and storage space was at a premium – schools had on occasion to be requisitioned for this task.

The Pakistani Eastern Command viewed the prospect of taking on the Indian Army with alarm. The original garrison, 14th Division with four brigades, had been reinforced with three divisional headquarters and 28 battalions from West Pakistan, but most had arrived without heavy equipment. When Niazi replaced Tikka Khan he discovered he had only one armoured and six artillery regiments in support. Niazi adopted a forward defence policy with 9th Division at Jessore, 16th Division at Bogra, the 14th and 39th Divisions in the east, 93rd Brigade in the north and the skeletal 36th Division headquarters in reserve controlling the counter-insurgency war around Dacca with a couple of battalions and paramilitary forces. Each division had one or two towns designated as fortresses which were to form the heart of the sector defence; little attempt was made to arrange mutual support and no arrangements were made for a fighting withdrawal in the event of the forward positions becoming untenable.

Towing tanks and ferrying troops

India began its offensive on 4 December. The main plan was to infiltrate and get behind Pakistani positions; there was no definite plan to take Dacca. The Indian forces enjoyed good intelligence through the cooperation of the local population and the Mukti Bahini. For river crossing, the Indians had PT76 Soviet amphibious light tanks, but the PT76 overheated after 30 minutes in the water, and some of the rivers needed a three-hour crossing. In those cases the tanks had to be towed across, and the main burden fell on helicopters to make assault crossings and establish air bridgeheads. Local craft and steamers were often commandeered to ferry troops and equipment.

In the west, II Corps under Lieutenant-General T.L. Raina and XXXIII Corps under Lieutenant-General M.L. Thapan made good use of their Soviet T55s and PT76s. Thapan thrust south towards Rangpur and Dinajpur with four brigades while a fifth struck eastwards from the Ballurghat salient. Within three days the Pakistani 16th Division had been split in two, but the advance met fierce resistance. Bogra did not fall until 15 December, the 'fortress' of Rangpur succumbing the following day.

Further south, Raina sought to avoid a pitched battle for Jessore, where the bulk of Pakistan's 9th Division was located; he determined on an enveloping operation striking in the north with the 4th Mountain Division from Darsana to isolate the enemy by taking Jhenida and Magura, with its ferries across the Madhumati River, while his 9th Infantry Division and the bulk of the armour and paratroops moved to isolate Jessore from the south. 4th Mountain Division

Below: An Indian 2nd Lieutenant, armed with a Sterling 9mm sub-machine gun, observes the progress of the Indian advance. The main hindrance to this advance was the difficulty of crossing the numerous rivers in East Pakistan. Right: Indian troops bring up prefabricated sections to repair a blown bridge. Below right: Pakistani troops prepare to destroy a bridge during their retreat. In spite of these attempts to halt the progress of the Indian Army, the obstacles were all overcome within a matter of days, and the Indian Army rode triumphantly into Dacca (bottom right).

manoeuvred quickly over dirt tracks to take Jhenida on 7 December, and on the same day the 9th Infantry Division entered Jessore unopposed – the Pakistanis having abandoned a strong position the Indians considered might take a week to overcome. II Corps failed to exploit its advantage swiftly enough, however, and the Pakistanis were able to muster stout resistance at Kushtia, where 4th Mountain Division's advance was blocked until 11 December. Still, the Pakistani 9th Division gradually dissolved in confusion, the majority of its surviving troops concentrating around Faridpur on 15 December.

In the east, India's IV Corps achieved spectacular successes, for the Pakistani commanders had not expected a major attack in this region. The 8th

Mountain Division attacked towards Sylhet in the north, the 57th Mountain Division struck through Akhaura in the centre, and the 23rd Mountain Division advanced on Chandpur, Kilo Force being assigned Chittagong. In the north Pakistan's 14th Division was quickly pushed back, although an attempt to create an airhead by helicoptering in a Gorkha battalion proved premature and the Gorkhas were isolated for a day. In the event the Pakistani garrison was able to escape across the Meghna but blew up the Ashuganj bridge before the evacuation was complete, leaving a brigade on the wrong side of the river. Further south, Pakistan's 39th Division disintegrated in the face of the fast-moving Indian advance. The three Indian divisions reached the Meghna on 9 December and almost immediately established a bridgehead across the river at Ashuganj. Thanks to the initiative of local officers and men, troops were built up in the bridgehead, being ferried across the mile-wide river by helicopter and steamer.

On to Dacca

Meanwhile, in the north, 101 Communications Zone had made remarkable progress, although General Gill was injured on the second day when his jeep ran over a mine. Gill was replaced by Major-General G.C. Nagra, whose force was strengthened by the addition of 167th Mountain Brigade. The advance southwards took Jamalpur on 9 December and Mymensingh on 11 December. To block Pakistani forces falling back on Dacca, the Indians staged a parachute drop on Tangail during the afternoon of 11 December, which was followed by a confused night battle with retreating troops continuing into the following morning. The Pakistani retreat was inhibited but not stopped. Nevertheless the Indian advance continued and by 14 December one of Nagra's battalions had discovered a metalled road which led directly to Dacca and was unguarded.

On the same day India's 57th Division, which had moved forward from the Ashuganj bridgehead, began shelling Dacca and Niazi's position was desperate. His score of Sabre fighters had been destroyed or neutralised and the Indian Air Force ruled the skies, flying 1978 sorties during the campaign. At sea an Indian task force built around the carrier *Vikrant* blocked all hope of escape while on land Niazi's forces were in tatters, short of supplies, disorganised and demoralised. On 15 December Nagra's troops began entering the suburbs of the city from the north. Nagra had once been military adviser to the Indian high commission in Karachi and had come to know Niazi quite well. He now sent him a personal message: 'My dear Abdullah, I am here. The game is up. I suggest you give yourself up to me and I'll look after you. Gandharv.' After some confusion, the final surrender was completed on the afternoon of 16 December.

Some 57,000 troops and 18,000 paramilitary personnel surrendered at the end of the 12-day campaign, which restored the Indian Army's prestige after the setbacks of the 1960s. But although the taking of East Pakistan was executed swiftly, it should not escape notice that there were serious deficiencies in Indian planning, the most serious being the failure to focus the effort on seizing Dacca, whose capture was almost an afterthought. Still, the Indian Army had performed well in action, manoeuvring with skill and verve despite the unfavourable terrain. **E.R. Hooton**

Red river-crossing
Soviet tactics and equipment

One of the most complex operations of modern war is the forcing of a defended river line. It has played a crucial part in two wars since World War II – the Indo-Pakistan War of 1971 and the Egypt-Israel campaign of the 1973 Yom Kippur War – and would be one of the keys to success in a war between the Warsaw Pact and Nato in Europe, should such a conflict ever occur. Central Europe is criss-crossed with rivers – in 1965 a Soviet study concluded that an advance into the West would encounter obstacles ranging from a small river up to 20m (66 feet) wide every 10-20km (6-12 miles) to a waterway wider than 300m (1000 feet) every 250-300km (155-190 miles). Consequently, both Nato and the Soviet Union have been forced to develop tactics and equipment for river-crossing, but it is the Soviets who have given it the most attention, and it is countries using Soviet equipment and tactics – for example India and Egypt – which have practised river-crossing most successfully in recent times.

The Soviet forces have a considerable degree of hard experience on which to build, stemming from World War II. They showed considerably greater facility in coping with river-crossing than did their German enemies: crossing the 600m (2000 feet) wide Dniepr River in 1941 along a front of 480km (300 miles), the Wehrmacht was able to add only one pontoon bridge and one ferry to the seven bridges they captured; forcing the same river during their advance in 1943, the Red Army built 57 road bridges, nine foot bridges, and operated several ferry sites along a 320km (200 mile) stretch – a crossing every 7km (4 miles) compared to the Germans' effort of one every 53km (33 miles).

According to Soviet military doctrine, river obsta-
cles must be overcome rapidly, with no pause in the tempo of operations. Their tactics include seizing crossings in advance using airborne or heliborne troops or forward detachments – that is, all-arms groupings infiltrated through the enemy deployment to race ahead of the main body and secure ground vital to an uninterrupted advance. The Indian Army's 1971 campaign in East Pakistan provides an excellent example of the type of operation envisaged by the Red Army. Despite the fact that the width of the major waterways with which they were confronted was measured in kilometres rather than metres, the Indians managed, through a combination of speed, flexibility and manoeuvre, to exploit the weakness in Pakistani deployment and largely avoid having to take the numerous water obstacles by force.

When an opposed crossing is unavoidable, Soviet doctrine holds that success depends on observing certain principles. Thorough reconnaissance is vital to establish the width, depth and current, and to discover the nature and slope of the banks and bottom. Potential fording, snorkelling, ferrying and bridging sites are identified, along with suitable concealed waiting areas for troops and crossing equipment. Reconnaissance of the obstacles starts long before the manoeuvre units arrive: long-range patrols and aircraft may well have kept it under observation for days, and divisional medium reconnaissance including engineer specialists, aim to arrive up to a day ahead of the main body. Above all, the emphasis is on efficient organisation and maintaining momentum.

Speed and surprise are essential. Bridgeheads must be seized before the enemy has time to organise an effective defence and reinforced before any counter-attack is mounted. Where there are insufficient

There are three basic elements in Soviet river crossing methods. First of all there is the emphasis on rapid and efficient bridge-building. Left: A pontoon bridge built over a Hungarian river during Warsaw Pact exercises in 1971. The second element is the provision of vehicles that can act as ferries for other equipment. Below: Soviet GSP amphibious vehicles which are used to carry heavy weapons (these models were in fact captured by the Israelis from the Egyptians in 1973). Thirdly, there is the amphibious capability of weapons designed to operate on land. Right: The PT76 light tank can swim across water obstacles at 5km/h (3mph). Bottom: T72s fitted with the snorkel attachment that allows them to ford shallow rivers.

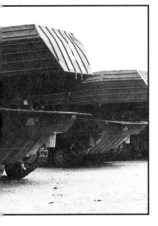

aircraft available for an airborne or heliborne assault or infiltration through enemy positions is impossible, Soviet advance guards are trained to cross the obstacle straight off the line of march. Only if attacks from the line of march failed would the Soviets organise an assault with detailed preparation.

The aim of the Soviet formations is to try to cross water obstacles on a broad front. A division has at least two regiments in its first wave, and each regiment attempts a passage at two points at least. Multiple crossings reduce the likelihood of large and vulnerable concentrations of troops. They also greatly complicate the intelligence picture for the defence in the crucial early stages while bridgeheads are being established: the enemy, unable to identify the main area of threat, finds it difficult to make decisions about the deployment of reserves. Crossings are supported by the maximum available firepower, both direct and indirect, and close air support. At all levels, second echelons are fed in through the more successful assault units and sub-units but are not used to reinforce where crossings have failed.

In accordance with their stress on speed and momentum, the Soviets will not pause to consolidate bridgeheads. Second echelons are ordered to press on deep into enemy territory. To facilitate as rapid a build-up as possible on the hostile bank, tactical bridges are built to replace the slower initial crossing methods such as ferries and amphibians. The tactical bridges are, in turn, replaced by more permanent structures so that tactical bridging equipment is released for use in further assault crossings. Crossing sites are choke points vulnerable to air attack. Consequently dense air defences are established at the outset, with divisional assets (SA-6 or SA-8 missiles) well forward, reinforcing regimental ZSU-23-4 anti-aircraft guns and SA-9 or SA-13 missiles.

The high priority accorded to river crossings from the march has led the Soviets to develop an amphibious capability in equipment. Among the many vehicles that can swim without preparation (although not if the banks are too steep – over 12 degrees in some cases rising to a maximum of 27 degrees in others) are the BRDM scout car and anti-tank guided missile derivatives; the BMP, BTR-60PB and MT-LB armoured personnel carriers (APCs); the 2S-1 self-propelled howitzer; and the SA-8, SA-9 and SA-13 air defence systems. In addition, with 15 minutes preparation, all medium tanks can snorkel across rivers which have firm beds and exit slopes not over 30 degrees; alternatively, they can be winched across underwater. In the 1971 campaign against Pakistan, the Indian Army demonstrated the value of amphibious vehicles through their imaginative use of their PT76 light tanks in forward and outflanking detachments – even if the river-crossings were often too wide for the tanks to traverse under their own power. Two years later, the rapid build-up of Egyptian strength on the East Bank of the Suez Canal during the Yom Kippur War owed much to their PT76s and BTR-50PK APCs.

Pontoons and ferries

Non-amphibious vehicles are catered for through the deployment of a large variety of crossing equipment. Each Soviet manoeuvre regiment carries four heavy truck-mounted bridges (TMMs), each 10m (33 feet) in length, which can be joined together to form longer bridges (capable of taking 60 tonne loads). MT55 or MTU20 tank-launched bridges, with spans of 18m (60 feet) and 20m (66 feet) respectively, are held on the scale of one per tank battalion. With these resources, regiments can cope with minor rivers, but they will be reinforced by elements of the divisional engineer battalion if faced with a major obstacle, bringing more TMMs and a range of other equipment: PTS amphibious transporters which can carry almost 12 tonnes and tow a PKP floating trailer which can take a field gun; GSP amphibious ferries, assembled in five minutes, which are used to get tanks and ZSU-23-4s onto the enemy bank as soon as possible after the assault waves of APCs; and PMP pontoon bridges, carried in sections which can be assembled at a rate of 10m (33 feet) per minute or alternatively be used as heavy ferries. Moreover, the Soviet Army

stresses improvisation using local means found near the crossing site if specialist equipment is not available in sufficient quantity. In the war for Bangladesh, indeed, civilian boats and ferries supplied by a friendly populace were the main crossing equipment.

In 1973 the Egyptians gave an excellent demonstration of what could be done with Soviet crossing equipment. The Suez Canal is about 18m (60 feet) deep and between 180m and 220m (600 feet and 730 feet) wide, with an embankment 20m (65 feet) high and 10m (33 feet) thick on the Israeli-controlled side. The Egyptians launched 16 assault crossings along the entire 170km (105 mile) length of the canal. In under five hours gaps had been created in the embankment and amphibious tanks, amphibious APCs and medium tanks on GSP ferries were crossing the waterway. Between six and nine hours after the beginning of the assault, the Egyptians established 50 heavy ferries and 12 bridges over the canal; 24 hours after the start of the operation, about 500 of their tanks were in Sinai. To cover the crossing the Egyptians pushed large numbers of infantry with manpack anti-tank guided missiles and hand-held anti-tank weapons over the canal and landed several strong groups by helicopter deep into Israeli positions. While these forces held off the Israeli armoured counter-attack, dense air defences made Israeli aerial reaction both expensive in casualties and ineffectual – not a single bridge was knocked out.

Whereas the 1971 Indo-Pakistan war and the 1973 Yom Kippur War proved the effectiveness of Soviet equipment and tactics, the Nato equivalent has not been seriously battle-tested. For the present, the Soviet Army remains the master of modern river-crossing techniques.   **Charles Dick**

Below: The Soviet doctrine for the swift exploitation of any bridgehead established in hostile territory involves the forward deployment of support weapons to cover the crossing points. Here, ZSU-23-4 radar-controlled mobile anti-aircraft guns move across a newly built bridge. The ZSU-23-4 is armed with four 23mm anti-aircraft guns.

Key Weapons

THE M4 SHERMAN

The long and successful career of the M4 Sherman medium tank in the post-World War II era is something of a paradox. For a tank that was woefully undergunned and poorly armoured by 1944 standards – an easy victim for predatory German Panthers and Tiger tanks – it was surprising that the Sherman survived so well that it could be included in the AFV inventories of a number of nations right up until the 1980s. The key to the Sherman's success lay in those most important – though often forgotten – constants of weapon design: simplicity, reliability and adaptability.

The M4 Sherman entered US Army service in 1942 and, although it weighed little more than 30 tonnes and was armed with a low-velocity 75mm gun, it soon became the main battle tank of the Allied armies, equipping both American and British armed forces. In the face of rapid technological developments forced upon tank design by the war, the Sherman underwent a series of improvements to increase armour protection, uprate the power plant and provide a better main armament.

Those Shermans with the original welded hull were designated as the M4, while those with the simpler-to-manufacture cast hull were known as the M4A1. Both types were powered by an adapted aircraft engine, the air-cooled Wright/Continental R-975, but as demand for aero engines was so great, an alternative power plant was sought. The M4A2 utilised a welded hull and was equipped with twin GMC 6-71 diesel engines, but this model was quickly superseded by the M4A3 which was powered by a Ford GAA V-8 petrol engine. The M4A3 had a welded hull and became the standard model in US Army service, being produced in greater numbers than any other variant. A continuing shortage of engines led to the M4A4 which was powered by five six-cylinder car engines; connected by a single crankshaft this multibank engine necessitated an increase in hull length and a re-spacing of the bogie wheels. Although more complex, the M4A4 had a more reliable engine than the other Shermans. Most of this type were exported to Britain under the lend-lease system.

The Sherman's gun proved a major problem. The 75mm M3 gun – which equipped most Shermans for the Normandy landings in 1944 – was clearly inadequate, having little effect against the opposing German tanks. This was replaced by the 76mm T1 which was a considerable improvement, although no match for the Panther's high-velocity 75mm Kwk 42 L/70, for example. The most striking improvement to the Sherman's fire power was developed in Britain when the long-barrelled 17-pounder (76.2mm) anti-tank gun was grafted onto a number of Shermans. Known as Fireflies, these Shermans had an armour-piercing capability to match the best of the German tank guns. In order to improve the US armoured division's high-explosive capability a number of M4 and M4A3 Shermans were up-gunned to take a 105mm howitzer and these tanks were reserved in headquarters companies to provide divisional fire support.

Unfortunately for the Sherman crews, the tank provided little armoured protection and even with the use of appliqué armour it could easily be penetrated by anti-tank weapons. This weakness was compounded by the stowage of ammunition in the hull sponsons so that once hit the Sherman had a tendency to burst into flames; they were known to the Germans as 'Tommy

cookers'. Attempts were made to overcome this problem by incorporating water jackets which surrounded the ammunition, so that if penetrated the chance of combustion was reduced. Those tanks fitted with water jackets were given the suffix 'wet'.

All these improvements considerably increased the Sherman's weight and mobility was reduced. The narrow tracks and vertical volute suspension – developed from the 20-tonne M2 – were unsuited to the more than 30-tonne Sherman and so towards the end of the war the HVSS (horizontal volute spring suspension) and wider T80 track were adopted, which restored the Sherman's cross-country mobility. Tanks so modified received the suffix E8 and were known by the Americans as the 'easy eight'.

Given the tank's adaptability it is hardly surprising that a number of Sherman variants emerged. The American interest in self-propelled artillery led to the M7 self-propelled howitzer. Mounting a 105mm M2 howitzer, the M7 utilised an M3 (later an M4) chassis and an M4A3 hull. A special feature was the ring-mounted anti-aircraft machine gun set on a raised corner of the superstructure, whose pulpit-like

Previous page: The most advanced of all the many Sherman types is the Israeli M51, seen here during the Yom Kippur War. Above: A British M4A4 Sherman Firefly fitted-out with a 17-pounder anti-tank gun, the only really effective armament against German tanks. Below: An M4 Sherman DD (duplex drive) tank with its flotation screen lowered. Like other early types this tank has VVS (verticle volute spring) suspension and narrow tracks. Opposite page top: A battery of M7 Priests, taken into Israeli service during the Six-Day War. Opposite centre: A Sherman hit by a land mine. Opposite below: An M4A3E8 of the Canadian Army prepares fire from fixed positions in Korea.

appearance led the M7 to be nicknamed the Priest. The British and Canadians took a number of M7s and converted them to take the 25-pounder howitzer and in so doing renamed them the Sexton. The M10 tank destroyer used the M4A3 chassis and was armed with a 3in M7 high-velocity gun which gave it a strong anti-armour capability, although its open-topped turret left the crew vulnerable to shell splinters. In British service the M10 was fitted with the 17-pounder and redesignated the Achilles.

By 1945 the Sherman was the most numerous tank in the US Army and remained so in the immediate postwar era. The outbreak of the Korean War in June 1950 saw the Sherman returned to the battlefield. American reinforcements were rushed to Korea to buttress the wavering South Korean Army and by August a Sherman-equipped tank battalion had arrived. The Shermans used in Korea were the

M4A3E8s and were evenly matched against the T34/85s of the North Koreans and Chinese.

Once the frontline had stabilised along the 38th Parallel, open tank warfare was a rarity, and the Shermans were employed in breaking up massed infantry attacks and acting as mobile artillery to destroy enemy bunkers and fortified emplacements. The smaller calibre of the Sherman's 76mm gun made it less effective as a 'bunker-buster' than the 90mm guns of the M26 Pershing and M46 Patton tanks. But the Sherman had a major advantage over the more powerfully armed tanks: its low ground weight and small size proved highly useful in traversing the mountainous terrain of Korea where lack of good roads and unstable bridges hampered the progress of heavy tanks. Consequently the Shermans could be sited on commanding hilltops to dominate the surrounding countryside. The heavy expenditure in ammunition caused by the Shermans acting as static artillery led to the addition of ammunition racks, welded onto the rear hull so an additional 40 rounds could be carried.

After Korea the Sherman was replaced in the US Army by newer models and a number of surplus tanks were exported to friendly nations including France, who used the M4 in their war against the Viet Minh in Indochina. The French had problems with the Sherman, in so much as the tank's ground pressure was found to be too high for much of the Indochinese terrain and it was eventually replaced with the lighter M24 Chaffee.

The Sherman has been exported worldwide and beside Britain and France the major users of this versatile tank have been the Israelis, who have undertaken major development programmes to update the Sherman so it can cope with the battle conditions encountered in the Middle East.

During the 1948 war the Israelis managed to procure a few war-damaged M4s as well as a number of 'demilitarised' Shermans mounting 105mm howitzers. At the conclusion of hostilities Israeli agents scoured arms dumps throughout the world and by the mid-1950s a sizeable number of Shermans had been delivered to Israel. They were a mix of all the variant types; the Israelis' main problem was to find a uniform main armament that was equal to the T54s of the Soviet-backed Arab armies.

The French supplied a number of surplus M4A1s

Right: Two M4A3E8s of the US Army travel up a stream in South Korea in May 1952. Both vehicles have HVS suspension and additional sand-bag armour, a useful device for dissipating the effect of hollow-charge projectiles. The Sherman in the foreground has a split hatch for the loader while the one in the background has a small oval hatch.

Below: A line of Israeli Shermans advances along a desert road on the Egyptian side of the Suez Canal during the Yom Kippur War. The main armaments are traversed to the rear for travelling purposes.

Left: Israeli soldiers crouch down alongside an M1 Super Sherman during the assault on Mount Scopus, Jerusalem, 1967. Below: An M4A3E8 of the US Army fires on communist positions with its 0.5in machine gun in support of an infantry attack.

mounting 3in guns, which were renamed M1s or Super Shermans by the Israelis. While the export of Super Shermans to Israel was being conducted the French began secretly to cooperate with the Israelis to upgun the basic Sherman with the high-velocity 75mm CN 75-50 gun, which with a muzzle velocity of over 1000mps (3300fps) was considered one of the most effective tank guns in existence at that time. Designed for the AMX13, a number of modifications had to be carried out to make it fit the Sherman turret. The new tank was designated the M50 and a company of these tanks took part in the Sinai campaign of 1956. After the 1956 war a number of further modifications were carried out and by the end of the decade M50s were being supplied to Israel on a regular basis. The old Continental engines, which powered most Israeli Shermans, were replaced by the more durable 460hp Cummings diesel engines which could be fitted into the M4A3 hulls with ease.

The M50s saw action in the Six-Day War of 1967 where they scored a notable success when an M50-equipped unit destroyed a Jordanian armoured brigade armed with the more advanced M47s. The M50 had proved itself an effective battle tank, able to handle the Soviet-built T54/5 and the US M26 and M47 tanks but the constant need for more powerful main armaments led to the development of the M51.

While the 75mm gun of the M50 fired simple armour-piercing ammunition, the idea behind the M51 was to use the French 105mm CN 105 F1 gun which could fire a specially designed HEAT (high explosive anti-tank) round. Fitted with a complex anti-spin device, the HEAT round had a very high muzzle velocity and was able to penetrate the armour of any tank fielded by Israel's Arab opponents. The long-barrelled CN 105 F1 proved too large for the Sherman turret and the Israelis compromised by shortening the barrel to reduce recoil space, and by using the larger cast hulls of the M4A1 they were able to squeeze the gun in.

The M51 also featured improved ammunition storage facilities, white light and infra-red searchlights and smoke projectors. All these improvements brought the tank's weight up to a heavy 39 tonnes but with the Cummings engine, HVSS suspension and wide tracks the M51 could reach an acceptable maximum speed of 45km/h (28mph) with a range of

Above: A unit of Israeli M50s patrols the Sinai desert. The M50 was based on the M4A3E8 but was armed with a high velocity French 75mm gun. Left: An unsuccessful Egyptian attempt to uprate the Sherman's firepower: an AMX13 turret grafted onto an M4 hull.

M4A3E8 Sherman Medium Tank

Crew 5
Dimensions Length 7.52m (24ft 7in); width 2.68m (8ft 8in); height 3.43m (11ft 3in)
Weight Combat loaded 32,284kg (71,153lb)
Engine Ford GAA V-8 water-cooled in-line petrol engine developing 500hp at 2,600rpm

Performance Maximum road speed 48km/h (30mph); range (road) 160km (99 miles); vertical obstacle 0.6m (2ft); trench 2.29m (7ft 6in); gradient 60 per cent; fording 0.92m (3ft)

Armour Min-max 12mm-75mm (0.46-2.9in)
Armament One 76mm main gun; one 0.3in M1919A4 machine gun co-axial with main armament; one 0.3in M1919A4 machine gun in ball mount in bow; one 0.5in M2 machine gun mounted on turret roof; one M3 smoke mortar in turret roof

270km (170 miles). The M51 represented the Sherman in its most advanced form and it is doubtful whether the tank could be further developed and yet still remain a Sherman. Israel still uses M50 and M51 Shermans in reserve and has supplied M50s to the Christian militias in Lebanon. It seems likely that the Sherman will remain a combat vehicle for some years to come.

Giap's new strategy

North Vietnam prepares its offensive

In 1972 President Nixon was standing for re-election in the United States. Four years previously the North Vietnamese Tet offensive had had a decisive influence on American politics. President Johnson had already decided not to stand for re-election by the time the offensive broke, and in its aftermath the American people, disillusioned with repeated claims of American success in the war, had supported Richard Nixon's policy of reducing the American commitment to Vietnam. In three years the American military strength in South Vietnam was reduced by over 500,000 men, and most of the remainder were due to leave during 1972. The policy of Vietnamization meant that the South Vietnamese forces now bore the brunt of the war on the ground, although the Americans retained a crucial role in the air war, but Vietnam was still a burning issue in the United States, and an offensive at such a politically sensitive time might well find the US response at its most uncertain.

External politics influenced North Vietnam in another respect. Nixon had pursued a policy of detente with the two major communist powers, the Soviet Union and China. He had had considerable success and was due to visit Peking in February 1972 and Moscow later in the year. North Vietnam depended on the Soviet Union and China for supplies, particularly arms, to continue the war and a rapprochement between the United States and North Vietnam's backers might be followed by a reduction in their assistance.

Internally the North Vietnamese were also facing serious problems. Although the Tet offensive had been a considerable propaganda success it had been dearly bought in terms of human lives. The communist leadership had often been prodigal with the lives of its troops but resources were not unlimited. In particular the losses of the Tet offensive had drastically reduced the cadre of trained Viet Cong guerrillas in the South. Dedicated, trained leaders could not be recruited in sufficient numbers within the South and the gaps had to be filled with regular troops from the North Vietnamese Army (NVA). The scale of guerrilla activity in the South was inevitably reduced during this period of rebuilding.

It would be an exaggeration to talk of defeat for the North, but all in all the picture was not encouraging, and the North Vietnamese leadership must have been aware that time might no longer be on their side. During 1971 they therefore began to plan a major conventional offensive against the South. Preparations were probably under way when Le Duan, first secretary of the Vietnamese Communist Party, visited Moscow in the spring of 1971. Certainly, deliveries of heavy weapons from the Soviet Union increased dramatically during late 1971. The deliveries included tanks, especially T54/55s, and heavy artillery, such as the long-range 130mm field gun. To counter American air power, more surface-to-air missiles (SAMs) were sent, including for the first time the man-portable SA-7.

Below: ARVN troops prepare to evacuate a wounded comrade on Route 13, the road to An Loc. For over a month the forces defending the area around Loc Ninh and An Loc were hammered by intense NVA artillery bombardments and armoured assaults and at one stage in the siege over 25 per cent of the ARVN defenders at An Loc were wounded. However Giap's decision to spread his forces along four axes of attack denied him a decisive superiority on any one front and by mid-May, with the aid of massive US air support, the NVA onslaught on An Loc was brought to a halt.

Left: Vo Nguyen Giap, veteran North Vietnamese strategist and architect of the 1972 invasion. Above: Nixon meets South Vietnamese Vice-President Ky in Paris in 1969. Despite the withdrawal of over 500,000 US troops between 1969 and 1972, Nixon continued to stress the US commitment to the South and steadfastly refused to contemplate the ousting of Ky and President Nguyen Van Thieu (right) as had been demanded by the North as a condition for peace.

Getting these weapons to North Vietnam was the least of the planners' problems. They had to be deployed to the South, not only into the demilitarized zone (DMZ) which split the country, but along the Ho Chi Minh Trail through Laos and Cambodia. More than this, considerable stockpiles of ammunition and fuel had to take the same route, exposed both to the enemy's reconnaissance and air attacks. Only after the monsoon ended in October was the Trail fully usable by vehicles, so the build-up was slow, giving the Americans and South Vietnamese time to react.

Statistics and reality

Further evidence of North Vietnamese difficulties comes from the statistics so eagerly collated by the Pentagon's representatives in South Vietnam. By their estimates guerrilla strength in the South had fallen from 250,300 effectives in 1968 to 197,700 in 1971. The Hamlet Evaluation System (HES) figures suggested that 84 per cent of villages were secure in government control, compared to only 47 per cent in 1968. Viet Cong activity was also much more local-ised and was now concentrated into 10 provinces, containing just over a quarter of the South Vietnamese people. These statistics were encouraging for the Americans and did reflect a real change in the fortunes of the two sides. However, they also disguised some significant aspects of the reality on the ground. The government forces had won a temporary tactical advantage but they were still a long way from winning the whole-hearted support of the population. Most people would support whichever side seemed to be winning at the time but would try not to compromise themselves totally for fear of a change in the tide. In many areas the local forces and the Viet Cong had reached a tacit understanding for a quiet life. Such areas showed up in the HES figures as 'secure' for the government because of the lack of fighting, but often contained main-force Viet Cong battalions and regiments.

Detailed examination of the South Vietnamese armed forces would also reveal discrepancies be-tween the figures and the reality. On paper the South Vietnamese Army (ARVN) was an impressive force, excellently equipped, with 11 divisions and a total strength of 410,000 men. Another 14,000 served in the Marines, while 43,000 sailors manned 1680 craft, mostly small riverine vessels. The air force contained 51,000 men operating more than 1000 aircraft, in-cluding over 500 helicopters. The ARVN carried out almost all of the allied offensive action on the ground and the South Vietnamese Air Force flew 3300 of the 4000 allied air strikes in February 1972. In addition there were local militias, the Popular Forces (PF) (248,000 strong) and Regional Forces (RF) (284,000 strong), and finally more than four million were nominally members of the People's Self-Defense Force, supposed to defend their own villages.

Yet the combat effectiveness of the forces was extremely variable. There were some excellent units, but they were the exception rather than the rule. One of the major problems was the quality of leadership. The South Vietnamese officer corps was largely composed of the better-educated middle and upper classes, mostly town-dwellers, while the rank-and-file soldiers were overwhelmingly peasants; there was in consequence an almost unbridgeable gap between officers and men. Poor leadership was a major factor in the exceptionally high (and climbing) desertion rate in the ARVN – 140,177 men deserted in 1971, compared to 116,064 in 1968. Even more worrying was the fact that regular combat units suf-fered most. Their desertion rate was 35.6 per 1000 each month, compared to 10.7 per 1000 in the RF and 7.9 per 1000 in the PF. Although few deserters actually went over to the enemy as opposed to going home, the ARVN was effectively losing a third of its manpower each year, making it almost impossible to maintain coherent, well-trained units.

An additional problem was that only a small pro-portion of soldiers had the technical background to cope with the sophisticated weapons which the Amer-ican government supplied in such abundance. In particular it was difficult to convince the Vietnamese of the necessity for routine maintenance work. The

Above: ARVN troops aboard a US-supplied M113 APC. Although well-armed, the ARVN's combat efficiency was marred by a lack of technical training in the use of modern weapons.

Below: ARVN forces set up a firebase in the Central Highlands. Earlier in the war firebases had provided invaluable support for anti-guerrilla operations, but they were outgunned by the Soviet-supplied 130mm field gun used by the NVA.

mutual support.

American military manpower in Vietnam at the end of March 1972 was only 95,000 men and was scheduled to be reduced to 69,000 by the end of April. The major ground combat formations left in the country were the 196th Infantry Brigade on port security duties at Da Nang in the north and the 3rd Brigade, 1st Air Cavalry Division, an airmobile task force based near Saigon. In addition there was the 1st Aviation Brigade, with several hundred helicopters under command, also based near Saigon. In each of the four ARVN Military Regions an American Regional Assistance Command was located, providing advisers and logistic support for the ARVN. (There were also two South Korean divisions in South Vietnam, although their strength was reduced from 48,000 to 38,000 men during February.)

American air strength had not yet been reduced to the same extent. Some 20,000 men of the United States Air Force (USAF) remained in Vietnam and another 27,000 were based in Thailand. Other units within the Pacific area could operate in Vietnam, notably the B-52s on Guam. By the end of March, when the North Vietnamese attack began, the USAF had 60 F-4 and 23 A-37 ground-attack aircraft in Vietnam. In Thailand there were 161 F-4s, 16 F-105s, 15 A-1s, 10 B-57s and 52 B-52s. In both countries there were about 30 AC-119 or AC-130 gunships. The South Vietnamese Air Force had about 160 purpose-built attack aircraft (mostly A-1s and A-37s), backed by less sophisticated machines which could be converted to rudimentary strike capability.

consequence was that the percentage of tanks, armoured personnel carriers and aircraft operational at any one time was disturbingly low.

As one would expect, the Vietnamese had absorbed American tactical doctrines along with their weaponry. Thus the ARVN relied heavily on firepower and technology. In particular, they had adopted the American system of 'firebases' – small artillery positions scattered throughout the country to give instant fire support to the infantry. The Americans had developed the system to meet the threat of a guerrilla war when they were fighting an enemy that possessed little more than smallarms. In more conventional warfare against a foe that had effective heavy artillery, the firebases were to prove too weak to defend themselves and too dispersed to provide

A build-up at the border

Once the 1971 monsoon had finished in October, American and South Vietnamese intelligence agencies began to report a build-up of North Vietnamese forces around the borders. It was estimated that 120,000 men had moved down the Ho Chi Minh Trail from October 1971 to February 1972, accompanied by considerable quantities of heavy equipment. Air photographic reconnaissance revealed nearly 8000 lorries loaded in North Vietnamese depots at the end of 1971, waiting for the trails to dry out in Laos. Although American bombing of Laos and Cambodia was persistent, the North itself had been largely spared since 1968, and new roads were built south from Hanoi and Haiphong, while two fuel pipelines were laid as far as the DMZ. The political workers within the North Vietnamese forces stepped up their activity and the Hanoi papers called for a decisive victory. From all these indicators it was not difficult to conclude that North Vietnam was planning an attack and it was even possible to guess approximately where the blow would fall. However, anticipating the exact timing remained a problem.

Some believed that the North would attack at the height of the American presidential campaign or even wait until 1973 when the American withdrawal would be almost complete, but most people expected the attack to coincide with Tet (the Vietnamese New Year) in mid-February, as it had in 1968. As the date approached, the Americans increased their air power in the theatre, particularly in B-52 heavy bombers. The aircraft carrier *Constellation* temporarily joined the *Coral Sea* and the *Hancock* in the Gulf of Tonkin in February; each ship carried an air group of 90 planes, a considerable weight of firepower. On 12-13 February the air forces launched a maximum-effort strike

Left: A corporal of the North Vietnamese Army on his way to the fronts of the South. Giap's massive commitment of men and war material to the invasion was to cost the North some 100,000 soldiers killed.

Below: By early 1972 the ARVN had been excellently equipped by the US to counter the threat of an all-out attack from the North. The recoilless rifle, M79 grenade launcher, flak jacket, webbing and hand grenade equipping this ARVN infantryman are all of US origin.

North Vietnamese forces 1971-72

Army 480,000 personnel organised into 14 infantry divisions, one artillery division, two armoured regiments and 20 independent infantry regiments. 110 T34 and T54 medium tanks, 300 PT76 light tanks, 550 field guns. 35 SAM battalions each with 6 SA-2 launchers

Navy 3000 personnel. Approximately 45 vessels

Air Force 9000 personnel. 165 combat aircraft

Source: IISS, London

against targets in the Central Highlands and repeated the effort in the DMZ on 16-17 February. South Vietnamese ground forces also launched spoiling attacks. The effect of these strikes was hard to assess, but when February passed without a major assault, the defenders of South Vietnam began to relax. The United States ended its alert, which had confined troops to barracks, on 2 March.

In fact, the North Vietnamese were able to exploit the attacker's classic advantage of the initiative in order to achieve surprise. They had decided to attack in the early part of the year, before the monsoon began again. By doing so they expected to affect the American presidential campaign. Furthermore a major defeat for the ARVN could convince the Americans that Vietnamization had failed and that a negotiated withdrawal was essential. The impact of the debacle would be even greater if substantial American forces were involved. Although this decision limited North Vietnam's options somewhat, they still had a large degree of tactical flexibility. They could afford to delay their blow until they saw their enemies lower their guard. The attack was finally timed for Friday 30 March, coinciding with Easter weekend when many American and Vietnamese decision-makers would be away from their offices.

The plan worked out by General Vo Nguyen Giap, the North Vietnamese minister of defence, involved several simultaneous thrusts in four main areas. In the north the old capital of Hue was the objective – four

Above: A flight of US Air Force F-4 Phantom fighter bombers streaks through the skies over South Vietnam. US close air support was provided by some 600 fighter-bombers and 100 B-52s and was to prove the decisive factor in the repulse of the North Vietnamese offensive.

divisions would attack on two axes south across the DMZ, two more divisions would strike eastwards from Laos, and while these thrusts converged on Hue, somewhat further to the south another division was to advance on Da Nang. In the Central Highlands two divisions were to aim for Kontum. Meanwhile, three divisions were to attack down Route 13, through Loc Ninh and An Loc towards Saigon. The fourth area to be attacked was the Mekong Delta, where one division was to attack from the 'Parrot's Beak' and another nearer the coast of the Gulf of Thailand.

Superior Soviet artillery

Giap aimed to achieve surprise not only by the timing of the attack but also by its scale and by the use of heavy weapons. Several hundred tanks were to support the assaults, although North Vietnam had rarely used tanks in the South before. Several Soviet artillery pieces that had not previously been seen in Vietnam now made an appearance. They included multi-barrelled rocket launchers, the D-20 152mm howitzer and most notably the M-46 130mm field gun. The latter, with a range of 34,000m (37,200 yards), was considerably superior to any allied piece in Vietnam.

Giap has been criticised for dispersing his forces too much and thus giving his enemies the chance to concentrate against individual elements; and it may well be that the North Vietnamese general, although a master of guerrilla operations, was too enmeshed in

the requirements of small-scale war to think as effectively on the wider plane of conventional warfare. It is certainly true that the dispersal of effort was a major reason for the halting of the Northern forces. Had one of the divisions that attacked near An Loc been available in the north then Hue might well have fallen, and a process of irreversible panic affected the shaky structure of the South Vietnamese state. It is just as likely, however, that given the limited logistic support available to him, Giap could not support larger forces on any of the main axes of attack. He was, therefore, forced to hope that the cumulation of assaults would undermine resistance.

There is also another point that presumably entered Giap's calculations. This was that if the Americans did decide to react in force, then they had the resources to halt almost any strength of attack. But if the attacks were spread, then the chances were that when the offensive ground to a halt the NVA would remain in possession of large areas of territory – useful bargaining counters or possible stepping-off points for further attacks. And if the struggle became protracted, then the greater discipline and cohesion of the NVA units would give them the advantage in a war of attrition during the summer. In the event the fighting did go on for several months, and the presence of large NVA formations on South Vietnamese soil was to be the crucial issue in the final round of peace talks that was to take place later in the year.

Michael Orr

Into the South

The communist offensive, 1972

The long-expected North Vietnamese offensive against the South began on 30 March 1972. After such a long period of anticipation the defenders of South Vietnam had lowered their guard and they were also surprised and staggered by the scale of the attack. Two hours after midnight South Vietnamese Army (ARVN) positions south of the demilitarized zone (DMZ) were struck by over 5000 shells and rockets. Soviet 130mm field guns out-ranged the American-supplied 105mm and 155mm howitzers in the isolated firebases near the DMZ, and one of the bases, Camp Carroll, received 2000 rounds within the first few hours. On the heels of the barrage came three North Vietnamese Army (NVA) regular divisions – 40,000 men. They were accompanied by 200 T54/55, T34 and PT76 tanks, which had little difficulty in overrunning the South Vietnamese positions.

The ARVN I Corps, comprising three divisions and two brigades, as well as the Regional and Popular Forces (not intended to face a conventional assault), were rocked back by the intensity of these first attacks. The area close to the DMZ, strategically very vulnerable to attacks from Laos, had deliberately been held rather lightly by the South Vietnamese, with the inexperienced 3rd Infantry Division. It was not surprising therefore that by 2 April most of the northernmost province of Quang Tri was in enemy hands. However, the NVA did not have everything its own way. Within the I Corps area the 20th Tank Regiment was on exercise when the invasion started. The 20th was a new unit, equipped with three squadrons of M48 tanks and an integral infantry company, trained to travel on top of the tanks and provide close support. It had recently completed a gunnery camp and had just begun a final tactical test. It was moved immediately to the front line and by the night of 1/2 April it was between Cam Lo and Dong Ha, just south of the Mieu Giang River. Just after dawn NVA tanks were seen approaching Dong Ha and the regiment deployed to prevent a crossing of the river. About noon another NVA column was reported south of the river and threatening the regiment's flank from the Cam Lo direction. However, a well-laid ambush destroyed two T54s and nine PT76s and drove the survivors back northwards. The regiment held its position, although it was denied air and artillery support for most of the day – the US Air Force was conducting a search-and-rescue mission for air crew near Cam Lo and imposed a no-fire zone covering most of the area.

Actions such as the 20th Tank Regiment's battle for Dong Ha ensured that the ARVN managed to hold a defence line along the Cua Viet River and its tributary the Mieu Giang. A strip of territory 16km (10 miles) wide had been lost to the NVA, from which they continued to probe the Southern defence. On 9 April, for example, the 20th Tank Regiment fought another battle against North Vietnamese tanks in which 16 T54s were destroyed.

While the attack through the DMZ was developing, the eastward thrust from Laos towards the northern coastal cities was also getting into gear. The advance of the NVA 324B Division along the A Shau Valley had sent thousands of refugees into Hue. But on this axis the veteran ARVN 1st Infantry Division was deployed and NVA progress was much slower than the refugees' flight. The Bastogne firebase lived up to its name and was a major obstacle to the NVA advance for 25 days until it was evacuated on 29 April.

Whereas in the northern provinces a heavy offensive had been expected, in the area just to the north of

The speed and scale of the NVA offensive caught the South Vietnamese off their guard, but US air power and stout resistance by some of the heavily-armed ARVN formations soon blunted the advance. Above: NVA regulars advance on Kontum at speed behind a T54/55 tank. Above right: NVA troops step warily forwards past the bodies of dead South Vietnamese Rangers. Below: NVA T54 tanks knocked out by the ARVN 20th Tank Regiment near Cam Lo. Right: American-supplied M48 tanks played a leading role in ARVN resistance to the initial onslaught.

Saigon, intelligence had not revealed the extent of communist build-up, and the first assaults caught the ARVN units in the region totally unprepared. The first wave fell upon the troops stationed near Tay Ninh, and NVA use of armour and heavy artillery led to rapid successes after the first round of fighting on 2 April. ARVN forces were sucked in to the defence of Tay Ninh, but this had been merely a feint. The real attack came on 5 April, when the town of Loc Ninh to the northeast was suddenly overrun. The garrison was overwhelmed and there were very few survivors.

The road to Saigon – Route 13 – was now open to the invaders. Reinforcements were rushed to the next main town on the line of advance – An Loc – which was attacked on 13 April. The siege was a minor epic, but the North Vietnamese did not handle their greatly superior forces well. Intense artillery bombardments, with as many as 7000 rounds being fired in a day, turned the town into rubble, but that just made it easier to defend. NVA tanks were committed to the street fighting and proved vulnerable to the M-72 LAW (light anti-tank weapon). Notwithstanding NVA errors, however, the situation at An Loc was very serious by 23 April – and on that date yet another axis of the offensive made itself felt, this time in the Central Highlands.

The attacks in the Central Highlands had been delayed by US and South Vietnamese air strikes, but they took the same form as those in the north and towards Saigon. Overwhelming firepower was brought to bear on firebases, and the town of Tan Canh, blocking the northern route to Kontum, was soon in communist hands. The bleak prospect of the country being cut in two was, therefore, now adding to the worries of the South Vietnamese government. Tan Canh was a serious loss, not merely because of its strategic position, but because the garrison there had panicked and fled at the approach of the NVA tanks. One of Giap's main objectives was being realised: the ARVN was looking decidedly shaky. In the southernmost part of the country, too, offensives along the coast and out of the Parrot's Beak also made progress and added to the range of South Vietnam's problems. For the first couple of weeks, then, the communist offensive generally achieved its objectives.

South Vietnam's defence was hindered by the weather, which greatly restricted flying time. As long as the American air forces were largely unable to fly, the North Vietnamese made steady progress. But, crucially, the South Vietnamese did not crumble. The ARVN, although shaken, did not break, and the Americans continued to give support. Aircraft reinforcements were quickly flown to Vietnam. Two aircraft carriers, *Kitty Hawk* and *Constellation*, joined the *America* and *Enterprise* on station within a few days and two more, *Midway* and *Saratoga*, were deployed from the eastern Pacific and the Atlantic. Thus there were always four carriers available throughout the summer of 1972, while two others in rotation were resting or replenishing. More than this, President Nixon had decided by 5 April to resume air strikes on the North. He told his advisers, 'The bastards have never been bombed like they're going to be bombed this time.' Giap's hopes of an early

Below: An ARVN artillery battery in action on the Central Highlands front. These 155mm M114 howitzers were effective, but nonetheless the NVA's Soviet-supplied artillery in general out-performed the ARVN's American equipment. Note the soldier on the extreme right fusing the large shells.

victory, therefore, had not come to fruition.

After a period of steady attrition throughout the middle of April, the North Vietnamese attack rose to new peaks towards the end of the month, and more elements of the ARVN began to crack under pressure. New gains were made by the North Vietnamese in the Central Highlands, and the ARVN 22nd Division, having born the brunt of the assault by the NVA 320th and 2nd Divisions, began to dissolve as it withdrew to Kontum. The South Vietnamese high command decided to relieve it and reform the division in the rear. In its place the 23rd Division was squeezed into Kontum just one day before the NVA arrived in force.

Covering the killing ground

The NVA tactics were to establish road blocks on the roads leading into Kontum. It was said that a typical road block would be in platoon strength; one section would cover the killing ground on the road, with another section giving covering fire. These would be standard elements in any army's approach to ambush tactics. What made the North Vietnamese tactics unusual was their practice of placing a third section in depth with orders to shoot if the forward sections withdrew too quickly.

Having isolated Kontum, the North Vietnamese brought their long-range artillery up into the hills which surrounded and dominated the city. Then sappers infiltrated the city and seized key points. Finally, on 25 May, tanks and infantry joined in the assault. Once again the NVA's tanks suffered heavily in the confined space of the town from light anti-tank weapons and the sappers were gradually winkled out of their positions. Skilled though

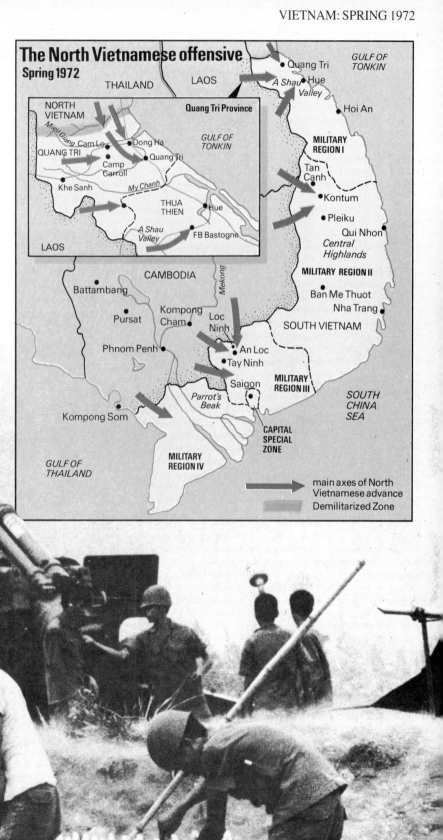

The North Vietnamese offensive Spring 1972

GULF OF TONKIN

LAOS

THAILAND

Quang Tri · A Shau Valley · Hue

Hoi An

MILITARY REGION I

Quang Tri Province

NORTH VIETNAM

Mieu Giang Cam Lo · Dong Ha

QUANG TRI · Camp Carroll · Quang Tri

GULF OF TONKIN

Khe Sanh · My Chanh

THUA THIEN

Hue

LAOS

A Shau Valley · FB Bastogne

Tan Canh

Kontum · Pleiku

Qui Nhon

Central Highlands

MILITARY REGION II

CAMBODIA

Mekong

Ban Me Thuot

Nha Trang

Battambang

Pursat

Kompong Cham · Loc Ninh

SOUTH VIETNAM

Phnom Penh

An Loc · Tay Ninh

Saigon

MILITARY REGION III

Parrot's Beak

SOUTH CHINA SEA

Kompong Som

CAPITAL SPECIAL ZONE

GULF OF THAILAND

MILITARY REGION IV

→ main axes of North Vietnamese advance

Demilitarized Zone

they were in many aspects of warfare, the NVA had little expertise in the combination of tanks and infantry, and extended attacks against prepared positions were not their forte. After four days the North Vietnamese fell back and the threat to the Central Highlands was ended.

The dangers in the north and south reached their peak late in April. The siege of An Loc continued. Attempts to relieve the city by road failed and South Vietnamese paratroopers had to be landed to reinforce the garrison. Some 20,000 soldiers and civilians were trapped in the town, but air-dropped supplies enabled them to hold out for 22 days until 3 May. American air power played a vital role, providing not merely resupply but the whole range of firepower from B-52 strikes to gunship operations. The gunships proved particularly valuable because of the accuracy with which they could deliver their fire. Individual houses could be targetted by the ground controllers during the street-fighting in the city.

The greatest threat to South Vietnam came in the north, however. When the second phase of the North Vietnamese attack began on 27 April, soon after news arrived of the attacks in the Central Highlands, the raw 3rd Division finally began to disintegrate. The Cua Viet River line was breached and Dong Ha fell. Bad weather limited air support in the region, so the NVA were able to press on to Quang Tri City. On 1 May their tanks broke into the defences on the north of the town, while at the same time the 3rd Division's flank was exposed by a failure of coordination among higher commanders. The divisional commander, Brigadier-General Giai ordered a withdrawal, but when he and his staff were evacuated by helicopter, panic spread and the withdrawal turned into a rout. The road back to Hue was already jammed by refugees and the North Vietnamese added to the panic and terror by shelling the road, causing 20,000 civilian casualties. An ARVN sergeant's account conveys the atmosphere of the retreat: '. . . the road was crowded with so many people, civilians and soldiers, that we could only crawl along. It was like everybody in the area was on that road and communist shells were exploding everywhere. A shell fell about five yards in front of our jeep, damaging a tyre and wounding a comrade in the leg. We abandoned the jeep and ran . . . . Soon we saw communist tanks, I ran towards the sea, then doubled back, and finally got to a safe place, I had run all day, without stopping, and my feet were covered with blisters.'

Dealing with deserters

Military discipline broke down completely and by 3 May broken, fear-stricken soldiers of 3rd Division were spreading panic in Hue. President Thieu saw the situation for himself on the next day and ordered draconian measures to restore the situation. Brigadier-General Giai was relieved of command and later court-martialled for abandoning his position in the face of the enemy. The commander of Military Region I was also sacked and replaced by Lieutenant-General Ngo Quang Truong, one of the country's most experienced soldiers. Truong quickly took a firm grip of the situation. He ordered that deserters and looters were to be shot and rallied the defenders of Hue. Thieu also sent reinforcements to the area, including the Marine and Airborne Divisions which were the ARVN's elite formations. The South Vietnamese line was stabilised 40km (25 miles) north of

Flight from Quang Tri

'Around noon the first bunch of fleeing soldiers started arriving at the My Chanh bridge. All in all it was a pretty unedifying spectacle. Some were drunk and kept firing wildly into the air. The line of lorries and army vehicles roared on south as if the devil himself were at their heels. Some deserters tried to hide their shame and embarrassment by fooling round and chasing dogs and chickens. On our way back to Hue, our Citroën was stopped by three grim-faced soldiers who fired their M16 rifles into the air until we pulled up. All three squeezed into the front beside the driver, and we drove off again. We gave them cigarettes to try and calm them, and the further we got from the front the friendlier they became. When we reached the outskirts of Hue they excused themselves, very formally, for their bad manners, thanked us for the lift, and stood waving goodbye until we disappeared from view. It wasn't really so surprising; they belonged, after all, to a very civilised race.

'As we expected the imperial city was in the grip of the collective hysteria defeat always brings in its wake. Two-thirds of the population flowed out along the 'dreary road' in a swaying mass, pushing carts and carrying bundles, battling their way towards the harbour at Da Nang. There was something eerie about the sight of this mass of humanity, sweating and groaning under their loads, moving south in virtual silence . . . . Even in despair they retained their dignity. That night in Hue the red glow of artillery fire lit up the dark sky over the river. Then shots rang out. Marauding troops had started looting and burning the market, irate because the local shopkeepers had refused to hand over their stocks of alcohol. The military police were trying to control the mob – hence the sound of shooting. We could hear the dull explosions of underwater mines going off down by the river. They were supposed to stop the North Vietnamese frogmen blowing up the one vital bridge across the Perfume River.'

Peter Scholl-Latour, Death in the Ricefields

Left: ARVN airborne troops celebrate a local success – they have just driven North Vietnamese soldiers out of the burning building behind them, during the struggle to retake Quang Tri City in the late summer of 1972. By this time ARVN morale was much improved.

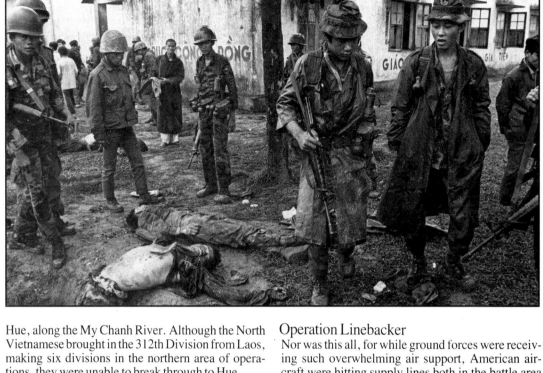

Right: The fighting in 1972 took a fearful toll of the North Vietnamese. Here, South Vietnamese troops, including the distinctively dressed Rangers (centre right), stand over the bodies of two North Vietnamese soldiers at Dong Ha on the northern front.

Left: A lone refugee carries her belongings down the long road from Quang Tri City to Da Nang as ARVN troops head the other way. It is reckoned that the fighting of 1972 created about 970,000 refugees.

Below: Two South Vietnamese soldiers sit amid the ruins of Quang Tri City after its recapture in September 1972, watching smoke rise from an air strike further north where fighting continues.

Hue, along the My Chanh River. Although the North Vietnamese brought in the 312th Division from Laos, making six divisions in the northern area of operations, they were unable to break through to Hue.

By the end of May the North Vietnamese offensive was running out of steam on every front. There had been no general collapse in the South Vietnamese Army, and the firepower provided by the Soviet-supplied tanks and artillery had been out-matched by the volume of American air and naval power. More than 25 warships of the US Seventh Fleet were available in the Gulf of Tonkin. They delivered 161,000 tonnes of ammunition to ground targets by September. Once the bad weather of early April had passed, the volume of air support was unprecedented – in March 1972, 4237 fixed-wing strike sorties were flown in South Vietnam and in May the figure was 18,444. About 700 US fighter-bombers and 170 B-52s were available to provide these strikes.

Operation Linebacker

Nor was this all, for while ground forces were receiving such overwhelming air support, American aircraft were hitting supply lines both in the battle area and, under the operational code-name 'Linebacker', north of the DMZ. There can be little doubt about the effectiveness of this air offensive.

The North Vietnamese would have been stretching their logistic support to the utmost whatever happened, but the scale of American air interdiction meant that the NVA's guns began to run out of ammunition and its tanks out of fuel. The initiative passed to the ARVN, which could now conduct a set of counter-attacks to regain lost ground.

Fighting continued throughout the summer months, with mixed results. At the end of June an ARVN offensive was launched north of Hue, resulting in the retaking of Quang Tri City by the middle of September. The ARVN also scored successes in the northern districts of Binh Dinh Province, east of Kontum. But the NVA troops were skilled warriors in defence and proved tenacious in holding the ground they had won. In some areas they even launched further attacks during the summer; Que Son, south of Da Nang, fell to such an assault in August and had to be retaken in September. Nevertheless, Giap's hopes of taking over South Vietnam in one fell swoop had been dashed, even though the presence of large NVA concentrations within the South remained a considerable threat to the South Vietnamese government.

For the communists, the cost of the offensive was high. About 100,000 North Vietnamese soldiers were killed. South Vietnamese casualties were less than half that figure and were more than made good by the 84,000 recruits who completed training between May and July. General Giap's men paid the price for a plan that ignored the basics of traditional military strategy. His forces were not concentrated sufficiently and he forgot that the South Vietnamese had the advantage of interior lines of communication. Most significantly of all, the North Vietnamese underestimated American will-power and the capabilities of American air forces. The offensive had shown that as long as the US air umbrella remained, the NVA could not take the South.
Michael Orr

An Loc '72
The ARVN holds out

The battle for control of An Loc was the most protracted single episode of the North Vietnamese Army (NVA) offensive that began on 30 March 1972. During the following months headlines throughout the world tended to be dominated by events in the north of South Vietnam – the fall of Quang Tri City on 1 May being the low point for the South Vietnamese Army (ARVN) – but in reality the battle for An Loc proved to be the key to the whole campaign.

The NVA offensive began on Good Friday with a massive artillery attack on ARVN positions throughout Quang Tri Province, and virtually the whole of the northern part of the province had fallen by the time the second part of the communist effort, in Tay Ninh and Binh Long Provinces in the Parrot's Beak and Fish Hook area to the north of Saigon, began to unfold on 2 April. The attack in Tay Ninh was diversionary, designed to tie down ARVN units while the communist main effort was made in Binh Long Province against Loc Ninh (a district capital), Quan Loi and An Loc. Secondary status, however, did not prevent communist forces in Tay Ninh securing Lac Long on 4 April and inflicting a sharp, if local, defeat on government forces outside Tay Ninh City on the following day.

These successes left the communists free to infiltrate and attack Binh Long from the west, just as the main effort in the south began with an advance by the 5th Viet Cong Division on Loc Ninh. The town came under siege on 5 April, and despite its garrison being given round-the-clock air support, it was lost by the ARVN on 7 April. That same day the 7th NVA Division cut Route 13 behind An Loc while other communist units forced the ARVN to evacuate Quan Loi, a small town and airfield on the high ground to the east of the town.

By 7 April, however, the South Vietnamese authorities had taken the decision to stand and fight for An Loc. Despite the seriousness of the situation in the north and the obvious danger of other enemy offen-sives elsewhere, Saigon had little option but to fight for a provincial capital just 90km (56 miles) from the capital. On 7 April two ARVN Ranger battalions were rushed to An Loc to support units from the 5th Infantry Division already in the city, and on 10 April two more units were airlifted into An Loc. Finally, on 13 April, President Nguyen Van Thieu committed his own guard, the 1st Airborne Brigade, to An Loc with orders to fight to the last man for the town. There were

Above: ARVN troops prepare to move into combat after landing at An Loc. Opposite above: Panic-stricken ARVN troops rush a helicopter in an attempt to flee An Loc early in the siege. Opposite below: Elite ARVN troops race towards An Loc.

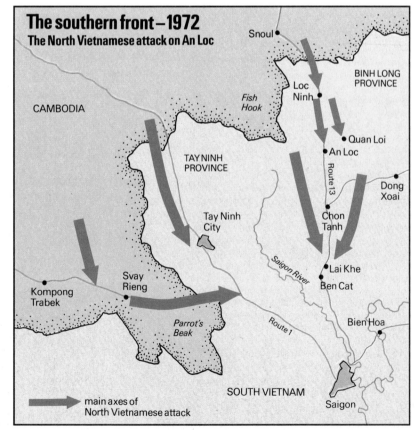

The southern front – 1972
The North Vietnamese attack on An Loc

Snoul · Loc Ninh · Fish Hook · CAMBODIA · BINH LONG PROVINCE · Quan Loi · An Loc · TAY NINH PROVINCE · Route 13 · Dong Xoai · Tay Ninh City · Chon Tanh · Saigon River · Lai Khe · Ben Cat · Svay Rieng · Kompong Trabek · Parrot's Beak · Route 1 · Bien Hoa · SOUTH VIETNAM · Saigon

→ main axes of North Vietnamese attack

however, two obvious problems attached to Thieu's decision to fight for An Loc: the defenders had little in the way of artillery support and the ARVN had no overland line of communication into the town.

The communists' softening-up barrage began on 12 April and the following day the 9th NVA Division made an unsuccessful effort to take the town in the face of pulverising attacks delivered by Huey Cobras and B-52 bombers. The communist formations spent the next day regrouping in readiness for the renewal of an attack that on 15 April carried them into the outskirts of An Loc. In the face of continuing attacks by fighter-bombers, AC-119 Stinger and AC-130 Spectre gunships, however, the attackers could neither consolidate nor expand their gains, and the communist toeholds were quickly eliminated by the defenders. After that date the communist forces settled down for a siege and strengthened their anti-aircraft defences in order to try to cut An Loc's last remaining link with the outside world.

As early as 12 April, at the very start of the battle, the South Vietnamese had been forced to end their attempt to resupply An Loc by Chinook helicopters, but with the airfield closed, they and the Americans had little choice but to try to maintain An Loc by low-altitude low-speed drops by transports such as C-130s. The first five American Hercules so committed were damaged, one being lost, before this particular effort was discontinued on 19 April in favour of high-altitude radar-controlled parachute drops. With

a restricted dropping zone and many parachute malfunctions, however, most of the supplies that were dropped fell into enemy hands. On 23 April the low-level missions were resumed, only to be abandoned again three days later in favour of night drops.

By this time government forces had begun a sortie towards An Loc to relieve the town. The approach of the relief force provoked the communists to launch their biggest single artillery attack to date on 27 April, but this and subsequent attacks were held and the ARVN broke into An Loc on 5 May. Nevertheless, with communist forces still astride Route 13, An Loc remained dependent on aerial resupply, although, with better parachutes and guidance techniques, this situation was improving.

This partial lifting of the siege, and obvious ARVN preparations for another relief sortie, forced the communists to abandon siege tactics in favour of a renewed attempt to overrun An Loc's garrison by sheer weight of numbers. On 9 May probing attacks were resumed, and American gunships found that increased enemy flak forced them to altitudes at which they could no longer provide the telling support that had characterised their April operations. On 11 May communist infantry, backed by a battalion of Soviet-made tanks and a heavy artillery attack, made a major assault. The Americans, however, concentrated every B-52 bomber in Southeast Asia in defence of An Loc. Pre-planned patterns of bombing shattered this attack and beat off further assaults on 12 and 14 April. Thereafter NVA forces moved away from An Loc in order to block the progress of the relief columns, and it was not until 7 June that the city was relieved for a second time. Communist forces were not cleared from An Loc and the immediate countryside until 12 June. The siege was declared to be at an end on 18 June.

Superficially the successful defence of An Loc was a major achievement by the ARVN, a large-scale communist attack having been thwarted and the process of Vietnamization having been vindicated after a very shaky start. This was true enough, but the real significance of the events was too easily missed. Communist forces hung on around An Loc for three months in the face of fearful air attack, and by

The hail of metal

'In the combat zone between the two hostile armies all hell had broken loose. US fighter-bombers circled overhead then plummeted like hawks before releasing their load of napalm and explosives. How did the North Vietnamese infantry manage to endure and survive this appalling hail of metal for weeks on end?.... The South Vietnamese never used infantry to overcome enemy resistance. Instead they waited until the enemy had been worn down and crushed by air and artillery bombardment. This tactic cut no ice with Hanoi's seasoned troops on Route 13.

'The North Vietnamese front line was dug in right where the napalm bombs sent up black puffs of smoke and fountains of mud rose high in the air. They were careful not to give away their position by returning fire.... While all this was going on the encircled stronghold of An Loc was clearly visible through binoculars about 12 kilometres away.... It seemed incredible that, with the colossal reserves of men and equipment the army of the South had at its disposal, it could not dislodge those few hundred North Vietnamese.'

Peter Scholl-Latour, Death in the Ricefields

mid-June An Loc was as isolated and vulnerable as it had been at any time since April. With the communists holding the surrounding countryside, Route 13 remained closed, and in August all ARVN bases between An Loc and Chon Thanh, 30km (19 miles) to the south along Route 13, had to be abandoned. By September fighting along the road had crept to within 65km (40 miles) of Saigon.

The fact of the matter was that, although between April and June An Loc had been flattened, with perhaps half of its 20,000 inhabitants and some 10,000 communist troops killed, the basic position in Binh Long remained unchanged. The communist sanctuaries across the border remained intact, communist control of the countryside was unbroken, and the ARVN remained overcommitted and too weak to resist attack unless provided with massive American air support. The full consequences of this dependence were to be seen when anticipated American air support did not materialise in April 1975.

H.P. Willmott

Below: An ARVN soldier clambers over a knocked-out NVA T55 tank. NVA tanks seemed to pose a serious threat, but in built-up areas they proved vulnerable to light anti-tank weapons and in open countryside were exposed to air attack.

In October 1981 it was announced that 100 Rockwell B-1B bombers were to be ordered for the United States Air Force (USAF) as part of an ambitious strategic forces modernisation programme. The new aircraft was needed to take over from the B-52 Stratofortress as a manned strategic system capable of penetrating the Soviet Union's air defences. The elderly B-52s were long overdue for replacement as low-level bombers.

The quest for a successor to the B-52 had proved to be a long and tortuous process. In the early 1960s North American Aviation produced the XB-70A Valkyrie, which was intended to defeat Soviet defences by flying higher and faster than any enemy interceptor or surface-to-air missile. Yet Soviet technological developments overtook this design and when it became clear that the Valkyrie would stand little chance against a new generation of interceptors and missiles (notably the Mach 3 MiG-25 Foxbat), the XB-70 project was cancelled. Strategic bomber design then changed direction and sought to produce an aircraft capable of defeating enemy air defence systems by flying at low level under radar beams, so that the enemy would be given only the shortest possible warning of its approach.

North American's successor company, Rockwell International, produced just such a bomber in the B-1A. This was a four-engined, variable-geometry winged aircraft capable of flying at very low altitudes - as low as 30m (100ft) - at high subsonic speed, or of reaching over Mach 2 at altitude. Apart from its considerably improved flight performance over the B-52, the new bomber could lift one-and-a-half times the payload on a long-range mission and take off in half the distance. A short take-off run is of considerable advantage to a strategic bomber because it allows the time taken for a scramble take-off to be cut to a minimum, and enables the bomber force to be dispersed to numerous auxiliary airfields in time of crisis, thus making it difficult for Soviet target planners to knock out the bomber force on the ground.

Despite the B-1A's indisputable advantages over the B-52, it seemed that this new bomber design was to go the way of the Valkyrie, when in June 1977 the US government cancelled the 240-aircraft production programme in favour of the ALCM (air-launched cruise missile). However, it became apparent that the ALCM was no real substitute for the manned bomber but rather a useful adjunct to it. Compared to the

bomber, an ALCM lacks flexibility as, for example, it cannot be re-targetted after launch or react intelligently to enemy defence measures. Consequently when it was decided to deploy both bombers and ALCMs, the B-1 was a ready-made manned bomber system, with four prototypes under test from the earlier programme, and so the obvious choice for the USAF.

The USAF's manned bomber mission would typically involve a scramble take-off followed by a rendezvous with an in-flight refuelling tanker aircraft when the bomber would take on a full load of fuel. It would afterwards set course for its assigned target, flying at an economical cruising speed of Mach 0.85 at high altitude, until it approached the edge of the Soviet air defences, when it would drop down to around 60m (200ft), maintaining a speed of Mach 0.85. What is immediately apparent from this mission profile is that the B-1A's Mach 2-plus capability was entirely superfluous for its primary strategic mission. Accordingly the new production batch of B-IBs have been designed to possess a maximum speed of only Mach 1.2. This has allowed the complex engine inlet system of the B-1A, with its computer-controlled moveable ramps, to be replaced by a much simpler fixed inlet system.

Although the resemblance between the B-1A and B-1B is close, there are several other significant differences between the two aircraft. The B-1B's structure is lighter yet stronger, enabling the gross take-off weight to be increased from the B-1A's 179,000kg (395,000lb) to 216,500kg (477,000lb), with the increase being made up of either additional fuel or weapons. The reduced maximum speed of the B-1B has allowed a simpler wing sweep mechanism

Previous page: A B-1 trundles out onto the runway prior to take-off. Top: The second prototype B-1A is prepared for a test flight. Enormous care was taken to ensure that the B-1 incorporated all the latest advances in aviation technology. Above: The B-1 mock-up, unveiled to public view in November 1971. Built primarily from wood the mock-up was used by the air force and Rockwell as a manufacturing guide for the real thing.

to be designed for this variant. Another move towards simplifying the complex original design has been the substitution of individual crew ejection seats for a jettisonable crew escape capsule where the entire crew compartment would have been blasted away from the airframe by two solid-fuel rockets, the capsule then descending to earth under three parachutes.

The most significant change of all between the two B-1 variants is the reduction of the B-1B's radar signature by an appreciable amount. The B-1B's radar section is only one-tenth that of the B-1A, a reduction achieved by applying various aspects of 'stealth' technology to the design; for example, areas of the aircraft which act as good radar reflectors – engine inlets, nose radome, wing roots and tail assembly – have either been re-designed to reduce this characteristic or coated with radar-absorbent material.

The B-1 is an advanced design both structurally and aerodynamically. Carbon fibre composite materials are used in the construction of the tail fin, wing flaps and weapons-bay doors to reduce weight without compromising strength. Most of the airframe is built from aluminium, except that the undercarriage is steel and the aft portions of the engine nacelles and the wing pivot pins are constructed of titanium. The fuselage and wings are shaped to blend together, with the engines paired in nacelles beneath the fixed inner sections of the wing. The wing's outer panels can be varied between a fully forward position of 15 degrees sweepback and 67.5 degrees when fully swept. A low-altitude ride control senses gusts acting on the aircraft and applies automatic control corrections by means of small foreplanes mounted ahead of the cockpit section and by the lower half of the rudder. This system not only reduces pilot workload when flying at low level where gusting can be frequent, but it also improves overall crew efficiency by giving them a smoother and less tiring ride.

The internal arrangement of the B-1 is compact, with a great deal of the wing and fuselage occupied by fuel cells. The B-1B can carry a maximum internal fuel load of over 47,600kg (105,000lb), providing an intercontinental range which can be further extended by in-flight refuelling. The crew, comprising the captain, co-pilot, offensive and defensive systems operators, are grouped together in a pressurised compartment which provides a shirt-sleeves working environment. Most of the remaining internal volume of the fuselage is given over to various avionics systems and to internal weapons storage. The original B-1A design incorporated three internal weapons bays: two adjoining ones forward of the wing centre section and a third aft. In the B-1B, however, to accommodate AGM-86B ALCMs internally, the dividing bulkhead between the two forward bays has been made removable, so that one long bay can be created. External hardpoints beneath the fuselage can carry additional weapons, and if needed, auxiliary

Above: A B-1 in flight with its wings fully swept back. Variable geometry wings were considered essential for this high-speed low-level bomber. Below: A B-1 claws its way skyward. Despite being smaller than the B-52 the B-1 can carry a far greater bomb load.

Left: A B-1 prototype banks over to port, its wings fully forward. Right: A B-1 takes on fuel in mid-air. Typically the B-1 would be air-refuelled before setting out on its mission, in order to replace the large amounts of fuel used on take-off. Below: A B-1 depicted in level flight. Bottom: Testing procedures are carried out on a B-1 on the ground.

U.S. AIR FORCE

fuel tanks can be fitted in the weapons bays. Possible armament combinations include up to 38 free-fall nuclear bombs or nuclear-armed AGM-69 SRAMs (short-range attack missiles), 24 of them carried internally. The maximum load of AGM-86B ALCMs is 22, with eight carried on an internal rotary launcher in the forward weapons bay. A heavy load of conventional bombs can be carried, including up to 128 500lb Mk 82 bombs.

The B-1B's complex avionics can be classified as either offensive or defensive. The former includes the highly-accurate inertial primary navigation sensor, the Honeywell ANS-131 standard precision navigation gimballed electrostatic aircraft navigation system. In addition, there is a Doppler navigation radar, a FLIR (forward-looking infra-red) sensor for all-weather viewing of targets or navigational waypoints, and a range of communications equipment including an ASC-19 satellite communications set. Data transfer and the control of power distribution between the B-1B's great array of electronic equipment is handled by the EMUX electrical system, which it is claimed saves the need for more than 130km (80 miles) of conventional electrical wiring.

The defensive avionics, so essential for the effective penetration of enemy airspace, comprise the ALQ-161 ECM (electronic counter-measures) system and the ALQ-153 tail-mounted warning radar. The ALQ-161 is a computer-controlled threat-warning and jamming system which will pick up enemy radar signals and automatically initiate the appropriate jamming. In addition to chaff and flare dispensers, the B-1B has a large number of additional jamming transmitters which can operate against different radar threats simultaneously. The warning radar will pick up enemy interceptors and missiles to enable effective counter-measures to be initiated against them. The entire system is monitored by the defensive systems operator, who if he wishes can operate the counter-measures systems manually.

The B-1 will depend for success upon a combination of low operating altitude flying, stealth technology and electronic counter-measures to enable it to penetrate Soviet air defences. The USAF believes that these measures will be effective against any projected Soviet air defence system until well into the next century, by which time the new Advanced Technology Bomber will be established in service.

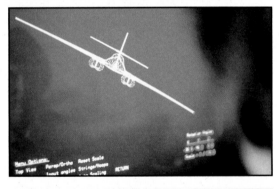

Top: The complex avionics that would confront the offensive weapons-systems operator. Much of the information is presented to the operator in digital form. Above: Two of the B-1s four 30,000lb F101-GE-100 turbofans. Right: A computer drawing of the B-1 during the design stage. Below: A mock-up of the B-1's complex cockpit.

Rockwell B-1B Bomber

Type Supersonic long-range strategic bomber
Dimensions Span (fully spread) 41.67m (136ft 8in); length 44.81m (147ft); height 10.3m (34ft)
Weight Maximum take-off 216,500kg (477,000lb)
Powerplant Four 13,600kg (30,000lb) General Electric F101-GE-102 augmented turbofan engines

Performance Maximum level speed Mach 1.25
Range 9815km (6100 miles)
Ceiling 18,300m (60,000ft)

Armament 38 free-fall nuclear bombs or nuclear armed AGM-69 SRAMs, 24 carried internally, up to a weight of 56,160kg (115,000lb). Alternatively, 22 AGM-86B ALCMs can be carried

Linebacker

The deployment of US air power in Vietnam, 1972

When the North Vietnamese invaded the South on 30 March 1972 the Americans, despite considerable force reductions since 1969 and a concurrent policy of Vietnamization, were still committed to the protection of their allies in Saigon. For domestic political reasons that commitment could no longer take the form of ground troops, but with nearly 400 United States Air Force (USAF) strike aircraft stationed in Thailand, South Vietnam and the western Pacific, and an ability to reinforce these numbers with speed, President Richard Nixon retained the option of a formidable response to the invasion. The fact that North Vietnamese Army (NVA) units mounted their attacks at a time of year when cloud ceilings might be low enough to hamper air operations, and advanced beneath a powerful protective shield of surface-to-air missiles (SAMs) and anti-aircraft artillery (AAA), implied that they were fully aware of the threat.

As soon as he received news of the invasion, Nixon acted with a ruthless determination that his predecessors had often lacked, ordering an immediate air reinforcement to the Vietnam theatre. By 4 April USAF and Marine F-4 squadrons had begun to deploy from Japan and South Korea to bases in Thailand and South Vietnam, the former USAF radar and communications infrastructure in the South had been reactivated and a special long-term air reinforcement programme, code-named 'Constant Guard', had been initiated. By the end of May USAF and Marine air strength in Southeast Asia had risen to 700 machines, of which nearly 400 were F-4 and F-105 strike aircraft and 170 were B-52 heavy bombers, backed by a host of reconnaissance, forward air control (FAC) and transport planes, as well as helicopters and remotely-piloted vehicles (RPVs). In addition, four US Navy carriers, each with 90 attack aircraft on

board, had taken up positions off the Vietnamese coast and the training and re-equipment of the South Vietnamese Air Force (VNAF), itself some 1500 aircraft strong, had been accelerated. It was an awesome display of force, made even more so by the addition of newly-developed technology, including the first-generation of Paveway LGBs (laser-guided bombs) – 900kg (2000lb) weapons which could be delivered with pin-point accuracy onto targets illuminated by a laser beam. They were symbolic of the enormous gap that existed between the NVA and its American-backed enemy.

Once deployed, American air power could carry out a wide range of tasks. Reconnaissance aircraft (usually RF-4Cs) had already monitored the build-up of NVA forces before 30 March and they continued to report on the location and scale of enemy attacks throughout the campaign. They were aided over the battle area itself by slow-moving, low-flying FACs and even, occasionally, by RPVs, although use of the latter devices was not yet general. Without the in-

Below: A Cessna A-37B Dragonfly launches its rockets against ground targets. The Cessna was transferred to the South Vietnamese Air Force in 1970, and was extensively used in both reconnaissance and close-support missions. Bottom: A Douglas A-1E Skyraider unleashes some of its ordnance against a suspected NVA position. The Skyraider could carry up to 3630 kg (8000lb) of armament on 15 hardpoints. The weaponry could range from bombs, napalm and rockets to depth-charges, mines and torpedoes.

Right: A B-52D, flaps down, approaches a runway at U Tapao airfield in Thailand. The B-52s based in Thailand were one of the major elements in the aerial power that the USA could deploy in the Far East and Southeast Asia.

Below right: Civilians survey the destruction wreaked by the short but intense US bombing campaign of December 1972. From 18-30 December (with a pause on Christmas Day) over 20,000 tonnes of ordnance were dropped on Hanoi and Haiphong.

Precision bombing

When B-52s were used on interdiction missions in South Vietnam, they had nothing to fear from enemy action, but remarkable skills were demanded to achieve the requisite level of accuracy. A five-second delay in the release of a bomb load from 11km (seven miles) high would give a totally unacceptable half-mile error in targeting. In effect, the B-52s bombed by remote control: ground radar stations manned by three controllers checking and double-checking one another's work led the three-aircraft B-52 'cells' onto their target and gave the order for bomb release to the lead plane when sure of the accuracy of the location. Journalist Michael Getler describes the feeling of remoteness from the realities of war on a B-52 mission north of Saigon in 1972:

'"Bomb doors open," a yellow light flashed in the darkened cockpit. "Five, four, three, two, one, hack," came the ground controller's voice over the radio and the lead B-52 unloaded 66 500lb bombs.

'A precise number of seconds later, the radar navigator . . . hit the bomb switch in our plane. The huge jet shuddered slightly as 66 more bombs were released, 42 from the bomb bay and 24 from the wings. It took seven seconds.

'Another yellow light and "bombs released" flicked on in the cockpit. In the navigator's compartment lights went out one by one, telling him that all the bombs had dropped free and none was hung up on the rack . . . .

'We banked to the east, arching back to the sea before the first bombs had even reached the ground. It takes about a minute for bombs to hit from seven miles up. Flashes bounced off the clouds . . . . It was the only hint of the spectacle that was going on below us.'

formation thus provided, often at great personal risk to the aircrew involved, the full weight of destructive air power – the main advantage enjoyed by the allies – could not have been delivered.

Because of the weather problems, this power tended to be exercised most forcibly by B-52s from Thailand and Guam, flying in three-aircraft 'cells' which could devastate a preselected 'box' measuring 1km by 3km (0.6 miles by 2.5 miles) even through cloud. On more then one occasion NVA forces, massing for an attack, were caught in such a 'box' and decimated, and the availability of the B-52s – operating at altitudes which made them virtually invulnerable to air defences – meant that strikes of this nature could be repeated almost at will. On 11/12 May, for example, as the battle for An Loc to the north of Saigon reached its height, B-52 'cells' arrived over the disputed area every 55 minutes for nearly 30 hours, effectively blunting the NVA assault.

But such attacks were, by their very nature, indiscriminate – NVA forces could be destroyed only if they happened to be in the preselected 'box' – and more precise battlefield targets had to be left to close-support aircraft such as F-4s, F-105s, AC-119 and AC-130 gunships or attack helicopters. These were potentially vulnerable to anti-aircraft defences and initially found it difficult to operate effectively through the persistent cloud and mist, although in a remarkable display of flexibility a workable system was soon developed.

Firepower and GRADS

Whenever ground troops called for support, the target would be located by the ubiquitous Cessna 0-1 Bird Dog or Rockwell OV-10 Bronco FACs and the attack aircraft would then be called down. Preceded by F-4s or F-105s dispensing 'chaff' or deploying electronic countermeasures (ECM) equipment to confuse SAM radars, the attackers would launch LGBs, cluster-bombs or conventional ordnance to devastating effect. In the northern provinces alone, between 1 April and 15 August 1972, an estimated 285 NVA tanks were destroyed from the air, some of them while literally on top of South Vietnamese Army (ARVN) positions. For even more precise work, taking out individual buildings or enemy posts, the gunships could deploy 20mm, 40mm and 105mm firepower and were available both day and night, while US Army UH-1B Iroquois helicopters, equipped with TOW (tube-launched optical-tracked wire-guided) anti-tank missiles and 2.75in rockets, also put in an appearance. Against such a weight of fire, the NVA attacks could make little real progress.

But this was not the only advantage enjoyed by the South Vietnamese. The key to ARVN success in 1972 lay in its ability to defend existing locations, denying momentum to the enemy advance; without the transport and resupply capabilities of air power this would have been impossible to organise effectively. During the initial stages of the campaign, threatened outposts were reinforced or, if no longer tenable, evacuated, using helicopters and fixed-wing transports. Thereafter, as the battle progressed, beleaguered ARVN positions were resupplied with food, munitions and fuel – the latter carried in special 17,000-litre (4500-gallon) 'bladders' in the cargo bays of C-130s – and, if completely cut off, sustained by paradrops using the newly-developed GRADS (ground radar aerial delivery system) technique. Despite teething troubles,

Above: A bridge cut by the US air raids of 1972. The fact that the NVA was engaging in a more conventional form of warfare in the spring of 1972, making great use of armour and artillery support, meant that it needed a much greater volume of supplies than previously. This made it more vulnerable to US interdiction bombing than ever before.

GRADS enabled 90 per cent of supply drops into An Loc in May and June to reach the defenders and on one unique occasion a C-130 even managed to deposit its load directly on top of that from a preceding aircraft. Such impressive accuracy was clearly of crucial importance to the maintenance of ARVN defences.

By comparison the NVA could not guarantee its supply chain, for while the invasion was being blunted in the battle area, the Americans adopted a deliberate policy of air interdiction, designed to cut the invaders off from their bases in the North. Close to the battlefield, this involved B-52s hitting transportation choke-points – in the northern provinces of South Vietnam in May, for example, 45 bridges were destroyed between the demilitarised zone (DMZ) and the front line – while further north across the border similar targets were hit in a campaign which gradually grew in intensity. Within three days of the invasion, US aircraft were authorised to bomb military installations up to 40km (25 miles) north of the DMZ, under the operational code-name 'Freedom Train', and by mid-April the target area had been extended as far as the 20th parallel. On 8 May, as the latest round of peace talks in Paris broke down, Nixon went one stage further and released a substantial part of his air capability over the whole of North Vietnam (except for a narrow buffer along the Chinese border) in what was known as Operation Linebacker.

At first sight this looked like a repetition of the unsuccessful Rolling Thunder campaign of 1965-68, but in reality there were considerable differences. In the first place, the basic aim of Linebacker – to reduce North Vietnamese capability to wage continued war against the South – was a realistic goal. The conventional offensive the North Vietnamese were now waging was vulnerable to air interdiction because it required 10,000 tonnes of supplies a week to sustain. By comparison, in 1967 it was estimated that only 400 tonnes a week sufficed to feed the communist war effort in the South. Nixon's decision to allow the mining of North Vietnamese ports effectively halted the flow of war materials from elsewhere in the communist bloc. By the middle of the year Soviet and Chinese freighters had been forced to off-load their cargoes outside Vietnamese territorial waters, transferring supplies to barges in an operation which sometimes took a month to complete. When this coincided with the destruction of rail and road links between China and Hanoi, the North Vietnamese faced the problem of sustaining a major campaign in the South from a dwindling stockpile of supplies.

Secondly, Linebacker did not suffer from the disadvantage of tight political control which had so bedevilled Rolling Thunder, for few targets were restricted and local air commanders were allowed to exercise a marked degree of initiative. Only within the population centres of Hanoi and Haiphong were the targets subject to specific political approval, but even then it took little to gain the necessary authorisation. Finally, with the introduction of Paveway LGBs and other 'smart' weapons, the Americans were at last able to guarantee the accurate destruction of targets in the North, replacing the bludgeon effect of Rolling Thunder with strikes of almost surgical precision and avoiding, to a large extent, the political problems of damage to civilian areas.

Even so, the campaign was not without its problems, chief amongst which was the threat of substantial air losses from North Vietnamese defences, for by 1972 Hanoi possessed a sophisticated SAM and AAA capability as well as an air force containing over 200 MiG fighters. The Americans countered this by developing an elaborate 'strike package'. At the centre were the attack aircraft – usually 32 F-4s equipped with LGBs and conventional bombs – protected by a further 20-40 aircraft which included F-4 or F-105 Wild Weasels (to search for SAM sites), special hunter-killer teams (to suppress ground defences) and fighters fitted with Sparrow or Sidewinder air-to-air missiles (to take on the MiGs). A pair of RF-4C

B-52s over Hanoi

Linebacker II from 18-30 December 1972 brought the first and so far the only full-scale encounter between America's strategic bombers and a Soviet air defence system. Previously B-52s had been carefully kept away from high-risk areas; their missions over Laos and Cambodia were largely unchallenged.

Massed raids into the heart of the Hanoi air defence system were bound to be a different proposition. The B-52s were to attack in three waves of 49 bombers, flying in mutually-supporting three-aircraft cells at over 9000m (30,000ft). Manoeuvring was to be kept to a minimum in order to avoid mid-air collisions in the crowded airspace and to increase the accuracy of bombing. It was thought that pre-strike attacks on MiG fighter airfields, the laying of a chaff corridor and the B-52s' own electronic countermeasures (ECM) equipment would ensure survival.

On the first night three B-52s were lost to North Vietnam's SA-2 missiles. There were problems with chaff, which was dispersed by high winds, and by the sharp post-target turn the bombers had to make – a vulnerable

moment when their ECM became less effective.

On the second night no B-52s were lost and the third night's bombing was approached with confidence on an identical pattern. In nine hours, however, the Americans then lost six B-52s to SA-2 missiles. All but one were downed during the post-target turn. The decision was taken to continue the bombing at a reduced level, and a hasty post-mortem was conducted on the operation so far. After discussion, tactics were revised: evasive manoeuvres and varied approach runs were adopted, along with a more shallow post-target turn, and the B-52Gs, which had less effective ECM than the B-52Ds, were dropped from the Hanoi raids. Bomber casualties immediately fell.

After the Christmas Day bombing pause, on 26 December another new tactic was adopted. In the space of 15 minutes 120 B-52s attacked Hanoi and Haiphong, saturating the air defences by sheer quantity and achieving meticulous coordination – although two bombers were lost. By 28 December North Vietnamese missile stocks were low and the attacks were proceeding with virtual impunity by the time the campaign was halted.

reconnaissance aircraft would be available to take post-strike photographs, while A-7s or F-4s, protected by yet more fighters and Wild Weasels, dispensed 'chaff' to create a SAM-free corridor. Further out, EB-66s would conduct standoff ECM jamming and an RC-121 (code-named 'Disco') would act as an aerial command post, relaying weather and target information from a US Navy control ship ('Red Crown') in the Gulf of Tonkin. KC-135 tankers refuelled the strike package as it went in and came out of the target area and HH-53 helicopters were on call to rescue downed air crew. It was a formidable force, in which the ratio of support to attack aircraft could be as high as 5:1, and when it is added that B-52s were also hitting the North (although not the Hanoi-Haiphong area), the scale of the Linebacker raids may be easily appreciated.

Taking out the bridges

The results were impressive. By 23 October, when Nixon suspended bombing north of the 20th parallel in response to a breakthrough in the peace negotiations, North Vietnam had absorbed 155,548 tonnes of bombs, delivered by a total of 41,653 aircraft sorties. In the process, the Americans had lost 44 warplanes but had inflicted widespread damage on the enemy's supply network. War-related industries and existing stockpiles of material had been hit, with repeated attacks on vehicle repair shops, POL (petrol, oil, lubricant) storage facilities, truck parks and military warehouses, and the replenishment of such supplies from outside sources had been curtailed, chiefly by the destruction of road and rail links between Hanoi and China, Haiphong and the DMZ. Crucial to this success was the new-found ability to destroy bridges using smart bombs; by the end of May Hanoi had been effectively isolated, having lost 13 rail bridges to the northwest and northeast, four towards Haiphong and several more to the south. Included amongst them were the notorious Paul Doumer and Thanh Hoa bridges, scenes of unsuccessful and costly raids during Rolling Thunder. By 13 May both had been cut by 'smart' bombs and were to remain out of service for the rest of the year. This helped to prevent the movement of supplies from China and the distribution of material to front-line units, contributing significantly to the halting of the NVA advance in the South, but still the bombing continued, hitting airfields, anti-aircraft defence sites and even thermal power plants before the halt on 23 October.

The most concentrated bombing of the North was, however, still to come. As the peace negotiations once more stalled, Nixon threatened the North Vietnamese with massive destruction if they did not accept the US proposals. No agreement was forthcoming, and on 18 December Nixon released his full air strength for a short, sharp campaign of destruction over the North. Unofficially known as Linebacker II, the campaign was to last for 11 days only.

About 20,000 tonnes of bombs were dropped during Linebacker II, chiefly onto Hanoi and Haiphong, and for the first time the B-52s were allowed to participate without restriction. Despite poor weather and a formidable air-defence problem – the North Vietnamese launched nearly 1000 SAMs and committed their entire force of MiG fighters to the fray – the bombing was sustained, accurate and deadly, imposing more damage on the North than all the raids of the previous eight years. In Hanoi the Gia Lam railyard was devastated, barrack buildings at Bac Mai were levelled (it was during this attack that a nearby hospital was inadvertently hit) and warehouses at Yen Vien and Van Dien were destroyed; in Haiphong twenty 190,000-litre (50,000-gallon) oil tanks were flattened and at Thai Nguyen a power plant was put out of action. By comparison, the Americans lost 26 aircraft (including 15 B-52s) but virtually wiped out the opposing air force and remaining SAM and AAA systems to achieve complete air supremacy. By 30 December an estimated 80 per cent of the North's electrical power production and 25 per cent of its POL storage facilities had been destroyed, leaving the bombers short of worthwhile targets.

Linebacker II was a stunning display of surgical air power which indicated that the Americans now had the ability to impose selective and devastating damage upon an enemy state even under the constraints of limited war. Nixon pulled the bombers back below the 20th parallel on 30 December – they were to continue hitting supply lines and SAM sites between there and the DMZ for another two weeks – and a peace agreement was eventually signed on 23 January 1973. The successful blocking of the 1972 invasion and the impact of the Linebacker raids had enabled the United States to withdraw from an unwanted commitment with at least an element of self-respect. If it had not been for the air weapon even that would have been impossible to achieve. **John Pimlott**

Below: US Phantoms from the carrier *Coral Sea* unleash their bomb loads over North Vietnam. The Phantom was a superb multi-role aircraft, with a capacity to carry bombs and missiles up to a maximum weight of 7258kg (16,000lb).

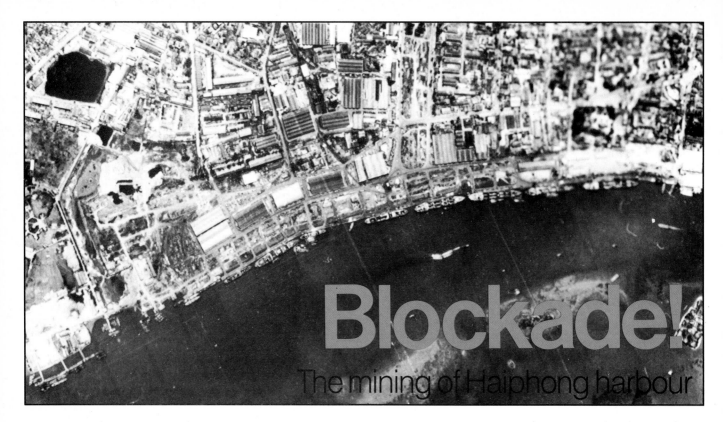

Blockade!
The mining of Haiphong harbour

Within two weeks of the armed forces of North Vietnam crossing the demilitarised zone in the spring of 1972, US B-52s were bombing deep into North Vietnam for the first time since November 1967. Just before dawn on 17 April, 100 aircraft including 20 B-52s crossed the North Vietnamese coastline and began bombing runs against the fuel dumps, truck parks and warehouses around the port city of Haiphong. Haiphong was the nerve centre of the North Vietnamese maritime foreign-supply infrastructure, being the main port of entry for arms and equipment shipped from the Soviet Union and other communist supporters of the Hanoi regime. By massive interdiction of the North Vietnamese supply and storage centres, it was hoped to starve the North Vietnamese Army (NVA) of the arms and ammunition necessary to maintain the pressure of the three-front offensive launched against the South.

By early May, however, the bombing campaign against the railways, bridges and supply roads of the North had shown little effect in halting the NVA advance. Quang Tri City had fallen and Hue, Kontum and An Loc were hard pressed. As the policy of Vietnamization seemingly crumbled despite massive US air strikes in support of South Vietnamese ground forces, the prospect of out-and-out defeat in Vietnam loomed before the Nixon administration. It was thus that President Nixon decided to gamble with a tougher long-term move and mine the harbours of Haiphong and six other key North Vietnamese ports – Cam Pha, Hon Gai, Thanh Hoa, Vinh, Quang Khe and Dong Hoi. Although the mining would have no immediate effect on the progress of the war since the NVA had enough stocks to keep the war going for several months, it reasserted American credibility and commitment to the South while also making it quite clear to the Russians that if they went on supplying huge stocks of war material to the North, the United States was prepared to take measures that might well affect the Soviet Union directly. The mining operation was

therefore intended as a complement to the escalated bombing campaign while also providing a future block to further Soviet supplies of arms and equipment.

On 8 May 1972, in a special television broadcast to the American nation, Nixon announced his new move. All entrances to North Vietnamese ports were to be mined, denying direct access to ships of all nations; countries with ships already in port had 72 hours to leave in safety before the mines were activated. At the time of Nixon's announcement there were 36 ships, of which 16 were Soviet, at anchor in Haiphong harbour. As the deadline for the mines' activation drew closer, six of the Soviet ships steamed out of harbour, while a number of others en route for the port were diverted.

Jeopardising relations

The decision to mine the harbours had not been taken lightly. Such action represented a serious escalation of the current US role in Vietnam, while also potentially jeopardising relations with the Soviet Union and Nixon's forthcoming visit to Moscow to sign the SALT agreement with Brezhnev on 22 May. It also put at risk the newly-forged links with China established by Nixon's February 1972 visit to Peking. In the United States Nixon's new measures were greeted with considerable scepticism within the administration. The military option of blockading the North had been considered on a number of previous occasions but had always been dismissed as too risky, if not ineffectual. CIA reports had concluded that supplies could easily be diverted to road, rail and air links, which past experience had shown capable of surviving all-out bombing. The North Vietnamese would, in any case, still be able to use small vessels to unload cargo freighters out beyond the minefields. Nixon, however, chose to ignore these arguments and the counsel of a number of his senior advisers, fearing that Hue would fall while he was in Moscow and that

Below: Soviet freighters unload war material at the docks in Haiphong. The US was always unwilling to bomb the harbour directly, for fear of sinking Soviet vessels and provoking a major international confrontation, and this led to the decision to mine the approaches instead.

both the reality of America's commitment to its South Vietnamese allies and the prestige of the US presidency would suffer irredeemably.

As soon as his order to mine the ports was transmitted to the commanders of the aircraft carriers USS *Kitty Hawk* aand USS *Coral Sea* stationed in the Gulf of Tonkin, carrier-based US Navy A-7 Corsairs flying at around 3000m (10,000 feet) seeded the harbours of the seven ports with the mines. Two types of mine were deployed, the 230kg (500lb) Mark 53 sweep-obstructor and the larger 900kg (2000lb) Mark 55 bottom mine. Since parachutes would leave a tell-tale marker as to their location, the mines were equipped with rotochutes which slowed their descent from the carrier aircraft and stopped them drilling too deeply into the silt of the harbour bottom. In the shallower water the mines were weighted to sink to the bottom, while in deeper water buoyant mines with mooring cables were laid.

Unlike the contact mine which detonates when struck by a vessel, the mines used to blockade the North were of the influence type. These were equipped with sophisticated electronic sensors to respond to a number of types of vessel 'signature' – its magnetic field distortion, its acoustic signals emanating from the turbines and propellors, and pressure changes in surrounding water created by its displacement. The Mark 55 was manufactured in a number of models which responded to one, two, or a combination of all three 'signatures'. Such a combination, along with the inclusion of an on-board computer, made the mines extremely difficult to clear. A minesweeper could pass the mine, emitting all the 'signatures' necessary to detonate it, while the computer delayed the explosion until a second vessel, perhaps a cargo-laden freighter which had been given clearance after the sweep, came into the mine's range. The inclusion of the computer also allowed the mines to be activated remotely long after the drop and similarly to be deactivated at a future date.

In the final analysis the mining of the North Vietnamese ports was to prove a success. Despite claims of 'brinkmanship' on Nixon's part, the Russians were not prepared to allow the situation in Vietnam to precipitate a confrontation, especially with the 22 May summit so close at hand. For the North Vietnamese, although significant quantities of war supplies could still be imported across the border from China, the 400,000 tonnes of extra cereals they required even in a year of good harvest still had to be imported by ship. The CIA reports which had warned that the North Vietnamese would unload freighters beyond the minefields were to prove correct, yet imports were severely hampered and despite good harvests in 1971 and 1972 food shortages were expected for 1973. The blockade could never be complete but as an adjunct to the bombing it severely restricted the possibility of North Vietnam continuing the war at the pace it had set in the Easter invasion.

Jonathan Reed

Left: An aerial photograph taken by a US reconnaissance aircraft showing the volume of shipping along the quayside at Haiphong prior to the controversial mining operation. Although Chinese war materials could still be imported by road and rail the mining of Haiphong and six other North Vietnamese ports of entry was to severely hamper the future inflow of supplies to the North from the Soviet Union.

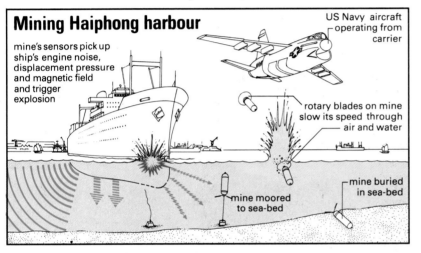

Mining Haiphong harbour

mine's sensors pick up ship's engine noise, displacement pressure and magnetic field and trigger explosion

US Navy aircraft operating from carrier

rotary blades on mine slow its speed through air and water

mine moored to sea-bed

mine buried in sea-bed

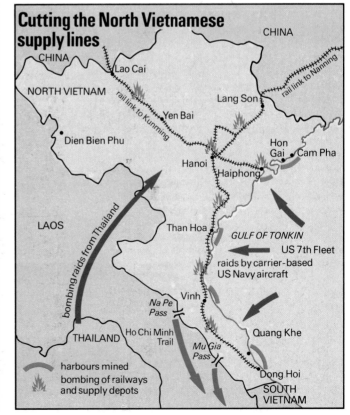

Cutting the North Vietnamese supply lines

CHINA

CHINA

NORTH VIETNAM

Lao Cai

rail link to Kunming

Yen Bai

Lang Son

rail link to Nanning

Dien Bien Phu

Hon Gai

Cam Pha

Hanoi

Haiphong

LAOS

Than Hoa

GULF OF TONKIN

US 7th Fleet

raids by carrier-based US Navy aircraft

bombing raids from Thailand

Vinh

Na Pe Pass

THAILAND

Ho Chi Minh Trail

Mu Gia Pass

Quang Khe

Dong Hoi

SOUTH VIETNAM

harbours mined
bombing of railways and supply depots

Sea War Vietnam

The role of the US Navy

It is not immediately obvious how seapower could have been so important to the United States in a conflict like the Vietnam War, fought over paddy fields and jungle against an enemy with almost no naval strength. Yet the US Navy was crucially involved from the outset, providing air power, cutting seaborne supply routes and carrying the war into the rivers and waterways of South Vietnam's interior. Seapower was instrumental in allowing the US to prosecute the war at all, with a huge logistic train that crossed the Pacific via Hawaii to the western seaboard of the United States. At peak, an average of 771,000 tonnes of supplies a month would take this route and new ports or vastly expanded off-loading facilities were constructed at six sites in South Vietnam, including Saigon and a huge new naval base at Cam Ranh Bay. The direct superior of the American commander on the ground in Vietnam was Commander-in-Chief Pacific (CINCPAC), an admiral of the US Navy with his flag at Pearl Harbor in Hawaii.

The story of large-scale US involvement in Vietnam in fact began at sea. Shortly after taking office in November 1963, President Lyndon B. Johnson authorised clandestine US Navy destroyer patrols (code-named 'De Soto') along the coast of North

Vietnam to gather intelligence and support South Vietnamese commando raids. It was while making such a patrol in the Gulf of Tonkin on the afternoon of 2 August 1964 that the US destroyer *Maddox* picked up three North Vietnamese torpedo boats on her radar. The ensuing engagement was slight in military terms – one torpedo boat was disabled and another damaged as the *Maddox* opened fire and aircraft from the carrier USS *Ticonderoga* came to her aid – but its repercussions were grave. After a somewhat doubtful report that the *Maddox*, now accompanied by the USS *C. Turner Joy*, had been attacked again by torpedo boats on the night of 4 August, President Johnson ordered the first direct air strikes on North Vietnam, and it fell to US Navy aircraft from the *Ticonderoga* and *Constellation* to carry them out. Air attacks on four North Vietnamese naval bases destroyed 25 torpedo boats and oil storage sites. Two days later the US Congress passed the Gulf of Tonkin Resolution, legalising further military involvement in Vietnam.

The Gulf of Tonkin incident, as it is known, was the only definite surface-to-surface engagement of the war, although a month later, when the De Soto patrols had resumed, the destroyers USS *Morton* and USS *Parson* again engaged what were believed to be

Above: A US naval convoy steams towards the eastern seaboard of Vietnam. The US Navy had several important tasks during the Vietnam War: the three most notable were the provision of gunfire support for operations inland; the prevention of seaborne resupply for the Viet Cong; and the use of carrier-borne aircraft on operations over North and South Vietnam.
Right: Drenched in the spray thrown up by his craft, a US soldier with an M60 machine-gun keeps a watchful eye for any communist activity on the river bank. Operations along the coast and inland waterways of South Vietnam were successful in lessening the flow of seaborne war material to the Viet Cong.

torpedo boats, firing 300 shells at radar-predicted targets, but there was no visual contact and neither ship was actually fired upon. The focus of US Navy attention was now switching towards a different role.

In late 1964 the US Navy began a huge build-up of naval airpower off North Vietnam. By early 1965 the Seventh Fleet was operating three carriers in Task Force 77 on Yankee Station, a rendezvous in the Gulf of Tonkin some 140 km (90 miles) off the North Vietnamese coast. On 7 February aircraft from USS *Hancock* and USS *Coral Sea* began the first of the Flaming Dart series of reprisal air strikes, soon to merge into the much larger Rolling Thunder air campaign against the North. Task Force 77 aircraft were heavily engaged through the spring and summer of 1965 attacking bridges, radar sites and ammunition depots, and on 17 June they were involved in the first aerial combat of the war when two F-4s from the carrier USS *Midway* engaged four North Vietnamese MiG-17s, shooting down two of them with Sparrow missiles.

In May, at the request of General Westmoreland, one of the four carriers on Yankee Station was despatched south to Dixie Station, 185km (115 miles) southeast of Cam Ranh Bay, to support ground forces in South Vietnam, while the number of carriers covering the North grew to five in June. Already by the end of 1965, US Navy pilots had logged 56,888 sorties from their huge floating airfields.

At first the US Air Force (USAF) and the US Navy prosecuted their operations largely in isolation, but in November 1965 the North was divided into 'route packages' of targets, the navy taking responsibility for three coastal regions. In June 1965 the US Navy began a three-year effort to destroy a primary target in Route Package 4, the Thanh Hoa railway bridge.

Thousands of tonnes of ordnance were aimed at the bridge, delivered by every kind of strike aircraft in the navy inventory – A-4 Skyhawks, A-7 Corsair IIs, A-6 Intruders, F-4B Phantoms, F-8 Crusaders and the big twin-engined A-3B Skywarriors. In March 1967 US Navy A-4s made the first attack using Walleye guided glide bombs, developed by the navy itself and equipped with a TV in the nose. All three bombs impacted but still the bridge stood until finally destroyed by the USAF five years later using the new generation of laser-guided bombs.

The Rolling Thunder campaign was totally unlike the carrier battles the US Navy had fought in the Pacific War against Japan between 1942 and 1945, when aircraft waged ship-to-ship warfare in a few spasmodic strikes. This was a sustained operation, carried out almost on a routine basis against extended land targets, with short periods of replenishment in between to replace the vast amounts of bombs and ammunition consumed and to give aircrew a break. A typical schedule might involve three days of air operations followed by one day stood down with replenishment from attendant supply ships outside the battle zone. The consumption rate of US Navy strike aircraft, fuel aside, was prodigious. Considering that an A-6 or A-7 could fly three sorties a day, each time lifting five tonnes of bombs, an air group of 36 could expend over 500 tonnes of bombs a day, rapidly exhausting a carrier's magazines.

Accidental explosions

It was not just strike warfare, of course. As the number of Rolling Thunder sorties progressed, so North Vietnamese air defence stiffened. US Navy Phantoms had to fly combat air patrols (CAPs), less in defence of the carriers than over strike target areas (known as TARCAPs), as well as barrier patrols (BARCAPs) to prevent enemy aircraft attacking friendly naval forces or infiltrating the returning strike group and attacking the carrier. In fact, despite Yankee Station being comparatively so close to hostile territory and hemmed in the Gulf of Tonkin by mainland China and the island of Hainan, no direct attack was made on the huge concentration of US naval power that operated there. It was accidents, rather than enemy action, that caused damage to the carriers, packed with aviation fuel and high explosive as they were. The USS *Ranger* was damaged by fire in 1965 and had to leave station, a fire on USS *Oriskany* in October 1966 killed 44, and in the worst incident extensive explosions on USS *Forrestal* in July 1967 killed 134 men and destroyed 21 aircraft.

While Yankee Station and Dixie Station were contributing to the air war, US seapower was also securing the continuous blockade of the South Vietnamese coastline with its thousands of miles of creeks, swamps and inlets, denying the Viet Cong their seaborne supply routes based on junks and fishing boats. Coastal Surveillance Task Force 71, established in 1965, was responsible for maintaining the blockade. Code-named 'Market Time', the operation was based on five surveillance centres and, by late 1966, nearly 100 fast patrol craft, reinforced by 30 US Coast Guard cutters and nearly 500 armed South Vietnamese junks, were patrolling the shoreline, stopping and searching any suspicious traffic. A paramilitary Junk Force had been organised with US assistance as early as April 1960 and mass production of armed junks was undertaken to tighten

the grip on infiltration. The last sail junks were disposed of in 1969.

A related programme was 'Game Warden', designed to push this kind of patrol up into the extensive rivers and waterways of the Mekong Delta and the Rung Sat – the swampy area between Saigon and the sea. The River Patrol Force operated specialised shallow-draught vessels ranging from light fibreglass craft to armoured assault boats mounting heavy automatic weapons and flamethrowers.

From late 1966 the navy's riverine operations were also extended to include cooperation with the US Army in its campaign against Viet Cong guerrillas in the Mekong Delta area. The Mobile Riverine Force of monitors, artillery barges and barrack ships carried the 9th Infantry Division into some of the most difficult fighting seen in Vietnam. The navy also developed Sea-Air Landing (SEAL) assault platoons carried by UH-1 helicopters and 'Seawolf' helicopter gunships to operate in the interior.

Operation Sea Dragon

The Rolling Thunder air offensive which took the war to the North was mirrored at sea by Operation Sea Dragon, begun in October 1966. US warships sought out military targets in North Vietnamese coastal waters, although the rules of engagement forbade action against non-military targets, including vessels carrying Soviet military material into Haiphong harbour. Shore bombardment was only permitted in

response to attacks by North Vietnamese coastal artillery concentrated in the area. Sea Dragon operations were at first limited to waters below 17° 30' north, but the zone was moved up to 20° north in February 1967.

Along the South Vietnamese coast, shore bombardment in support of ground forces began in 1965. The burden of these operations was borne by World War II-vintage eight-inch gun cruisers including the USS *Canberra*, *Boston*, *Des Moines* and *Newport News*, joined by the rocket-firing Carronade and River-class bombardment ships of Inshore Fire Support Division 93. But the most spectacular contribution was made by the de-mothballed battleship USS *New Jersey*, taken out of reserve in mid-1967 and recommissioned on 6 April 1968. After her deployment to the western Pacific in September 1968 she was on the gun line off South Vietnam for a total of 120 days, with 47 days being the longest sustained period at sea. The *New Jersey* fired 5688 rounds from her nine 16-inch guns, each capable of throwing a projectile weighing 1225kg (2700lb) over a range of 39km (23 miles). While off Vietnam she also fired some 15,000 rounds from her five-inch secondary armament.

In March 1969 the *New Jersey* was withdrawn as part of a general running down of the US Navy's operations. Air strikes on the North had ceased in 1968, considerably reducing carrier activity, and Vietnamization led to the transfer of the coastal

Right: A Boeing CH-46 Sea Knight helicopter from the USS *Sacramento* prepares to lift a load of supplies from the deck of a supply ship. At the peak of operations in Vietnam, an average of 771,000 tonnes of supplies per month were landed from US ships.

Below: The unmistakable profile of a Vought F-8 Crusader preparing for take off from the USS *Constellation*. Inset bottom: The USS *Ranger*, an attack carrier, turns towards the Vietnamese coast during its cruise in the South China Sea.

surveillance and riverine effort to the South Vietnamese. By 1971 the South Vietnamese Navy counted some 850 patrol, coastal and riverine craft on its strength and nearly 100 destroyers, escorts, minesweepers and landing ships.

A display of naval power

The North Vietnamese offensive of March 1972 brought a final display of power by the US Navy, with extensive shore bombardments and air attacks. This time no fewer than six carriers were concentrated off North Vietnam, as President Nixon announced the resumption of the air strikes. The USS *Kitty Hawk* and *Constellation* arrived in April to reinforce the *America* and nuclear-powered *Enterprise*, followed by the *Midway* and *Saratoga* redeploying from the eastern Pacific and Atlantic respectively. US carrier aircraft struck the previously restricted target of Haiphong in April 1972, while aerial minelaying was undertaken in May. During the final bombing offensive of December 1972, US carrier aircraft joined B-52s in the large-scale Linebacker II raids.

After the ceasefire of January 1973, it may have seemed to some observers that American command of the sea, unchallenged by North Vietnam's tiny navy, had effectively helped in a successful defence of the South. But the events of 1975 were to prove that the whole costly operation had been for nothing, and the last act of US warships in Vietnamese waters was to act as landing pads for fleeing South Vietnamese who had managed to find a place in a helicopter as Saigon fell. For in many ways, the US Navy involvement typified American involvement in the Vietnam War as a whole. The massive weight of firepower and the ability to strike at will wherever it chose were the great advantages that the USA enjoyed; the problem was, of course, that they could not win the war.

Christy Campbell

Peace with honour?

American combat troops withdraw from Vietnam

Above: The inauguration of Richard Nixon for his second term of office as President. Nixon never allowed the communists in Vietnam to extract strategic advantage from the cycles of US political life. Indeed, his manipulation of the bombing campaigns of 1972 (above, Hanoi in flames after a raid) and the timing of the peace negotiations was marked by an ability to extract maximum political advantage.

On 8 October 1972 the North Vietnamese chief negotiator, Le Duc Tho, presented the Americans with a set of peace proposals which were immediately recognised by US National Security Advisor Henry Kissinger as at last offering an acceptable basis for a peace agreement. But why did a breakthrough come at this point after almost three years of seemingly futile negotiations? And why was a peace agreement not finally reached until more than three months later, after the destructive fury of the B-52 bombing campaign known as Linebacker II?

The talks which opened in Paris in January 1969 between the Americans and the South Vietnamese government on one side and the North Vietnamese and South Vietnamese communists on the other, were some of the most unproductive negotiations in the history of diplomacy, never becoming more than a sterile round of propaganda statements and manoeuvres. The secret meetings between Kissinger and Le Duc Tho, begun in the autumn of 1969, on which the real hopes of a settlement rested, also proved fruitless as long as the two sides felt an advantage could still be gained on the battlefield.

On the face of it, there were always grounds for agreement, on the simple basis that the US administration of Richard Nixon wanted to get its forces out of Vietnam and the North Vietnamese wanted them to leave. But the two sides could find no common ground on major issues. The Americans wanted to link a withdrawal of US forces to a withdrawal of North Vietnamese troops from the South, yet Hanoi incredibly refused to acknowledge that such troops were even there. The North Vietnamese demanded that a military ceasefire be accompanied by a political solution in which President Thieu would be replaced immediately by a coalition government comprising elements of the Saigon regime, members of the Provisional Revolutionary Government of South Vietnam set up by the communists in June 1969, and representatives of the so-called 'Third Force' of non-communist South Vietnamese opponents of Thieu. The Americans refused to abandon Thieu, regarding the proposed coalition government as the prelude to a total communist takeover.

Behind the proposals and counter-proposals lay the simpler logic of power. The Americans hoped that their policy of Vietnamization would eventually enable them to leave Vietnam without making any concessions to the North, since the South would be strong enough to defend itself. The North Vietnamese still expected that the steady decline in the American will to fight would finally give them an outright military victory.

During 1970 and 1971, the Americans made some concessions in the face of almost total North Vietnamese intransigence. Crucially, in October 1970 President Nixon first mooted the idea of a ceasefire-in-place, making it clear that if the terms were right the US would withdraw while the communists remained in control of areas of the South. The Americans also came some way to meet the North Vietnamese political demands by proposing a coalition council to supervise elections in Vietnam – a much less powerful substitute for the demanded coalition government in Saigon. But the North Vietnamese clearly felt they had no need to accept a compromise that would leave South Vietnam and Thieu a reasonable chance of survival.

The events of the 1972 Spring offensive transformed the situation in two ways: firstly, it showed the North Vietnamese that they had no chance of military victory as long as the South Vietnamese Army (ARVN) was supported by US air power; secondly, the advances made by the North Vietnamese Army (NVA) gave the communists control of a substantial part of South Vietnam with some 150,000 troops installed there, thus making the prospect of a ceasefire-in-place much more attractive. By October another factor had entered their calculations – Nixon was almost certain to be re-elected to the presidency in November, and after re-election they feared he would be much tougher to negotiate with.

Le Duc Tho's proposal on 8 October was carefully timed to make an agreement possible before the presidential elections. It accepted in substance the American bargaining position already established: there would be a ceasefire-in-place, followed within 60 days by an exchange of prisoners and the withdrawal of US forces. Under the principle of 'two administrations, two armed forces and two zones of control', South Vietnam would remain divided until elections could be held under the auspices of a coalition National Council of Reconciliation and Concord. In effect, the demand for a political solution to accompany the military solution was dropped. Probably both sides realised that the proposed elections were unlikely ever to be held.

Peace at hand?

By 18 October, after discussion of technical details, the Americans and North Vietnamese had reached agreement, but when Kissinger took the peace terms to President Thieu he turned them down flat. Thieu did not trust American assurances of military intervention should the North break the ceasefire, and he insisted that the proposed National Council was only a coalition government in disguise. The Americans then informed Hanoi that there would be a delay while Thieu's agreement to the terms was obtained; not surprisingly the North Vietnamese felt cheated. Nevertheless, on 26 October Kissinger made a public declaration that 'peace is at hand'.

Given the dependence of the Saigon government on American financial and military support, it seems difficult to believe that the US administration could not have forced Thieu to accept the agreement had the Americans themselves been wholeheartedly behind it (indeed, an American ultimatum was to secure Thieu's compliance the following January). But it is possible that Nixon and his advisers could see advan-

Below: Civil Defence had been one of the major concerns of the Hanoi government during the 'Rolling Thunder' bombing campaigns of the 1960s and in 1972 air defence measures against US air attack had to be revived once more, with constant training drills (as here) to enable the population to take cover with utmost speed whenever a warning sounded.

tages in delay, not only to wring concessions from the North Vietnamese but also to alter the military balance in the South's favour – enormous quantities of military hardware were pumped in to South Vietnam during November, December and January.

On 20 November the Americans put forward a revised set of proposals which differed from those originally agreed in October more in form than in substance. The North Vietnamese declared their readiness to accept the October terms but rejected many of the new ones, and they began to raise extra points of their own, notably concerning the fate of political prisoners in the South whose release had not been agreed on the same terms as military personnel. Kissinger has stated that it was his impression the North Vietnamese were being deliberately obstructive on a series of minor points of wording and technicalities; the North Vietnamese blamed the Americans for refusing an agreement they had accepted in October.

Demands and concessions

On 13 December the Americans withdrew from the stalemated negotiations and threatened North Vietnam with heavy aerial bombardment if the American terms were not accepted. On 18 December the most concentrated bombing of the North was initiated, wrecking a large part of the country's infrastructure and hence its war-making capacity. The announcement of the end of the bombing campaign on 30 December was followed within three days by the resumption of negotiations and within little over a week there was agreement in principle on a settlement, although finalisation had to wait a little longer.

The interpretation of these events remains controversial. According to Nixon and some other administration figures of the time, North Vietnam had been bombed to the negotiating table. It is difficult to square this view, however, with the facts of the agreement reached in January, which differed in no substantial respect from the North Vietnamese proposals of 8 October. After the December bombing it was the Americans, not the North Vietnamese, who made concessions, dropping most of their revised proposals of November, including the demand for

North Vietnamese troop withdrawals. This gives some credibility to Hanoi's contention that the bombing was an American defeat, forcing Nixon to accept the terms he had previously rejected, but militarily this version seems nonsensical given the undoubted effectiveness of the bombing campaign.

The truth is probably, in fact, that the bombing was not intended to affect the peace negotiations, but to satisfy two related goals. Firstly, by incapacitating the North for some time to come, it ensured the South a fair chance of survival; in this sense the bombing was a logical companion piece to the flood of US equipment that the ARVN was receiving. Secondly, it made it possible for Nixon to assert, whatever the truth of the matter, that the peace agreement was a settlement imposed on a defeated North Vietnam.

The obvious beneficiaries of the peace agreement signed on 23 January 1973 were the North Vietnamese. President Thieu only assented to the terms under duress, since an arrangement that left 150,000 NVA troops in South Vietnam augured ill for his regime's long-term survival. Although Nixon had given Thieu written assurances that the US would intervene again if needed, by the end of March all US forces were out of Vietnam and it would never be politically possible to send them back.

The terms of the treaty providing for the withdrawal of US forces, the exchange of prisoners and the initiation of a ceasefire were carried out, but none of the political clauses concerning elections and the National Council was ever implemented. Despite the arrival of an international team to supervise the ceasefire, its terms were constantly violated by the build up of armaments and small-scale fighting. Le Duc Tho and Henry Kissinger were jointly awarded the Nobel Peace Prize for 1973, but Le Duc Tho refused it on the grounds that there was no peace.

Both Nixon and Kissinger are adamant that the peace agreement was not intended to guarantee a 'decent interval' between the US withdrawal and the fall of Saigon, but rather to create a lasting South Vietnamese state. Yet both South and North Vietnamese knew that only endless US support could stop the North eventually imposing its own solution to the Vietnam problem by force. **Graham Brewer**

Below: Henry Kissinger is besieged by the world's press after the conclusion of the peace agreement between himself and Le Duc Tho, an agreement signed on 23 January 1973. By the end of March all US forces had withdrawn from Vietnam, though there existed written assurances to President Thieu that the US would again intervene if needed.

The
MIRAGE 2000/4000

The latest members of Dassault-Breguet's famous Mirage series are the Mirage 2000 multi-role fighter, which entered front-line service with the Armée de l'Air in 1984, and the larger and more powerful Mirage 4000. Perhaps the most noteworthy feature of both designs is the return to the tailless delta configuration of the original Mirages, after its abandonment with the swept-wing Mirage F1. The Armée de l'Air's 1973 requirement for a successor to the Mirage III called for a twin-engined multi-role fighter capable of undertaking both a high-altitude interception role and a low-level nuclear strike role. In 1975, however, French thinking on future fighter requirements changed and the Mirage 2000 project emerged as a single-engined fighter with a primary air defence role and secondary low-level strike capability. In spite of the loss of official interest – and financial backing – in the heavier fighter aircraft, this project was continued by Dassault as the privately-financed Mirage 4000, in the hope of attracting export orders.

The Mirage 2000 is in many respects an advanced-technology version Mirage III. The great advantages of the tailless delta design are its low wing loading, large internal volume for fuel stowage and thin aerodynamic section in comparison with a swept wing. However, these positive characteristics are offset by a poor sustained turning performance in combat, during which the wing acts as an aerodynamic brake, and by high approach and landing speeds. In the Mirage 2000 design these problems have been alleviated by producing an aircraft with negative longitudinal stability. This means that the Mirage 2000's centre of gravity is aft of the aircraft's aerodynamic centre. As a result of this, in order to pitch up the aircraft during a turning manoeuvre or landing approach, an upload on the elevons is required. (A tailless delta has control surfaces on the wing edge which combine the function of elevators and ailerons and are known as elevons). This will increase the wing's aerodynamic lift, whereas with a conventional

Previous page: Led by three Mirage 2000s is a Mirage 4000, its considerably larger wing area visible in this photograph. Above: A Mirage 2000 in the camouflage colours of the Armée de l'Air.

Below: Mechanics fit the Thomson-CSF radar, a multi-mode system capable of detecting airborne targets at high, medium or low altitudes.

Right: An underside view of a Mirage 2000 revealing an interesting range of ordnance. Eight 250kg (550lb) bombs are slung along the fuselage, while attached to wing hard-points are two 1700-litre drop tanks and two Matra 550 Magic short-range air-to-air missiles. Similar to the US Sidewinder the 550 Magic carries a 12.5kg (27.6lb) high-explosive warhead and has a maximum range of 10km (6.25 miles).

aircraft, which has positive longitudinal stability, a download produces the same pitch-up manoeuvre, but at the same time reduces the wing's lift. The practical results of the Mirage 2000's negative longitudinal stability can be seen by comparing its landing approach speed of 278km/h (173mph) with the Mirage IIIE's approach speed of 354km/h (220mph).

The theoretical advantages of negative longitudinal stability have been recognized for a long time, but its practical application had to wait the development of electronically-signalled 'fly by wire' control systems. A longitudinally unstable aircraft would be impossible for a pilot to fly using a direct mechanical linkage between the pilot's controls and the aircraft's elevons and rudder. In the Mirage 2000, the pilot's control movements produce an electronic signal which commands a computer known as the advanced automatic flight-control system to perform the required manoeuvres. The computer translates these commands into movements of elevons or rudder to produce the desired change in flight. Other advantages of the 'fly by wire' system are that the control surface movements respond to the pilot's commands more quickly than with a mechanical system and that the pilot cannot fly the aircraft beyond its design limits because the flight computer would ignore such instructions.

The Mirage 2000 is powered by a SNECMA M53 turbofan engine which consumes less fuel yet produces more thrust and weighs less than the Atar turbojet which powered the earlier Mirage aircraft. Early production Mirage 2000s were fitted with the 9000kg (19,840lb) thrust M53-5, but an improved M53-P2 engine has been developed which will be retrofitted to the early production models. The improved M53-P2 produces 10,000kg (22,000lb) of thrust and in addition to its greater maximum power it is also more efficient at low and medium altitudes than the M53-5.

Above: The wide variety of armaments available to the Mirage 2000. Included are Matra guided missiles, unguided rocket pods and 30mm DEFA cannon.
Below: A Mirage 2000 with Matra Super 530 and 550 Magic air-to-air missiles.

The wing area of the Mirage 2000 is appreciably greater than that of the Mirage III providing the aircraft with a low wing loading. The wing and fuselage are blended in a bulged fairing, providing increased internal volume for fuel stowage without any aerodynamic drag penalties. Control at high angles of attack and low air speed is improved by automatically actuated wing-leading and trailing-edge flaps, which increase the wing's camber under these conditions.

The flow of air over the vertical tail surfaces is also improved by fitting small strakes on the engine inlets, which help to prevent the vortices generated during high angle of attack manoeuvres from buffeting the tail surfaces. Another noteworthy aerodynamic feature of the Mirage 2000's design is the 'wasp waisted' fuselage shape which reduces drag at supersonic speed.

The avionics and armament fitted to the Mirage 2000 will vary according to its intended role. The first production aircraft to be manufactured are the Mirage 2000C multi-role fighters, while subsequent aircraft have been optimised for an air defence role and as the two-seat Mirage 2000N nuclear strike aircraft. It is possible that a reconnaissance variant will also be produced and Mirage 2000B two-seat conversion trainers have been ordered. The Mirage 2000C is fitted with a multi-mode Thomson-CSF RDM radar, which can detect airborne targets at high, medium or low altitudes. It can also be used to detect ground targets, for ground mapping, terrain avoidance and for target range finding. Other avionic equipment includes a SAGEM inertial navigation set, a pilot's head-up display, an Atlis II laser target designation pod, a radar warning receiver and ECM jamming systems. In 1986 the much-improved RDI radar will become available and it is to be fitted to the air defence version of the Mirage 2000, which will replace the Mirage F1 interceptor in service with the Armée de l'Air. The RDI will offer a considerable improvement in air-to-air detection performance over the RDM. For example, it will be able to detect a low-flying target at ranges of up to 50 nautical miles, whereas the RDM's range against such a target is only 20 nautical miles.

The two-seat Mirage 2000N is intended to operate at low-level and at high speeds in the tactical nuclear strike role and so will be fitted with an Antilope 5 terrain-following radar. It is to be armed with the ASMP (air-sol moyenne portée) medium-range air-to-ground missile, which carries a 150-kiloton nuclear warhead. Maximum range of the ASMP is some 80km (50 miles).

In the air-to-air combat role the multi-role and air defence versions of the Mirage 2000 can be armed with two medium-range Matra Super 530D missiles, which can both 'snap up' to engage high-flying targets, or 'snap down' to counter those at treetop height. In addition, two Matra 550 Magic short-range missiles can be carried and there are two built-in 30mm DEFA cannon. The Mirage 2000C has nine hardpoints for the carriage of air-to-ground ordnance, which can include free-fall or laser-guided bombs and the AS 30L laser-guided air-to-surface missile.

The Mirage 4000 is essentially a scaled-up Mirage 2000, powered by two M53 turbofan engines. With an operating weight in clean condition (that is, without external stores) of some 16,800kg (37,500lb) it is

Left: While one Mirage 2000 acts as an escort another takes on fuel from a French Air Force KL-135 tanker. In-flight refuelling has become a standard part of any long-range strike mission, to allow the aircraft to dispense with external fuel tanks and provide it with a worthwhile bomb load. Inset, below left: The Mirage 2000 as a strike aircraft, capable of carrying nuclear weapons. Inset below: An under-wing view of the Mirage 2000. Main picture below: A Matra Super 530 air-to-air missile is fired from a Mirage 2000. Replacing the unsatisfactory Matra R530 the Super 530 is a high performance air-to-air missile with a maximum range of 35km (22 miles). Guidance is by semi-active radar: the target aircraft is 'illuminated' by the launch aircraft allowing the missile's AD26 radar to home onto the reflected radiation.

appreciably heavier than the 9500kg (19,800lb) Mirage 2000. However, the increased power of twin M53 engines gives it a thrust-to-weight ratio of around 1:1 and its performance is also enhanced by the fitting of canard foreplane surfaces similar to those on the Israeli Kfir-C2. The Mirage 4000 has an improved range compared with the Mirage 2000 and much greater mission versatility. However, only a single prototype was built (first flying in 1978) and, in spite of unconfirmed reports of interest and even financial backing from Saudi Arabia, no export orders have been received for the Mirage 4000. As a result, the future of this expensive aircraft must remain in doubt, especially in view of the success of US aircraft such as the F-15 and F-16 which have been exported to a number of Dassault's old customers in place of the French Mirage series.

In contrast, the Mirage 2000 will serve in substantial numbers with France's Armée de l'Air, which has a requirement for around 250 fighters, and it has been ordered by the air forces of Egypt (20), India (40) and Peru (26). The prototype first flew on 10 March 1978 and deliveries of production aircraft to the Armée de l'Air began in 1983 – a year behind schedule. As a true successor to the popular Mirage III, the Mirage 2000 has a considerable export potential, particularly to the nations of the Third World.

Above and top: The Mirage 4000. Employing the same delta wing as the smaller Mirage 2000, the 4000 is powered by twin M53 engines and utilises canard foreplanes to improve performance. Despite the manufacturer's faith in the Mirage 4000 little interest has been shown in the aircraft.

Above left: The cockpit of the Mirage 2000 features the latest avionic equipment, including the Thomson CSF integrated head-up/head down display system. A major feature is the 'fly-by-wire' control system, making flying easier. Left: The pilot's view through the head-up display on the Mirage 2000. Essential combat information is transmitted to the pilot on the screen without distracting his attention from the outside environment.

Mirage 2000

Type Multi-role fighter
Dimensions Span 9m (29ft 6in); length 15.33m (50ft 3in); height 5.30m (17ft 6in)
Weight Empty 6400kg (14,080lb); normal take-off 9000kg (19,840lb); maximum take-off 15,000kg (33,000lb)
Powerplant One 9000kg (19,840lb) thrust SNECMA M53-5 turbofan with afterburner

Performance Maximum speed at sea level Mach 1.2, or 1472km/h (915mph); maximum speed above 11,000m (36,000ft) Mach 2.35 or 2495km/h (1550mph)
Range Tactical radius 700km (435miles)
Ceiling 19,800m (65,000ft)

Armament Two 30mm DEFA cannon and up to 5000kg (11,000lb) of ordnance, including Matra 550 Magic and Super 530 air-to-air missiles, ASMP and AS 30L air-to-surface missiles, laser-guided and conventional free-fall bombs

Loss of faith

The effects of Vietnam on the US establishment

It was, President Richard Nixon proclaimed, 'peace with honor'. Noticeably, he did not use the word victory about the Vietnam ceasefire that came into force on 27 January 1973. For it was, in effect, a thinly disguised American retreat. Over 56,000 Americans had lost their lives (46,500 in action) and well over 300,000 had been wounded in a vain attempt to save a regime that would, in a little over two years, succumb to the forces of the North. 'I had,' Nixon later admitted, 'no illusions about the fragile nature of the agreement or about the communists' true motives in signing it.' While the last remaining American troops, the cynical remnant of an army long since sick of a cause it could neither wholeheartedly pursue nor summarily reject, would be withdrawn, the North Vietnamese would flagrantly violate the Paris peace accords which America now lacked either the means or the will to uphold. The result was inevitable. 'We shall have to undergo more sacrifices, but we are sure to win total victory. This is an absolute certainty,' Ho Chi Minh had prophesied. And so it proved. The greatest power on earth was humbled; the efforts of five presidents, from Eisenhower to Ford, were unavailing and, as their successor Jimmy Carter put it: 'We were taught that our armies were always invincible and our causes always just, only to suffer the agony of Vietnam.'

For Americans generally, the Vietnam War represented a loss of innocence, while those who had run the war suffered a perhaps irreparable blow to their self-confidence, individually and as a caste. That military and political establishment which had guided America's destinies abroad since World War II on the basis of a general consensus of viewpoint, whichever political party was nominally in power, had come apart. Educated as often as not at Ivy League universities, perhaps partners in prestigious law firms or top executives in elite corporations, the members of this establishment moved in and out of government, rubbing shoulders with those members of the academic and business community who were equally fascinated by the exercise of political power. Significantly, few sought elective office and if they were civilians the temptation to show the military they could be tough-minded was a strong one. They were,

Top: President Richard Nixon addresses a joint session of the Houses of Congress. US political institutions found the long-running Vietnam War a thorny problem because it split the American people. The regular TV shots of US troops destroying civilian dwellings (above, a member of the 1st Cavalry burns down huts in a Vietnamese village) and the obvious horrors of the conflict (right, a child victim of the war) caused repugnance among millions of American citizens. The deep divisions which this opened up were difficult to accommodate within a democracy where foreign policy had traditionally been decided by concensus in the political world.

as one critic termed them 'the best and the brightest'. But they had been proved wrong over Vietnam. The consequence was that the assumptions of a generation would have to be rethought.

The commitment to South Vietnam had begun tentatively enough under President Eisenhower in the 1950s, when the general consensus was that 'politics stopped at the waterline' and any president could expect bipartisan support in his foreign policy. Moreover it was an axiom of American foreign policy, for Republican and Democrat alike, that communism had to be contained and that the domino theory applied in Southeast Asia: the fall of one nation to communism would lead ineluctably to threats to its neighbours. Still, Eisenhower conceded that there could be 'no greater tragedy than for the United States to become involved in an all-out land war in Asia', and if he began sending military personnel as 'advisers' the number totalled a mere 685 at the time he left the White House in early 1961. As a chief executive of vast military experience and authority, his policy was unlikely to face much opposition from a Congress in any case accustomed to following the president's lead.

The same might not have held true for the youthful President John Kennedy at the start of the 1960s, who escalated the commitment to some 16,000 'advisers' and promoted counter-insurgency; but his handling of the Cuban missile crisis of 1962 further burnished the aura of the president who alone had the knowledge to make instant and secret decisions shared only with senior officials, less servants of a republic than courtiers around a king. Whatever the Founding Fathers of the American constitution had originally intended when they had assigned to Congress the power to declare war, seemed in practice to have been superseded by the presidential role of commander-in-chief of the armed forces entrusted with the defence of the United States – an obligation liberally interpreted by successive presidents to justify, if necessary, military responses on their own initiative thousands of miles from home. Thus President Lyndon Johnson secured the Gulf of Tonkin Resolution of August 1964 not to authorise his actions but merely, in an election year, to demonstrate Congressional support. In agreeing to 'approve and support the determination of the president, as commander-in-chief, to take all necessary measures to repel any armed attack against the forces of the United States and to prevent further aggression', Congress was to see American military presence in South Vietnam rise to over 500,000 personnel within four years, while by the end of the Johnson presidency the United States had dropped more bombs on Southeast Asia than on Germany and Japan in the whole of World War II. There is a certain irony in that Johnson, scarcely an establishment figure by birth, education, or background, pre-eminently indeed in those terms the outsider, abandoned that shrewd horse-sense that served him so well in domestic politics and seemed over-anxious to earn the condescending approval of just that elite whose policies were to destroy him. For Vietnam became the acid test of establishment convictions, and the decision in early 1965 to escalate the war became the means to express them. These convictions included the belief in the invulnerability of American arms, the obligation to assume any burden for the cause of freedom and the unquestioned authority of the presidency. But the sense of imperial mission was to prove misplaced.

The 'arrogance of power'

Disillusionment set in early. Senator William Fulbright, who had steered the Gulf of Tonkin Resolution through the Senate at the president's behest, was soon criticising the administration's 'arrogance of power'. In August 1967 Nicholas Katzenbach, who was to serve both as attorney-general and under-secretary of state, told a Senate foreign relations committee hearing that things moved too fast nowadays for the president to be able to consult the Senate before starting a war. Appalled, Senator Eugene McCarthy argued that, 'In that case there's nothing left but to take it to the people.' Yet the political process seemed unavailing. Though Johnson abdicated the presidency in 1968 after 'dove' critics like McCarthy and Robert Kennedy had challenged him in presidential primaries, the ultimate beneficiary was Richard Nixon who, if he darkly hinted at a peace plan, was to escalate the war into Cambodia and Laos, whilst one third of the American deaths in the war were to occur during his presidency. For the first time since World War II, American foreign policy was coming apart, and such establishment verities as the need for a

Right: The direct controllers of US military might, the Joint Chiefs of Staff in 1972, the last full year of US involvement in Vietnam. Standing, left to right: Admiral Elmo Zumwalt, Chief of US Naval Operations, and General Robert E. Cushman, Commandant of the US Marine Corps; seated left to right: General William C. Westmoreland, Chief of Staff of the US Army, Admiral Thomas H. Moorer, Chairman of the Joint Chiefs of Staff, and General John D. Ryan, Chief of Staff of the US Air Force.

Lyndon Johnson (far left with General Westmoreland) inherited the mantle of an 'imperial presidency', but decided not to run in the 1968 election. His successor Richard Nixon successfully disengaged from Vietnam, but the methods he used tainted his whole administration and led to the Watergate scandal (left, Nixon with some of the infamous Watergate tapes). Nixon resigned to avoid impeachment, and his office devolved upon Vice-President Gerald Ford (right), who became the first president since 1932 to fail at the polls when seeking re-election.

Above: Senator William Fulbright. Chairman of the Senate Foreign Relations Committee in 1964, he was instrumental in having the Gulf of Tonkin Resolution passed through Congress, but by 1966 had become an opponent of the war.

powerful – its critics called it 'imperial' – presidency were being questioned.

One of the cores of the US belief in its mission to defend the free world had been the unquestionable integrity of its presidents – from Roosevelt, through Truman and Eisenhower to Kennedy – and the conviction that they were acting in the best interests of the American people. Vietnam destroyed that conviction, and left a moral vacuum.

Congress took up the challenge. It had become fashionable on the part of the political establishment to deride congressmen, though the military had often found them useful allies in increasing defence appropriations. From 1969 onwards, controlled by the opposition Democrats, Congress at last began to assert its prerogatives. In June 1970 it voted by a large majority to repeal the Gulf of Tonkin Resolution and to prohibit further use of US troops in Cambodia. Nixon complained that it was 'the first restrictive vote ever cast on a president in wartime.' Later a bipartisan resolution was introduced to remove all troops from Vietnam by 30 June 1971. Although the administration successfully disputed this infringement of executive power, it only served to underline the increasing isolation of the presidency – both the cause and the

effect of increasing secrecy in government. It was easier to circumvent opposition by stealth. Hence the secret air war against Cambodia in 1969 and 1970 or the attempt to stop publication of the Pentagon Papers (the Defense Department's secret study of government policy on Vietnam 'leaked' in 1971). Soon it led to paranoia about national security, the need to stifle dissent and to prevent leaks – and the road lay open to Watergate. Presidential abuse of power then stood revealed in all its ugliness.

Consulting Congress

Inevitably, despite Nixon's removal as a result of Watergate in August 1974, the moral authority of the presidency was tarnished and consequently faith in the president's role as commander-in-chief was weakened. In 1973, Congress passed a resolution prohibiting the use of public funds 'to finance combat activities ... over or from off the shores of North Vietnam, South Vietnam, Laos or Cambodia.' A War Powers Act of the same year, passed over Nixon's veto, forbade the president from committing troops into battle except after a declaration of war, and they had to be withdrawn within 60 days unless specifically authorised by Congress. Even in a national emergency, occasioned by an attack on the United States or its possessions, the president had to consult with Congress whenever possible before deploying forces – a requirement Gerald Ford was to find physically impossible when, in late March 1975 during Congress' Easter recess, the situation in South Vietnam began to deteriorate and he vainly sought the absent and widely scattered congressional leaders. In practice, of course, a president might still present congress with a *fait accompli* in a case where American lives might be jeopardised if support were not forthcoming. Still the message was clear enough: in future, presidents would have to tread more carefully. Thus Congress finally denied Ford further funds for a last minute transfusion for South Vietnam in 1975: 'I will give you large sums for evacuation,' said one Republican senator, 'but not one nickel for military aid.'

'No more Vietnams,' implicitly foreshadowed in the 'Nixon doctrine' of 1969 announcing more restrained foreign commitments, became a catchphrase whenever overseas intervention was mooted – in

Angola, for example, or Central America or the Lebanon. When US embassy staff were taken hostage by the Iranian regime in 1979, one reason at least why the Carter administration initially adopted a policy of gentle pressure and negotiation to secure their release was that Carter's secretary of state Cyrus Vance had, 15 years earlier, as deputy secretary of defense under President Johnson, supported the widening of the Vietnam War and lived thereafter with all of its consequences.

It was not the least of the war's ironies that the politicians should have thus learned the limitations of force. The US Army had, in many ways, performed creditably in difficult circumstances and could argue that it had never been fully allowed to prove its mettle. Of its professionalism there could be no doubt but this professionalism was not enough when the army was required to fight a counter-guerrilla war which had a political dimension. At the basic level of combat engagements, the army did not know how to cope in hostile terrain with an enemy who simply melted away into the countryside rather than risk a set battle. Even the numerical odds told against the Americans. This last might have seemed incredible to student protesters back on campus in America anxious to avoid a draft that had already taken thousands of their contemporaries, but in Vietnam terms it was literally true. The professional American Army believed that the success of its actual fighting men was ensured by effective support services so that back-up personnel outnumbered the actual combat troops. At times this could be as much as a ratio of 10 to one for infantry. Yet another calculation required at least a 10 to one ratio of counter-insurgency personnel to guerrillas if the latter were to be defeated; clearly even 500,000 American men were nowhere near enough to satisfy both formulae.

Massacres and My Lai

There were other calculations that went equally awry. How did you actually estimate success? Was an area successfully pacified simply because the Viet Cong slipped away until American forces themselves withdrew? Was so crude a yardstick as 'body-count' of much value against an enemy who always seemed to find replacements, when the numbers killed were likely to be inflated by junior officers anxious to

vindicate their patrols, when the bodies themselves – if they were real ones anyhow – were as likely as not to be those of innocent civilians? And what was happening to the American Army when such massacres as My Lai could occur, making Lieutenant William Calley almost the best-known soldier of the war? Did napalmed villages, defoliated jungle or the lunar landscape left by B-52 raids indicate the success of American arms and what cause justified such inhuman callousness? Clearly modern war required rethinking.

And if the American regular army was superbly professional and supremely well-equipped, what of the unwilling civilians drafted into a war they detested? Soon indiscipline was endemic to the extent that over-zealous officers risked being 'fragged' (attacked with grenades and fragmentation devices by their own men). Drug-abuse, a milder form of protest – and escape from the war – reached epidemic proportions, and contempt for the South Vietnamese allies one was supposed to be assisting was widespread. By the spring of 1971, former National Security Advisor McGeorge Bundy could conclude: 'extrication from Vietnam is now the necessary precondition of the renewal of the US Army as an institution'. When Nixon ended the draft in 1973 the professional military breathed a sign of relief.

The military were bloody but unbowed; in the

Above, left to right: Stills from the most notorious TV sequence from Vietnam – the shooting of a recently captured prisoner by the Saigon police chief in 1968. This flagrant disregard for any recognisable judicial process was the final confirmation for many Americans that the war was being fought on behalf of a regime that was not worth saving. Right: Students protest at the military involvement in Vietnam. Below right: A Vietnam veteran at the memorial to the US troops who died in a war which, in the end, can only be said to have delayed a communist takeover of South Vietnam, and which shattered the self confidence of the world's most powerful nation. Below: The final withdrawal from Vietnam for the US Army as the 21st Infantry Regiment furls its colours at Da Nang and prepares to leave.

aftermath of Vietnam they struggled to regain self-confidence and to reject the interpretation of the war as a defeat for the US armed forces. The chief object of their hostility was the media, and especially television, which army leaders saw as crucially responsible for the collapse of support for the war from the public and politicians. In September 1965 the news programmes had extended their nightly coverage to half an hour; thereafter Americans would have longer to watch with increasing horror and disgust the visually arresting images of war: the Saigon police chief blowing out the brains of a Viet Cong suspect, American soldiers setting fire to peasant dwellings, the napalmed child running naked down a road. As the credibility of military briefings to the press declined, a yawning gap opened up between the vision of the war being transmitted by the media and the image the US Army desired to present.

Muzzling the media

The message, as interpreted by the military, was that in future conflicts they would have to keep the media firmly under control. It was America's British allies who first had a chance to try out a new approach; during the Falklands conflict in 1982 the British forces rigorously – and on the whole very successfully – controlled the flow of images in such a way as to maintain credibility while minimising the adverse impact of the horrors of war. With the invasion of Grenada in 1983, the Americans tested their new hard line with the media, preventing any television coverage of the fighting, again with largely favourable effects on public opinion. Whether such techniques could have been applied in such a lengthy war as that in Vietnam must remain extremely doubtful.

For, if Vietnam was above all a political defeat, it was only so because of the inability of the military to achieve a victory within the terms of limited war that necessarily applied. No change in media coverage could have given the US armed forces the ability to defeat the Vietnamese communists or have turned the Saigon regime into a popular and stable government. The assumptions of American foreign policy which had perhaps been valid at the end of World War II – the invincibility of American arms, the duty to fight 'communist expansionism' anywhere in the world – had been proved outdated.   **John Kentleton**

Wild Weasels and

Technological developments of the Vietnam War

Throughout recorded history weapons technology – the refinement of existing weapons and the development of new ones – has been a crucial factor in the outcome and nature of warfare. Examples are legion: from the first use of iron weapons to the invention of the tank. In no war, however, was the development of weapons technology given quite so central a place as in the Vietnam War. The US military had decided to prosecute the conflict by applying its technical might, and rather than expend American lives, it preferred to find technological solutions to military problems. Whether this was the approach best suited to winning a limited war against a guerrilla army must remain an open question.

The most important weapon for the individual front-line soldier is, of course, his own personal firearm, and although the Vietnam War produced no wholly new equipment it emphasised weapons that could offer sustained fire against an unseen enemy in a jungle thicket, project a grenade in a village battle or destroy a bunker system. Among the US, South Vietnamese and allied forces, the most important smallarms were the M16 rifle and the M60 machine gun. Entering service as a replacement for the M14, the M16 came into widespread use in the late 1960s. It fired a 5.56mm projectile rather than the previously standard 7.62mm round, which meant that the weapon was lighter but did not have the range of its predecessor. It weighed 3.5kg (7.6lb), and was capable of single-shot, cyclic-burst or automatic fire. At first in Southeast Asia the M16 proved particularly susceptible to malfunctions due to the ingestion of mud and the like and was somewhat mechanically fragile, but these faults were partly rectified in a second model. The weapon's light weight made it an ideal rifle for the Vietnamese, a fact not lost on the Viet Cong who prized captured M16s highly. It is one of the many ironies of the war that equal value was given to the main Northern smallarm, the Chinese-built Type 56 rifle, by the Americans.

The 7.62mm M60 was introduced into service in 1960 and proved to be a tough and effective weapon. With a sustained rate of fire of 100rpm, the type was used as an infantry weapon, mounted on helicopters and river craft, and as both a fixed and a free-firing gun on tanks and APCs. Backing these 'standards', the US troops employed a wide range of other smallarms ranging from pistols through machine pistols and sniper rifles to such unlikely weapons as 12-bore shotguns. The various 'special' units had the widest range of such weapons, in some cases supplied through private purchase at unit level.

Higher up the scale, extensive use was made of a range of man-portable support weapons including mortars, recoilless rifles and grenade launchers. This last class of weapon was especially favoured as it could project 40mm grenades in excess of 100m (110 yards). The popularity of such weapons becomes readily apparent when it is realised that a fragmenta-

tion grenade delivered in this way could incapacitate anyone standing 25m (80 feet) from impact – an ideal weapon for jungle and street fighting.

The major grenade launcher was the M79, a single shot weapon which, in the hands of a skilled operator, could launch up to seven grenades per minute. Attempts were made to combine the M79 with the M16 in the form of the M203 introduced in 1970. Intended to replace the M79, the M203 was a cumbersome weapon which found little favour with its users.

The Viet Cong excelled in night-fighting, and a major objective of US technology was to redress this superiority. To this end, the AN/PVS2 individual weapon sight was introduced. Commonly known as the 'starlight scope', the PVS2 was designed to intensify the available background light to the point where shapes could be identified even in conditions of almost total darkness. Easily fitted to, for example, a standard M16, the PVS2 offered a range of vision of about 400m (1300 feet). In established positions such as firebases, the AN/TVS4 NOD (night observation device) offered a similar capability. Range was in the order of 1200m (4000 feet) and when combined with the highly portable AN/PPS5 surveillance radar

People Sniffers

Left: The view from inside the twin canopy of a Grumman A-6 Intruder. This aircraft was the US Navy's counterpart of the B-57G and was fitted with FLIR and LLTV. It was nicknamed the 'miniature B-52' by the Viet Cong due to its extensive weapons load, almost 30 per cent of its maximum land take-off weight.

Below: The Grumman OV-1 Mohawk. This fixed-wing aircraft is a unique STOL platform for carrying sensors over land battlefields and is mounted with APS-94 SLAR (side-looking airborne radar), auxiliary fuel tanks and bombs.

(range 5000m – 16,600 feet – against personnel), the TVS4 offered a high degree of night security for base areas.

Apart from the defence of established perimeters, the transport of men and supplies was a major problem throughout Southeast Asia. The forces of the South relied on standard trucks, APCs, helicopters and river craft as the terrain dictated, while those of the North used Soviet GAZ (Gorky Automobilova Zavod) trucks, bicycles and the infinitely flexible human back. But for operations in the Mekong Delta region, the Americans developed a whole new class of river-ine vessels for transport, patrol (the PBR MkII), fire support (ASPB MkI) and command and control (CCB MkI). In addition, considerable use was made of air- and ski-boats while hovercraft, such as the Bell SK-5, were operationally tested.

All these vessels were capable of operating in very shallow water, having drafts of no more than 60-90cm (2-3 feet). The PBR MkII patrol craft carried a crew of five and was armed, typically, with three 0.5in calibre machine guns, a 40mm grenade launcher and a 60mm mortar. The ASPB MkI was designed to provide suppressive fire during 'search and destroy' missions, an interdiction capability against enemy river traffic and a mine clearance platform. Crew comprised six men and armament was typically one 20mm cannon, two 0.5in and two 0.3in calibre machine guns, and two 40mm grenade launchers.

The workhorse of the war

Essential though these vessels were for operations in the Delta, without doubt the workhorse of the war for the American forces was the helicopter. The four most important that fought in Vietnam were the Bell UH-1 'Huey', the Boeing CH-47, the Bell AH-1 'Huey Cobra' and the Hughes OH-1 'Loach'. With the exception of the AH-1, all these aircraft had flown prior to the American involvement in the war and the concept of 'air mobility' was already well established. But the escalation of the fighting brought about many refinements and created a new weapons system, the 'gunship' helicopter.

The idea of arming a helicopter was not new and armed machines had been used operationally by the French in Algeria. Fire support for the landed infantry was a key component of 'air mobility' and the first UH-1A and UH-1B 'Hueys' to arrive in Vietnam during 1962 were field-modified into gunships. Neither model was ideal for the role, however, and both had been largely replaced by the UH-IC by the end of 1966. The new model was specifically developed as a weapons platform and featured revised rotor and vertical fin geometry combined with a modified hydraulic system. Over 700 examples of the 'C' were manufactured and it was capable of carrying 12 distinct armament sub-systems. These ranged from unguided rockets through various combinations of M60 machine guns and 7.62mm rotary weapons to

Unnecessary suffering?

The American decision to use airpower in a war of attrition against a widely-dispersed and lightly-armed enemy who exploited conceal-ment in difficult terrain, led logically to the employment of anti-personnel munitions which was to prove highly controversial.

The most notorious was napalm, a jellied petroleum first used for bombing in World War II, but never previously dropped in such quantity – almost 400,000 tonnes of napalm were expended in America's Indochina War, compared with 33,000 tonnes in Korea. Napalm bombs constituted about 10 per cent of fighter-bomber munitions in Vietnam and official rules restricting its use had little impact. White phosphorous munitions were often used in conjunc-tion with napalm, the spontaneous ignition of the phosphorous ensuring the ignition of the napalm. Phosphorous was also used to mark targets, to provide a smoke screen, and to set fire to houses and huts.

Both napalm and white phosphorous were heavily criticised by the anti-war movement for their effect on civilians. It was argued that the burns they caused constituted 'unnecessary suffering' as defined in the Hague Conventions. But the American forces claimed that these munitions were uniquely effective against en-trenched infantry, and resulted in no more suffering or 'collateral damage' than high explosives.

Another controversial anti-personnel technique was the use of 'improved conventional munitions', a refinement of the fragmenta-tion munitions concept. Developed in the early 1960s, these muni-tions comprised a container filled with submunitions; the container was fitted with a fuse set to explode before, during or after impact, according to the effect desired, scattering the submunitions over a wide area. These munitions included cluster bombs and 'beehive' artillery shells, the latter containing a payload of small dart-like

Above: A Douglas A-1E Skyraider drops phosphorous onto a VC position. The Skyraider could carry 3629kg (8000lbs) of ordnance.

flechettes usually scattered by an air-burst in a rain of deadly arrows.

Much criticism was direct at the American use of riot control agents, chiefly CS and CN gas, in military operations. Initially employed specifically for the clearance of tunnels, gas soon be-came a normal part of army munitions, with over 2.7 million kg (6 million lb) of CS gas used in 1969. Although it could be argued that tear gas is a relatively humane weapon, the use of any gas for military purposes appeared a dangerous step backwards towards the horrors of World War I.

The only area in which criticism led to the abandonment of a technique in the course of the Vietnam War, however, was in the case of herbicides. The American forces had begun experiments with defoliation in the late 1950s, using commercially available herbicides, and in 1962 programmes of defoliation and crop des-truction were initiated in Vietnam. By the end of 1970 spraying from the air had defoliated about 1.9 million hectares (4.7 million acres) of South Vietnam – 46 per cent of the total forest area – and destroyed crops over 195,000 hectares (480,000 acres). The military effective-ness of defoliation is not disputed, but crop destruction is widely held to have been counter-productive, alienating the peasant population without effectively denying the Viet Cong food supplies.

The curtailment of the programme came, however, as a result of research into the long-term effects of the principal defoliant used in Vietnam, Agent Orange. On 15 April 1970 Agent Orange was banned both in its military use in Vietnam and in its agricultural role in the United States after the revelation that it could cause genetic defects leading to malformations in new-born infants. Both defolia-tion and crop destruction were phased out completely by the end of June 1971.

The helicopter proved to be the most versatile weapon of the Vietnam War. It fulfilled a wide range of tasks, including defoliation (inset below, a Bell UH-1D releases its load of chemicals during defoliation operations in the Mekong Delta), and ground attack (below, the view from the doorway of a Bell UH-1 Huey showing the manually operated M60 in the hands of the door gunner and the pylon-mounted, electronically operated external machine guns).

40mm grenade launchers and, on two aircraft, TOW anti-tank missiles.

The UH-IC proved to be an effective weapons platform but it was still not perfect, and was to be superseded by the world's first purpose-designed attack helicopter, the AH-1. This machine carried a crew of two and was armed with two rotary machine guns – or one such weapon and a grenade launcher – in a nose turret, plus four weapons stations carried on stub wings. In service from 1967, the type proved to be very effective and apart from armament changes, was only subject to modification to counter the heat-seeking hand-held SA-7 SAM (surface-to-air missile) which was deployed by communist forces in the South from 1970.

Seeking out the enemy at night proved as much of a problem for the helicopter gunships as for any other system. The INFANT (Iroquois night-fighter and night-tracker) night-sighting equipment was one solution applied to the UH-IM (a re-engined UH-IC) type. INFANT comprised twin nose-mounted sensors feeding an LLTV (low light television) and a monocular image intensifier. These units were backed-up with laterally mounted combined infra-red viewers/searchlights; armament comprised two 7.62mm rotary machine guns and two rocket pods. Three INFANT 'Hueys' were operationally tested in Southeast Asia where they were used as 'pathfinders'. The system seems not to have been particularly successful and no wide-scale use was made of it.

Following on from INFANT, the US Army attempted to give the AH-1 an all-weather capability with the SMASH (Southeast Asia multiple-sensor armament system helicopter) programme of 1969. SMASH aircraft were fitted with a nose-mounted FLIR (forward-looking infra-red) sensor, a pod-mounted AN/APQ-137B radar (to starboard), the standard nose turret and a wing-mounted 20mm cannon and rocket pod to port. At least one SMASH AH-1 was completed but the American withdrawal overtook the programme and it was never tested operationally.

If little success was achieved in mating night sensors to helicopters, much more satisfactory results were obtained with fixed-wing types. Great use was made of infra-red sensors and LLTV for reconnaissance in such types as the OV-1 and the 'Patricia Lynn' RB-57s, but without doubt the most effective systems of this nature came together in three attack aircraft, the USAF's 'Pave Spectre' AC-130 and B-57G and the US Navy's A-6C TRIM (trails, roads, interdiction, multisensor) Intruder.

From 'Spooky' to 'Pave Spectre'

The 'Pave Spectre' was the ultimate development of a line of aircraft unique to the Southeast Asian war, the fixed-wing gunship. The idea originated in the AC-47 'Spooky' which was a C-47 transport fitted with a battery of 7.62mm rotary 'miniguns' along its port side. Such aircraft operated usually at night and on finding a target, banked in a circle, allowing a concentrated cone of fire to be laid down on a single spot. So successful was the AC-47 that further gunships were produced from C-119 and C-130 airframes.

Based on a C-130 airframe, the 'Pave Spectre' widened the concept of the gunship from the predominantly defensive role of its predecessors to an offensive one of interdiction along the Ho Chi Minh Trail. To fit them for this role, 'Pave Spectre' aircraft carried a vast array of sensors including FLIR, LLTV, tracking radar, a 2kW searchlight, flare dispensers and the 'Black Crow' direction-finder which homed in on the emissions from truck ignitions. The 'Pave Spectre' aircraft could attack a target with two 20mm Vulcan rotary cannon, two 7.62mm 'miniguns', two 40mm Bofors guns and in some cases, even a 105mm field piece.

Complementing this extraordinary aeroplane was the B-57G which likewise carried a battery of sensor systems with which to seek out targets in the dark. Developed under the 'Tropic Moon' programme, the B-57G carried FLIR, LLTV and a laser designator for its primary armament of four Paveway laser-guided bombs. Problems in hitting precision targets during the war hastened an already existing US programme aimed at developing television and laser-light

guidance for free-fall weapons. This work produced the 'electro-optical' Walleye for the US Navy and the HOBOS (homing on bomb optical system) for the USAF and the laser-guided Paveway, again for the USAF. All three weapons saw action in Vietnam with good results and B-57Gs consistently managed to deliver Paveways to within 4.5m (15 feet) of a given target in conditions of total darkness.

The last of the trio, the A-6C Intruder, was the US Navy's counterpart of the B-57G. Introduced in 1969-70 the A-6C was fitted with FLIR and LLTV, carried in an under-fuselage turret. The A-6C was used extensively against coastal traffic around the Mekong Delta at night or in bad weather.

Whilst these sensor-laden aircraft attempted to disrupt the communists' night-time activities in South Vietnam, Laos and Cambodia, similarly advanced technology was being brought to bear in the air offensive against the North Vietnamese heartland. During 1965, the first SA-2 SAM site was discovered in the North. This weapon, although intended for use against high-flying strategic bombers, posed a serious threat to the USAF's strike missions. It had long been known that the weak link in such systems was the tracking radar used for missile guidance and the American QRC-160 programme was utilised to provide jamming pods to counter these radars. This was a development of the utmost importance, for the USAF had never attempted to provide tactical aircraft with an ECM (electronic counter-measures) capability.

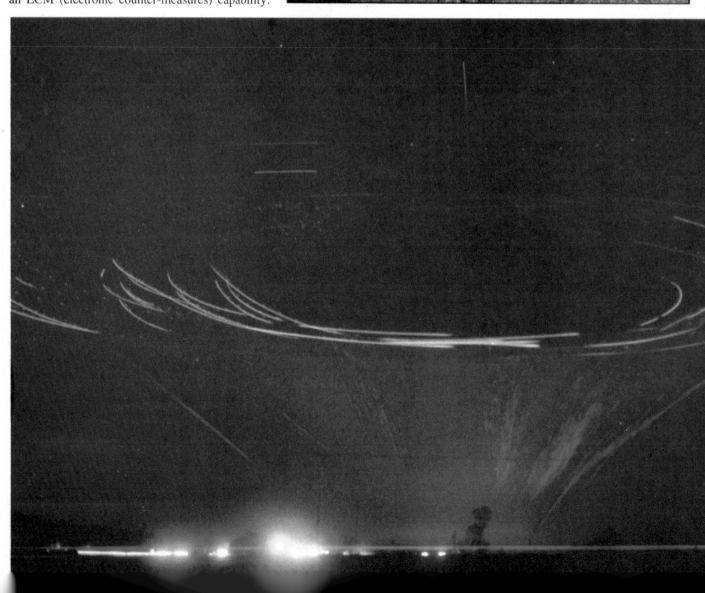

Above: US Marines with their M50 ONTOS. Although originally designed as a tank destroyer, the ONTOS was widely used in Vietnam in a fire support role. Left: A PACV moving at speed. Right: The M60, with a cyclic fire rate of 100 rpm, was a valuable weapon.

The Lockheed AC-130 mounted a 105mm howitzer, a 40mm cannon, two 20mm cannon and two 7.62mm miniguns (below, a minigun blasts away at ground targets). Usually operating at night, these aircraft, on finding a target, banked in a circle allowing concentrated fire to be laid down on a single area (left, a delayed exposure photograph shows the white circular movement of the aircraft and the red 'cone' of fire).

By 1966 the first fruits of QRC-160, the AN/ALQ-71 pod, had become operational and proved far more effective than its predecessor, the EB-66 'stand-off' jammer. The North Vietnamese response was to extend the frequency range of their radars and progressively to introduce the newer SA-3 missile alongside up-dated SA-2s. By 1969 the USAF was using ALQ-71 to cover the S-band frequencies, the ALQ-72 for the X band and the ALQ-87 for the C, X and Ku bands; such was the extent of the 'radio' war which had developed between the two sides.

Although jamming was only one response to the missile threat and not a complete answer, ECM had a major effect. The North Vietnamese needed to launch 194 SA-2s to achieve 11 'kills' in 1965 and 4244 SA-2s and SA-3s to achieve 49 'kills' in 1972. By the latter date, 86.6 missiles were fired for every aircraft destroyed, whereas back in 1965 the figure was 17.6.

This dramatic decline in missile efficiency was not only due to effective ECM and tactics but also to the introduction of 'Wild Weasel' SAM-suppression aircraft. Such machines, initially F-100Fs and then F-105s, F-105Gs and F-4Cs, were fitted with receivers which could both warn of illumination by a SAM radar and give a bearing on its location. The 'Weasels' acted as both decoys to lure the SAM sites into revealing themselves and as strike aircraft to destroy them. In this latter role, the major weapon was a new breed of missile capable of homing onto a radar signal. Two types, the AGM-45 Shrike and the AGM-78 Standard anti-radiation missile, were used in Southeast Asia with considerable success.

It is tempting with the benefit of hindsight to argue that technology served only to pull America deeper into the quagmire of Vietnam and actively prolonged the war. Without technological successes such as the reduction of the amount of men and weapons coming down the Ho Chi Minh Trail, then the failure of policies within South Vietnam would have been highlighted and the realities of the situation would have been much clearer, much earlier. What such insight would have resulted in must remain in the realm of speculation; but it is clear that technological innovation was at the very core of American involvement in Vietnam. **Martin Streetly**

Limited War

Keeping conflict below the nuclear threshold

The term limited war was first used by General George C. Marshall in May 1951. As US secretary of defense, General Marshall appeared before the Senate Committees on the Armed Services and on Foreign Relations concerning the military situation in the Far East. He was asked how he would describe the Korean conflict – would he call it a war or a police action? General Marshall replied, 'I would characterise it as a limited war which I hope will remain limited.'

The modern concept of limited war and the policies associated with it were first seen when the Cold War was spreading to Asia and the Soviet Union was beginning to achieve the capability to inflict considerable nuclear damage on the United States. It was the Korean War which really stimulated a debate in the United States about the nature of limited war. In contrast to the American experience of World War II, where the US had been fighting to defeat the enemy completely using maximum force, the US government sought only a partial or limited victory in Korea and deliberately restricted the nature and scope of its intervention partly to avoid direct armed confrontation with the Soviet Union and partly to avoid protracted war on the mainland of Asia that might weaken US forces in Europe.

The Korean War had compelled the American government to grapple with the problems of limited war because the task of defeating the invasion by North Korea was not one that could be undertaken by nuclear weapons without risking a world war or depleting US stockpiles of such weapons. And the limits placed upon the actions of the UN forces (which General MacArthur and then General Ridgway found very irksome) reflected the nature of a struggle which was always confined within certain bounds.

In fact, as far as the superpowers are concerned, all the wars since 1945 can be defined as 'limited' in that they have never ended in world war. There are four major criteria for coming to this definition. Firstly, there has been a geographical limitation: wars have been restricted to a particular geographical area of the world such as Korea, the Middle East or the South Atlantic. Neither of the world wars was limited geographically.

Secondly, there has been a limitation of objectives. World War II had become an unlimited war by 1943 because the Allies had adopted an objective of unconditional surrender. In contrast, from the perspective of the United States, Vietnam was a limited war because the objective was not the total defeat of the North.

Thirdly, there has been a limitation of the means by which wars are fought, with a restraint in respect of the mobilisation of national resources and the quality and quantity of the weapons used. The United States used only part of its massive conventional strength and none of its nuclear capability in Vietnam and the

Below: Royal Marine Commandos 'yomping' across the barren terrain of East Falkland, on their way to Port Stanley. It was the excellence of British troops and the ability of the naval task force to maintain itself thousands of kilometres from the nearest British bases that enabled the British government to prosecute a limited war in the South Atlantic in 1982, a war in which the hostilities were all confined to within a few hundred kilometres of the islands over which the conflict had broken out.

Above: It is the US government that has had most practical experience of limited war – in Korea and Vietnam especially. Nixon's visit to China in 1972 (above) was a breakthrough in international relations that occurred even while the Chinese were arming the North Vietnamese. While regular updates on the world's trouble spots (above right, Jimmy Carter is briefed on the Middle East) have been essential if presidents are to make the firm but measured responses that are needed to keep conflicts local in areas where over-reaction could have fatal consequences for the whole world.

same can be said so far of the Soviets in Afghanistan.

Finally, there has been a limitation of targets selected for attack. Under Robert McNamara's 1960s nuclear strategy it was envisaged that there would be a restraint on city targetting by US strategic nuclear forces and during the Vietnam War there was restriction on the areas of North Vietnam that could be bombed by the US air forces. During the Falklands War the British government limited its targets to exclude a direct attack on mainland Argentina.

A limited war can start out as such, however, and slowly develop by the course of events into something quite different. World War II began as a limited European war concerning the independence of Poland and yet developed into worldwide total war. The basis of limited war theory is, therefore, a concern with the problem of how to keep wars limited, and especially how to prevent them escalating into a nuclear conflagration.

The experience of the Korean War did not make limited war an integral part of US strategic theory, however. 'Massive Retaliation' to any communist

aggression was adopted as the basic approach of the Einsenhower administration. But in the late 1950s and early 1960s the dangers of 'Massive Retaliation' were pointed out by various theorists, and, retrospectively, the Korean War was assimilated into a body of thought that emerged as the dominant strand in the thinking of President John Kennedy's administration. Kennedy and his advisers believed that a new strategy of containment had to be adopted to meet the challenge of communism in the Third World and they set about strengthening US conventional and counter-insurgency forces to give the limited war capacity that containment required. Critics of this policy – which was chiefly associated with Secretary of Defense Robert McNamara – argued that the US and its allies would never have sufficient conventional forces to meet a Soviet conventional challenge in Europe; that the credibility of the nuclear deterrent was undermined by the emphasis on a limited war capability; and that a limited war capability in the Third World was an open-ended commitment which could prove disastrous for American power and prestige.

The US involvement in Vietnam, under President Johnson, with McNamara still secretary of defense, put the limited-war theories fully to the test. The objective of the American involvement was not the overthrow of the North Vietnamese government in a total military victory, but the dissuasion of the communists from continuing their effort to defeat the Saigon regime. As Henry Kissinger had said of limited war in a theoretical work of the late 1950s: 'It reflects an attempt to affect the opponent's will, not to crush it, to make the conditions to be imposed seem more attractive than continued resistance, to strive for specific goals and not for complete annihilation.' Dedicated to this political and psychological approach, the Johnson administration sought to impose tight controls on military action so that it would serve the political purpose.

The politicians also imposed geographical limits on their forces. Although covert operations and secret bombings on a large scale carried US military action into Laos and Cambodia, major incursions by ground forces were ruled out, as was an invasion of the North. Varied targetting restrictions on bombing of the North also applied – with the somewhat ironic result that the territory of America's ally, South Vietnam, was subjected to more unconstrained air attack than its enemy. Interdiction of supply lines from China and the Soviet Union was ruled out, as was the use of nuclear weapons.

The poker-playing principle

The limited war strategy dictated a graduated build-up of operations; theoretically each stage of the escalation would once more give the enemy a possible occasion to back down – the poker-playing principle. Under Johnson, the Americans were not even seeking to make the North Vietnamese negotiate, but rather to induce them to withdraw from combat.

Many US military leaders felt at the time – and still feel today – that this limited war approach denied them the chance of military success. The restrictions placed on operations beyond the borders of South Vietnam allowed the communists safe bases from which they could strike and to which they could withdraw. Despite the heavy bombing, the vital Ho Chi Minh Trail could not be cut without a massive incursion of ground forces across the Laotian frontier. The frequent bombing pauses and 'controlled escalation' of the Rolling Thunder campaign against the North made it ineffective. Some military leaders have argued that they should have been authorised to use maximum force immediately, wherever and whenever it was militarily necessary in order to defeat the enemy.

Both arguments for and against the use of limited war in Vietnam face insuperable problems. The military case fails to tackle the ineluctable problem of superpower relations; North Vietnam was an ally of China and the Soviet Union, and attacks on Soviet shipping, raids too near the Chinese border, or an invasion of the North might easily have brought Soviet or Chinese forces into the war, with incalculable consequences. At worst, an escalation to world nuclear conflict could have resulted. No American government could have felt that the cause justified such risks – Vietnam was not that vital to American interests.

But events clearly discredited limited war, at least in the case of Vietnam, as a means to achieve the containment of communism. Faced with an enemy whose will to win was implacable, prepared to make enormous sacrifices to that end, the United States was bound to lose the political and psychological confrontation of a limited conflict. Indeed, it was the North Vietnamese, holding the strategic initiative throughout, who imposed an escalation of the conflict that eventually induced the Americans to back down. In one sense, North Vietnam's strategy against US forces from 1965 to 1973 can be seen as itself a most successful exercise in limited war.

The other major flaw in the US limited war approach to Vietnam was that it resembled the 'maximum force' option in its dependence on the deployment of massive quantities of firepower to achieve its objectives. Yet the first necessity of a successful Vietnam policy would have been the establishment of a viable political and social system in the South – something that could only have resulted from an intelligent counter-insurgency effort. The limited war approach, with its reliance on signalling threats to a constituted political authority – in this case the Hanoi government – had no place for counter-insurgency as a 'hearts and minds' strategy. The limited war version of counter-insurgency could only be terror – convincing a population that guerrilla acts would be met with widespread destruction.

Under President Nixon the rules of limited war were somewhat changed, but the principle remained the same – Nixon was just a tougher poker player. His better relationship with Russia meant he knew exactly what he could get away with. The measure of success he achieved merely showed that, if limited war could not be a strategy for American victory, it could at least be the tactic for a negotiated withdrawal.

In the wider sphere of world politics, however, the Nixon-Kissinger foreign policy did make clear the successful side of limited war. In 1972 it was possible for Nixon to make a historic visit to Peking and to achieve a summit triumph in Moscow even while the Vietnam War continued – indeed the Moscow visit occurred right in the middle of the crisis over the mining of Haiphong harbour. Thus, although Vietnam appeared to demonstrate the failure of limited war as a technique for the containment of communism, it also revealed its continuing value as a part of superpower relationships.

Graham Brewer

Below: A Soviet convoy winds its way circumspectly through the mountains of Afghanistan. The Soviet Union has allowed itself to get dragged into a guerrilla war in Afghanistan, but has always resisted the temptation to escalate its involvement above a level of about 150,000 men. In Afghanistan, therefore, standard Soviet military doctrine, which stresses the use of overwhelming force to secure a given result in the fastest possible time, has been superseded by the more subtle constraints of limited war, for although the Soviets undoubtedly could commit more troops to this sparsely populated mountainous country, they evidently feel that there are good reasons why they should not.

Key Weapons
TACTICAL NAVAL MISSILES

Since 1945 the guided missile has become the dominant weapon on the ships of the world's navies, its greater range and accuracy largely replacing the conventional gun. A guided missile is simply a self-propelled shell with an explosive warhead which is fitted with equipment that can alter the direction of the shell, either by radio command from the launching ship or by the shell sensing the position of the target and automatically guiding itself. The ability of the missile to be guided onto its target allows for an extraordinary degree of precision so that a hit by a single missile can almost be guaranteed against a relatively small target tens of kilometres away.

The first naval missiles were adopted for use against aircraft, largely because guns were unable to deal with the greatly increased speeds of the new jet aircraft. Missiles designed to sink other ships were slower in being developed but the loss of the Israeli destroyer *Eilat* on 21 October 1967 – sunk by a Soviet-made Styx missile launched from a small Egyptian patrol boat – dramatically revealed the power of the ship-to-ship missile and instigated new interest in this type of weapon. As the submarine is regarded as the chief threat to surface ships it was only a matter of time before anti-submarine missiles came into being. Thus there are three main types of ship-launched missile: surface-to-air, surface-to-surface and surface-to-subsurface.

Naval SAMs (surface-to-air missiles) can be broadly divided into two categories. The first are long-range missiles for defence against high-altitude aircraft, and termed area defence weapons they are designed to protect a force before an attack actually materialises. The second category are close-range point-defence missiles whose function is to defend vessels at the point of attack and be able to knock out both high-speed low-level strike aircraft and approaching missiles.

Area defence missiles vary considerably in size, range and guidance methods, although the means of propulsion is usually standard, provided by a two-stage jet motor: a booster to blast the missile to the required speed and a sustainer to keep it in flight. One of the larger area defence SAMs is the US Talos missile which weighs 3175kg (7000lb), has a range of 120km (75 miles) and is guided onto its target by a combination of beam-riding and semi-active radar. In 1968, Talos missiles fired from the US cruiser *Long Beach* knocked-out two MiG fighters over North Vietnam at a range of 112km (70 miles).

The US Terrier and Advanced Terrier missiles are less than half the weight of the Talos but have a shorter range of just over 32km (20 miles). The Advanced Terrier has been replaced by the Standard missile which came into US Navy service in the early 1970s and utilised solid-state electronics and an exclusively electrical control system, thereby greatly increasing reliability. The Standard comes in two configurations: the MR (medium range) missile which has a range of 24km (15 miles) and the heavier ER (extended range) which can be fired to a distance of 56km (35 miles). A highly sophisticated weapon, the Standard can be used against aircraft and cruise missiles – even at low levels – and has the capability to be deployed in a surface-to-surface role.

A major problem in SAM defences is the danger of a ship being swamped by incoming enemy targets, as the SAM director can usually only handle one or two targets at any one time. The American Aegis system is

an attempt to solve the problem. Aegis employs an advanced electronic scanning radar which can look in all directions almost instantaneously, so that missiles can launch with a minimum of reaction time. Aegis employs an uprated Standard missile (the SM-2) available in MR and ER versions which has a two-way link guidance system for air-to-air command and improved electronic counter-measures resistance.

The first British area defence missile was Seaslug which after a slow developmental programme was fitted to the Royal Navy's County-class destroyers from 1961 onwards. Possessing a range of around 45km (28 miles) Seaslug utilised a beam-riding guidance system. The more sophisticated Sea Dart has since replaced Seaslug and in its Mk2 form has a speed of around Mach 3.5 and a maximum range of at least 80km (50 miles).

The Soviet Union has relied on SA-N-1 Goa missiles which are mounted on twin-round launchers and

Page 1503: A Sea Dart area-defence missile is launched from the deck of HMS *Invincible* in September 1980. Sea Dart was designed to have the capability to deal with both aircraft and low-flying missiles; experience in the Falklands suggested that the smaller Seawolf was more effective as an anti-missile missile. Left: A Sea Dart missile mounting. The Mk 2 Sea Dart has a maximum range of at least 80km (50 miles). Below left and inset: The Seawolf point defence missile. Capable of an extremely fast reaction to an enemy threat, Seawolf can score a direct hit on a target as small as a 4.5in shell at a distance of several kilometres in only five seconds. Six rounds are stored in the missile launcher at instant readiness and can remain there for long periods at sea without maintenance. Right: A Seaslug SAM blasts off from its launcher. Inset right: A Soviet SA-N-1 Goa missile is prepared for launch. Below: The advanced Standard missile – the variant with extended range – is test-fired from a US Navy frigate in April 1973. The Standard missile has a maximum range of 56km (35 miles) and is armed with a substantial high explosive warhead.

have a maximum range of 24km (15 miles). During the 1970s the advanced long-range SA-N-3 Goblet and the short-range SA-N-4 came into service and armed the more recently launched ships of the Soviet Navy.

Point-defence missiles often have only seconds in which to react and are directed either by radio command from a ship-board operator or more commonly by automatic guidance from a radio-command computer. As the ranges are usually short, between three and five kilometres (two and three miles), the missiles are quite small, needing little fuel and only a single stage motor. In many cases both the target (missile or aircraft) and the outgoing missile are tracked by separate radars which aim to guide the two together. The command guidance system is very difficult to jam as it operates through backward facing antennae on the missile control surfaces. The best known of the point-defence missiles is the British Seawolf, a small

and highly agile weapon which proved itself in the Falklands conflict of 1982, able to deal with the missiles that slipped through the outer defence rings of combat air patrols and area defence missiles.

While SAMs are obviously defensive in nature, SSMs (surface-to-surface missiles) are intended to fulfil a completely opposite function, in order to improve a vessel's offensive capability. Most SSMs were designed for use when the launching ship had spotted the target vessel by radar, which meant that the missile's range was about that of the ship's own radar horizon, a maximum of about 40km (25 miles). To overcome this problem of detecting over-the-horizon targets a third party is required – another ship or an aircraft (notably the missile ship's own helicopter) – which can act as a link between the two, thereby extending the missile ship's horizon.

Typically SSMs use a two-stage guidance system. Initially the missile is guided to the target by an

inertial navigation system, that is, the position of the launch ship and the target's estimated course and speed are fed into a computer which transmits a course and distance to the missile's navigation equipment, which guides it in the general direction of the target. To allow for alterations by the target vessel, the missile has its own terminal radar which comes into action only when the missile closes on its target. Once turned-on, the missile's radar searches for the target and when found locks on to it and guides the missile to its destination.

The advantages of employing an inertial navigation system as well as a terminally active system are twofold. The first, and most important, reason is that if the missile's radar were transmitting during the whole of the flight, the target ship would have time to pick up its transmissions and jam them. Travelling at sub-sonic speeds over long distances a missile can take two to three minutes to reach its target, ample time to initiate jamming measures. If, however, the missile's radar begins transmission only a few kilometres from the target, the enemy vessel has only seconds in which to respond. The second reason is that the missile's radar would have to be much larger and more powerful if it had to detect a target at 40km (25 miles), and the limited space in the missile would have difficulty holding the larger radar and its power supplies.

The US Harpoon is one of the more advanced SSMs, employing the usual inertial navigation and active terminal-homing guidance systems. Its radar is 'frequency agile' which means that it is constantly changing frequency making it very difficult to jam, and during the later stages of its flight it adopts a number of 'pop-up' manoeuvres making it a hard target to shoot down. Powered by an air-breathing turbo jet engine with a solid propellant and booster motor, it has a range in excess of 80km (50 miles).

France, Britain, Germany, Greece and Argentina, plus a number of other navies, have all adopted the French Exocet missile and it has been fitted in a variety of ship types as well as some aircraft. It has a two-stage solid propellant motor which gives it a speed of 1110km/h (690mph or Mach 0.9) and a range of 37km (23 miles). Like the Harpoon it is also a wave skimmer; after launch it drops down to just above sea level and continues its journey at this height, making it more difficult to detect by radar. It has the standard two-stage inertial navigation and active terminal radar homing system. The Exocet achieved

Above left: The French-built Exocet missile during launch. Above: A US Harpoon missile is fired from a speeding hydrofoil. The Harpoon is a highly versatile missile, capable of being launched from a wide range of platforms including even submarines. Left: The launch of an Israeli Gabriel anti-shipping missile, developed by the Israeli Navy as a counter to Egypt's Osa-class missile-launching vessels. Below left: A test firing of the Franco-Italian Otomat missile. Above right: A Penguin SSM is launched from a Storm-class fast missile craft of the Royal Norwegian Navy. Right and below: Soviet Osa-class vessels, armed with the SS-N-2 Styx missile, one of which sunk the Israeli destroyer *Eilat* in 1967.

considerable fame (or notoriety) during the Falklands campaign when the British destroyer HMS *Sheffield* was sunk after being hit by an air-launched Exocet missile. an Exocet was also responsible for the sinking of the *Atlantic Conveyor*, and the County-class destroyer HMS *Glamorgan* was damaged by a land-launched missile.

There are a number of other ship-to-ship missiles being produced in Europe. Italy and France have completed development of the Otomat, a similar missile to Exocet, but with a greater range of 80km (50 miles). It has been designed from the outset to be launched onto its target through aerial reconnaissance as well as by ship's radar. Italy has also developed the Sea Killer, a lightweight short-range missile (20km – 12.5 miles) employing a combined beam-riding/radio command system. Of a similar range is the Norwegian Penguin which is designed for use from patrol boats and supplements its standard first-stage inertial navigation system with a second-stage infra-red homing system.

The Soviet Union has shown considerable interest in naval cruise missiles, big, clumsy weapons which have a very long range and a large warhead (even nuclear) but which are reasonably easy to intercept. The SS-N-3 Shaddock is one such naval cruise missile and is estimated to have a maximum range of as much as 850km (530 miles) though a more modest 200km (125 miles) is considered an optimum range. The SS-N-2 Styx achieved instant fame when it sunk the *Eilat* in 1967 and remains the most numerous SSM in the Soviet Navy. The SS-N-9 is a more advanced missile and is thought to have a range of 110km (70 miles). The SS-N-11 is similar to the old Styx missile but makes use of modern manufacturing techniques; it has been exported to India, Finland and Iraq.

The Israeli Gabriel missile has, like the Exocet, seen combat service, and during the 1973 Yom Kippur War it sunk a number of Egyptian patrol boats. Manufactured in two sizes, the Gabriel has a range of 22km (13.6 miles) or 41km (25 miles) depending on the weight of the variant. The first missiles came into operation in 1970 and were installed on Israel's French-built Saar-class gunboats which can deploy two three-round launches and two single-round launches. The Gabriel can be launched in rough seas and has an all-weather capability.

Surface-to-subsurface missiles are sophisticated anti-submarine weapons, far in advance of the simple depth charge. The two main types are the American Asroc and Australian-British Ikara. Both are solid fuel rockets able to deliver acoustic homing torpedoes (although Asroc can carry a nuclear depth charge). Asroc has a range of 10km (6 miles) and when launched describes a ballistic trajectory, releasing its torpedo at a pre-set point over the water. Ikara is more advanced, in that the missile is guided in flight and both guidance and torpedo release are guided by a central computer receiving data on the submarine's position through the ship's sonar. The Norwegian Terne is a lightweight surface-to-subsurface missile with a limited range of just 3km (1.8 miles) and which delivers a 50kg (110lb) warhead.

Submarines themselves also fire missiles. Subroc is an American system, a submarine-launched two-stage rocket which is inertially guided and has a range of 56km (35 miles). Following its submarine launch, Subroc's rocket motor ignites underwater and the missile is then propelled out of the water to fly to a set

Above: An Ikara long-range anti-submarine missile is launched from a frigate of the Brazilian Navy. Ikara is a highly flexible weapon and it can be fitted with a number of acoustic homing torpedos, usually the US Type 44 lightweight torpedo.
Left: An Asroc anti-submarine missile and launcher.

point where it then releases a nuclear depth charge, primed to explode at a pre-set depth. Submarines can also fire missiles at surface ships, using modified SSMs. They are launched from the submarine's torpedo tubes, and then propelled to the surface like Subroc when the missile's own rocket motor is fired. The missile then flies on an inertially-guided programme until its own terminal radar takes over for final target acquisition. Typical examples are modified versions of the US Harpoon and the Soviet SS-N-15.

Guided missiles are singly the most important weapon available to surface vessels but it must be remembered that they are not suitable for certain kinds of action. In many cases the launching of an extremely expensive missile is an uneconomic proposition against small craft like patrol boats, where a conventional naval gun would do the job just as well. Equally, missiles cannot fire a warning shot across the bows of an intercepted vessel and are unsuitable for bombarding shore targets.

Above: The frigate USS *Brooke* fires an Asroc missile during trials in the Pacific. Besides a whole range of conventional torpedo warheads Asroc can also be armed with a nuclear depth charge.

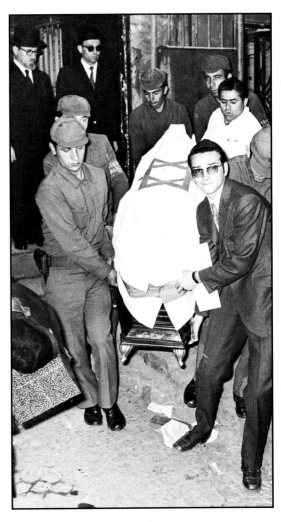

Terror international

Hostages, hijackings and bombings in the early 1970s

The wave of hijackings, bombings and assassinations that swept the world in the first half of the 1970s can now be seen to have marked the high tide of international terrorism. The roots of the upsurge lay in a coincidence between developments in the Palestinians' conflict with Israel and developments within the revolutionary left in the West and Japan. Its initial success was guaranteed by the unpreparedness of the authorities and their failure to produce an adequate response.

The Palestinians had first turned to terrorist acts outside the Middle East in 1968, when the Popular Front for the Liberation of Palestine (PFLP) initiated a series of hijackings and bombings against Israeli targets in Europe. Led by George Habash and his deputy Wadi Haddad, the PFLP adopted this strategy for practical and theoretical reasons: practically, it was much easier to hit soft targets like airliners than to attack Israel itself; theoretically, the PFLP interpreted the Palestinian cause as part of a global revolutionary struggle aimed at the whole capitalist world.

The peak of the PFLP's initial campaign was reached in September 1970 with the hijacking of three airliners to Dawson's Field in Jordan, an event which helped precipitate the attack on the Palestinians by King Hussein in which the Jordanian Army drove the Palestinian guerrillas out of his country. Known as Black September, this defeat for the Palestinians severely weakened their military position, forcing them to regroup in Lebanon. It might also have been expected to discredit terrorism, but this was not the case. The increasing hopelessness of the Palestinians' situation – unable to launch successful raids on Israel now they could not operate out of Jordan, and faced with the prospect of an unfavourable peace in the Middle East since Egypt had ended its War of Attrition against Israel – dictated a further resort to terrorism as the only technique which might still force the world to pay heed to their cause.

For the renewed terrorist campaign, the international revolutionary left offered them willing helpers. The failure of the student revolts of 1968 to achieve any significant change in Western societies had convinced some radicals that the only way forward was through terrorism. However, they lacked any experience in the use of firearms or explosives, coming as most of them did from comfortable and peaceful backgrounds in the urban middle class. Both the PFLP and Yassir Arafat's Fatah were prepared to offer courses at their guerrilla training camps, an opportunity snapped up by the would-be urban guerrillas who, in any case, fully approved of the Palestinian struggle. In return, they would in future help the Palestinians. Among the groups to train in Palestinian camps were the West German Baader-Meinhof Red Army Fraction, the Japanese Red Army, the Turkish Dev Gench, and some members of the IRA and of the American Weatherman group.

Above left: Two of the most important figures in the Middle East during the early 1970s were Yassir Arafat (seated front right), head of the PLO and in effect the spokesman and political head of the Palestinians, and Colonel Gaddafi (seated front left), ruler of Libya and supporter of many Palestinian groups, including those committed to terrorist campaigns. Above: The body of the Israeli consul-general in Istanbul is carried away after his murder by Turkish Dev Gench terrorists. Dev Gench had kidnapped the consul and demanded the release of Palestinians held in Turkey as a condition for his release. This incident was one of the first indications that Palestinian terrorists were cooperating closely with those in European countries.

Above: George Habash, head of the radical Popular Front for the Liberation of Palestine (PFLP). The PFLP openly proclaimed its belief in violence, and its commitment to world revolution gave it common ground with the European terrorists of the Italian Red Brigades and the German Baader-Meinhof group. The PFLP had a secure base in South Yemen and enjoyed control over a considerable number of guerrillas in Jordan before the events of September 1970, after which the Palestinian organisations were driven out of that country. Above right: Palestinian guerrillas in training.

The terrorists could also depend on varying degrees of support from certain national governments. The Soviet Union, although ready to dip its toe in these murky waters, was suspicious both about the political alignment and the tactics of the terrorist groups, many of which in their turn denounced Soviet-style communism. Russia's Cuban and North Korean allies were more ready to offer assistance, but despite holding meetings to discuss a strategy for world revolution, neither became much involved in the Palestinian-centred network. The main support came in the Middle East, from South Yemen (People's Democratic Republic of Yemen) – where the regime which had replaced British rule in Aden gave sanctuary to the PFLP – and Colonel Gaddafi's Libya. The military coup in Libya which had overthrown the monarchy in 1969 had given a radical regime control of the vast resources of an oil-rich state. Money from Saudi Arabia and the Gulf states might filter through to the Palestinian terrorists from contributions paid to the Palestine Liberation Organisation (PLO) – the umbrella grouping under which all the Palestinian groups operated – but only Gaddafi was ready to put the wealth of an oil state behind international revolutionary projects. He might at any moment withdraw support from an operation or an organisation which annoyed him, but Libyan money and arms made their contribution to terrorist acts from Belfast to Beirut.

The Western powers were woefully unprepared for the wave of terrorism that was about to strike them. There were few special forces trained to cope with terrorism and there was no concerted approach. Individual countries were too jealous of their own legal traditions and national honour to agree to a joint legal and military response. France, whose government policy was hostile to Israel, was particularly at fault, on several occasions catching terrorists in the act and then simply putting them across the nearest border so that they could kill again. A form of cooperation did grow up, largely on a personal basis, between the various police and army units actively involved in the fight against terrorism – Britain's SAS was one of the prime movers in this cooperation, lending men, equipment and techniques to other less well-trained forces. But it was not until after the Munich massacre of 1972 that the EEC set up machinery for multinational cooperation.

Allied to the lack of special forces and of a formal umbrella under which they could cooperate was the lack of will among governments around the world to combat terrorism. Except for the Israelis, they were rarely prepared to risk the death of innocent people by attacking hostage-holding terrorists – and this was probably the most effective weapon in the terrorists' armoury.

The first terrorist act of the new international campaign took place in Rotterdam on 14 March 1971. A mixed group of Palestinians and French leftists – including the glamorous Evelyne Barges – under the orders of the head of the PFLP's European network, Mohammed Boudia, blew up oil tanks belonging to Gulf Oil. Then, on 17 May, Israel's consul-general in Istanbul, Ephraim Elrom, was kidnapped and later murdered by the Turkish Dev Gench who demanded the release of all Palestinian 'fighters' held by the Turkish government. There was also a seaborne attack in the Red Sea on the Israeli tanker *Coral Sea* which was damaged by rockets fired by four men from a small boat who then took off at high speed for the safety of the South Yemen. It was said, but never proved, that they were American blacks who had joined the PFLP.

But it was not until 28 November 1971 that a new terrorist group revealed itself. Wasfi Tell, Jordan's prime minister, leading his country's delegation to the Arab Defence Council in Cairo, was shot dead in the quietly lush foyer of the Sheraton Hotel. When his murderers were arrested they not only confessed but boasted: 'We have taken our revenge on a traitor.' Tell was killed because of the part he had played in hounding the Palestinians out of Jordan in Black September and when the organisation that killed him claimed his death, that was the name it gave.

Next month Black September struck again, ambushing Said Rifai, the Jordanian ambassador to London, and riddling his Daimler with Sten-gun bullets as he drove through Kensington. Rifai's right hand was shattered by one bullet but none of the others touched him although, according to a passer-by, 'It was like a scene from a Chicago gangster film.'

The sudden appearance of this new and deadly group came as a surprise to Middle East experts. The known groups were easily identifiable and all had their own structure of command existing under the umbrella of the PLO. Black September was something new. It had no known headquarters or leadership, nobody acknowledged membership. And yet it had to have some sort of planning and logistics staff. The mystery was unravelled strand by strand, until eventually it became apparent that Black September did not exist as a separate identity and had no infrastructure for the simple reason that it was an integral part of Yassir Arafat's Fatah organisation. Arafat, who was of course the head of the PLO as well as of Fatah, distanced himself from Black September and even today refuses to acknowledge any responsibility for its activities. He saw his role as a political and diplomatic one, and knew that if he was identified with a terrorist group he would lose not only the support of the rich Arab countries which were financing the PLO, but also the sympathy of those nations on whom he was relying to get the Palestinians' cause heard in the world's council chambers.

But at the same time, in 1971 he was not strong enough to resist the demands of his young militants for revenge on Hussein and for matching the PFLP in the ruthlessness of its campaign against Israel. And so Black September was formed as a name only, drawing its recruits for individual missions from Fatah's ranks and being armed, financed and trained in great secrecy by Fatah itself. The men in charge were Abu Iyad, Arafat's own deputy, and Ali Hassan Salameh, son of Sheikh Hassan Salameh, legendary Palestinian leader killed fighting the Israelis in 1948.

The sound of gunfire

1972 opened as 1971 had closed – to the sound of Black September gunfire. On 6 February, five Jordanian workers – allegedly Israeli spies – were shot to death in Cologne and two days later in Hamburg a factory making electric generators for Israeli aircraft was heavily damaged by a bomb: both these attacks were claimed by Black September. But later in the month it was the PFLP which returned to the headlines. Whereas Black September was receiving large sums of money from Gaddafi, the PFLP was short of funds – Gaddafi opposed the PFLP's specifically Marxist ideology which was not part of his own Islamic revolutionary creed – so Habash's men hijacked a Lufthansa airliner to Aden and demanded a five million dollar ransom. The Germans paid up, but Habash only got his money after the South Yemen government had extracted a million dollars for landing rights.

Then in April it was back to Black September, who sent a mixed nationality team into Israel to carry out bombing attacks during the Easter pilgrimage season. It was led by Evelyne Barges who came equipped with a coat and toiletries impregnated with incendiary chemicals. The Israeli police were far more alert than their European equivalents, however, and the 'Easter commando' was arrested.

May 1972 was a critical month for the terrorists, involving an important meeting and two major operations. The meeting was called by the PFLP at its main camp in the Lebanon, and those present included

Below: Wasfi Tell, the Jordanian prime minister, who was shot in Cairo in November 1971 in retaliation for his part in the events of September 1970, during which the Jordanian Army forced the PLO to leave Jordan. This killing marked the debut of the 'Black September' terrorist group. Right: Jubilant scenes in a Cairo courtroom as four Palestinians accused of Tell's murder are released on bail.

The Munich massacre

At 0400 hours on 5 September 1972, two guards patrolling the Munich Olympic village, where athletes participating in the Games were quartered, saw eight men climb in over the perimeter fence carrying large bags. Since the men were dressed in track suits the guards assumed they were athletes returning from a night out – but they were in fact a Palestinian Black September commando, embarked on a mission to take the Israeli team hostage.

The Palestinians, armed with Kalashnikovs and grenades, swiftly moved into Building 31 where the Israelis were staying. After a short but violent struggle in which weightlifter Joseph Romano and wrestling coach Moshe Weinberg were killed, nine athletes and officials were taken hostage, the remainder of the Israelis escaping through windows or the rear door. The building was soon surrounded by 300 armed police and negotiations began.

West German Chancellor Willy Brandt contacted the Israeli government who made it clear that they would not comply with any of the terrorists' demands for the release of prisoners and that they did not wish the Germans to carry on negotiations in earnest. The Bavarian security forces set out to devise a plan to free the hostages, but an assault on Building 31 was ruled out as certain to lead to the Israelis' deaths. Finally it was decided to pretend to accept the terrorists' demand for a plane to fly them and their hostages to Tunisia, in the hope of mounting a successful attack on them before they boarded the aircraft.

At 2200 hours the terrorists bundled the hostages, trussed up and blindfolded, into a bus and they were driven to a nearby helicopter pad. Three helicopters took off for Fürstenfeldbruck, two carrying terrorists and hostages, the other carrying German negotiators. The two leading helicopters landed 150m (165yds) from the Lufthansa airliner provided to fly to Tunis, watched by five Bavarian police marksmen hidden on the roof of the control tower. Two terrorists walked over to inspect the inside of the plane while another two dismounted from the helicopters with the pilots; as the first two terrorists walked back from the plane, the police marksmen opened fire. Three terrorists were killed, but the others immediately began shooting the hostages and opened fire on the control tower, where a policeman was also killed.

The terrorists held out until just after midnight, when in a final gesture of defiance one of their number leapt from a helicopter and threw a grenade back into it, setting it ablaze. He and another terrorist were then picked off, and the remaining three were captured by security personnel in armoured cars. All of the hostages were found dead, tied up inside the helicopters.

The immediate consequence of the Munich massacre was a series of Israeli air attacks on Palestinian targets in Lebanon and Syria. Among its longer-term effects were the Israeli Wrath of God assassination campaign against Black September, the widespread development of specialist anti-terrorist squads, and, hardly surprisingly, a reluctance for some years ahead to try attacks on terrorists while they were actually holding hostages.

Above: A terrorist peers cautiously out of the room in which the hostages were held while a German policeman (right) also keeps watch. Top: The wreckage of one of the helicopters in which the hostages died. Below: The memorial service for the dead athletes.

A member of the Israeli Sayaret Matkal leads away one of the two female members of the Black September group that hijacked a Sabena airliner in May 1972. The aircraft was flown to Tel Aviv, and the terrorists tried to obtain the release of 317 Palestinians in Israeli gaols in return for the safety of the passengers on board the airliner. The Israeli authorities, however, had by now determined to use force against terrorists, and the plane was stormed by troops disguised as mechanics. The two male terrorists were shot dead, and one of the passengers died in the crossfire.

representatives of Black September as well as most of the Palestinians' international allies. It was the most advanced attempt to organise terrorism on an international scale and was soon to bear fruit.

But first, on 6 May, a Black September cell of two men and two women hijacked a Sabena airliner and audaciously forced it to land at Tel Aviv where they demanded the release of no less than 317 Palestinians held by the Israelis. This attempt goes down in terrorist history not only for its sheer cheek but also for the fact that it was the first hijacked airliner to be successfully assaulted by an elite group of anti-terrorist soldiers. The Israeli government opened negotiations with the hijackers, but under cover of the talks, members of the Sayaret Matkal, the Israeli equivalent of the SAS, disguised themselves as mechanics and stormed the plane. They killed the two male hijackers and captured the women; one woman passenger was killed in the crossfire. The Israelis thus demonstrated that they were willing to accept civilian casualties in order to defeat the terrorists, a principle which was slow to be accepted by the Western nations. The Israeli chief of staff, David Elazar, later said: 'We never proposed to hand over any prisoners to them. All our negotiations were playing for time until the right moment.'

Three weeks later, the PFLP sent in their Japanese allies on a kamikazi mission to Tel Aviv's Lod airport. The Japanese killed 26 people and wounded 76. Two of the terrorists died and the third, Kozo Okamoto, is still in prison.

But even the horror of Lod was surpassed in the public consciousness on 5 September when a Black September hit team, helped by German and French sympathisers, burst into the Israeli quarters in the Munich Olympic village, killed two of the athletes and took nine as hostages. All terrorism is theatre, a calculated attempt to seize the audience's attention. In this case the audience was the whole world, watching the Olympics on millions of television screens. The Games that the Germans had designed as

proof that they were now part of the human race again, cleared of all taint of Nazism, turned into a bloody shambles. All the Israeli athlete hostages were killed in a shoot-out dreadfully mismanaged by ill-trained, poorly-equipped Bavarian policemen. Five of the terrorists and one policeman also died in the fight.

Kill and counter-kill
After the Munich massacre no Palestinian could ever argue that the world had not heard of his cause, and while Munich did not have the lasting political effects which stemmed from the hijackings to Dawson's Field, it had immediate effects on the way in which the war against terrorism was fought. It forced the Germans – also fearful of the Baader-Meinhof gang – to accept that it was impossible to fight international terrorism with the fragmented police forces belonging to the individual states of the Federal Republic. Reluctantly, they came to the decision that responsibility had to be given to a Federal force and that it must be equipped and trained as an elite unit – a decision which horrified all those who thought that the days of elite troops controlled by central government were over for ever. It forced the reluctant European states to agree to a concerted effort to fight terrorism. And it caused Israel to launch its Wrath of God hit teams in Europe to search out and kill those Arabs the Israelis judged responsible for acts of terrorism, so bringing about a war of kill and counter-kill which was to rage through the streets of Europe's cities.

But before the first retaliatory blow fell, Black September scored another success. Dr Ami Shachori, agricultural consul at the Israeli embassy in London, was killed by a letter bomb. In the next few days some 50 letter bombs were intercepted, all posted in Amsterdam to Israelis in England. Soon after, a second batch started to arrive, posted in Malaysia. These were followed in November by others posted in India. The Israelis, who have much experience with letter bombs, retaliated in October when a series of such bombs, posted in Belgrade,

Right: Two members of the Libyan-backed National Arab Youth for the Liberation of Palestine are taken off a British Airways VC-10 in Amsterdam by Dutch police in March 1974, having released the crew and passengers and set fire to the plane.

Left: Ilitch Ramon Sanchez, 'Carlos', the man who inherited the mantle of Mohammed Boudia as the leader of international terrorism in Europe.

Left: One of the letter bombs that marked another stage in the terrorist campaigns of 1972.

Below: The German GSG9 anti-terrorist squad in training. GSG9 was set up in the aftermath of the Munich massacre, as the German government decided that it must recruit a specialised force to avoid a repetition of the bungled shoot-out in which the hostages died.

arrived on the desks of Palestinian leaders in Lebanon, Egypt, Libya and Algeria.

Later that month the expected hijack to rescue the three survivors of the Munich hit team took place. A Lufthansa plane from Beirut to Ankara was taken over by two terrorists who threatened to blow it up in mid-air if the men from Munich were not released. They were, flying off to a hero's welcome in Libya.

However, 1973 soon brought a setback for Black September. On 9 February Abu Daoud, one of Yassir Arafat's most trusted lieutenants, was arrested in Amman where he was leading a Black September mission to kidnap or kill Jordanian government ministers – and probably King Hussein himself. Abu Daoud sang like a bird to the Jordanians, giving for the first time an authentic account of Black September and detailing its links with Fatah. But what little indignation was caused by his revelations was wiped out 12 days later when the Israelis shot down a Libyan airliner which had strayed over Israeli territory during a sand storm, killing 106 people. Despite Israeli protestations that they feared the plane was going to be used as a suicide bomb aimed at Tel Aviv, the whole world was horrified.

Colonel Gaddafi of Libya swore vengeance. He was implicated up to the hilt in the next, brutal terrorist operation: the occupation of the Saudi Arabian embassy in Khartoum by eight Black September terrorists on 1 March, during a farewell party for American diplomat George Curtis Moore. They demanded the release of all Palestinian and Baader-Meinhof prisoners, Sirhan Sirhan, the man who murdered Robert Kennedy, and Kozo Okamoto, surviving member of the Lod killers. But US President Richard Nixon refused to deal with the terrorists and, following instructions radioed to the embassy from somewhere in Lebanon, the killers shot Moore,

the US Ambassador, Cleo Noel, and a Belgian diplomat, Guy Eid. Afterwards President Nimeiri of the Sudan released evidence proving Gaddafi's role in supporting the operation.

Khartoum was followed on 10 April by another Israeli raid on Beirut, this time by members of the Sayaret Matkal whose mission was to kill Palestinian leaders whose apartments had been pinpointed by Israeli agents. The Israelis killed 17 people, some of them innocent bystanders, but among them were three high-ranking guerrilla leaders.

The Israelis also continued their war of assassination in Europe and on 28 June they carried out a killing which was to have a profound effect on international terrorism. They blew up Mohammed Boudia, the leading Arab terrorist in Europe, the organiser of the Rotterdam raid, the sabotage of the German factories and the 'Easter commando', and back-up organiser for Munich. The importance of his death was that it opened the way for Ilich Ramirez Sanchez to take over as the leader of international terrorism in Europe. This pudgy Venezuelan lover of pretty girls and the good life was to become notorious as 'Carlos the Killer'.

Terrorism and world opinion

Three weeks later there was an extraordinary affair when a group of three Arabs and a Japanese led by an unidentified woman hijacked a Japanese Air Lines Boeing 747 en route from Amsterdam to Tokyo. It all went wrong when the leader killed herself as she dropped the grenade she was carrying. It seems that only she knew what they were supposed to do next, so after flying around the Middle East for four days, stopping at various airports and trying to get someone to tell them what to do, they eventually fetched up at Benghazi in Libya where the passengers were released and the plane blown up.

Incident followed incident through the summer: the Saudi Arabian embassy in Paris was occupied by five Palestinians who demanded the release of Abu Daoud; two Palestinians seized a train travelling from Czechoslovakia to Austria carrying Jewish migrants from Russia, and extracted a promise from Chancellor Bruno Kreisky of Austria that he would close down the transit camp for Russian Jews at Schonau Castle. But the terrorist scene was changing. Arafat and other PLO leaders were increasingly worried by the adverse effect of terrorism on world opinion. Attacks on moderate Arab targets, such as the Saudis, threatened the PLO's financial backing and countered Arafat's long-established policy of cooperation with all Arab governments.

As a result of the change of mood within Fatah, Black September had ceased to operate even before the Arab-Israeli War of October 1973. After the war, when Arafat saw the possibility of a Palestinian diplomatic victory, the prohibition on terrorism became stronger, although his deputy Abu Iyad was still not above the occasional terrorist act. The main thrust of terrorism after October 1973 came, however, from those who rejected the search for a diplomatic solution, such as the PFLP and Colonel Gaddafi, and was aimed at conservative Arab targets as much as at the Israelis. The post-October 1973 phase would be dominated by new figures – Abu Nidal and Carlos – as well as already familiar ones like Wadi Haddad and the Japanese Red Army. Much more blood would be spilt before the high tide of terrorism ebbed away.

Christopher Dobson and Ronald Payne

Fighting in fractions

The Baader-Meinhof terrorist gang

The late 1960s were heady years for the radical left in West Germany. The time seemed ripe for revolution: universities from California to West Berlin and from Tokyo to the Sorbonne were in ferment as the expanding student population demanded change at home and abroad. In West Germany one of the most popular causes was support for Iranians suffering at the hands of the Shah's brutal secret police, and a visit by the Shah to West Berlin on 2 June 1967 provoked rioting by student protesters, in the course of which a student named Benno Ohnesorg was shot dead by the police. It was to prove the spark that set off ten years of terrorism in West Germany.

At that time, despite their admiration for Che Guevara or the Viet Cong guerrillas, none of the student revolutionaries had formulated a plan for armed action. The initial mood was Utopian as leaders like Rudi Dutschke preached the abolition of 'the power of people over people'. In theory violence was approved of, both as a tactic for oppressed minorities and the downtrodden of the Third World to use against their rulers and as a form of 'personal cleansing', freeing individuals from fear, inhibition and constraint. But violence was interpreted as the throwing of stones and street-fighting with police rather than guns and bombs.

Two would-be revolutionaries in West Berlin drew fresh conclusions, however, from the shooting of Benno Ohnesorg and decided to embark on an urban guerrilla campaign: they were Gudrun Ensslin and Andreas Baader. In April 1968 they attacked two large department stores in Frankfurt with firebombs, afterwards announcing that the act was designed to

give the comfortable citizens of Germany a taste of Vietnam. 'We don't care about burnt mattresses', Ensslin is quoted as saying, 'We are worried about burnt children in Vietnam'.

A strong-minded woman, at that time 27 years of age, Gudrun Ensslin was the daughter of a Protestant pastor. Her commitment to the revolutionary philosophies of the New Left was greater than that of Baader who was largely pulled along in her wake. He was an art student drop-out who had failed at school and had made a vague attempt at being a potter. Dark and handsome, he moved into the revolutionary student world of West Berlin more through a desire to make love than an interest in politics, but through his involvement with Ensslin his commitment to revolution became total.

The Frankfurt fire raid brought a spectacular new recruit to the group – Ulrike Meinhof, a highly intelligent woman journalist, star columnist of the fashionable New Left magazine *Konkret*. A rich woman from the glittering intellectual cocktail set, she left her husband and, taking her twin daughters with her, went to live in a commune and plunged into the revolutionary underground. She was 28 at the time.

Joined by a lawyer, Horst Mahler, the group embarked on a campaign of bomb and fire raids against a variety of targets, but Baader was soon arrested at a road block in West Berlin and given a three-year sentence. The terms of his confinement were, however, extremely lax. Baader was permitted to visit libraries under guard in order to carry on 'sociological research'; and in May 1970 Ulrike

Above: Forensic experts collect evidence from around the murdered bodyguards of Hanns-Martin Schleyer after he was kidnapped by Red Army Fraction terrorists.

Meinhof and her colleagues made an armed attack on a library where Baader was studying. Meinhof and the man who became her lover made a stylish escape in a silver-grey Alfa Romeo, and the Baader-Meinhof gang was launched.

It was in the summer of 1970 that they first made contact with Palestinian terrorists – trained men with funds, weapons and facilities. They flew to Beirut and Jordan for a course at a Fatah training camp, where they made contact with many groups from other countries. Returning home with weapons and ammunition, they established safe houses, garages and communications networks. To finance their operations they embarked on a series of bank raids, a standard urban guerrilla tactic. For cars they favoured stolen BMWs because the initials coincided with theirs. They soon adopted the title Red Army Fraction (RAF), to indicate that they formed part of a world revolutionary movement. Their logo was a five-pointed red star with the initials superimposed on a sub-machine gun at the centre.

Under this sign the group began their urban guerrilla campaign in earnest in May 1972. They placed a series of bombs at the headquarters in Frankfurt of the US Fifth Army Corps, declaring the act was in retaliation for American action in Vietnam. They killed a colonel and wounded 13 other people. Two weeks later bombs killed three more soldiers at US Army headquarters in Heidelberg. Other assaults were launched against police offices and a devastating bomb attack was made upon the Axel Springer press building in Hamburg.

Six regional groups were now operational as the Red Army Fraction spread its networks throughout West Germany. Like-minded groups also proliferated, sometimes working with the Red Army Fraction and sometimes quarrelling with it. In a radical Berlin commune a new group came into being calling itself the Second of June Movement, a reminder of the date on which Benno Ohnesorg had been shot by the police. Among its early members was Bommi Baumann, one of the few actual working-class terror-

ists. Leadership was eventually taken over by Ralf Reinders as the group graduated from violent demonstrations to fire bombing and shooting.

As terrorist raids became more widespread and murderous a wave of alarm spread through West Germany. The federal government began tightening security. Special anti-terrorist squads were established, including the Grenzschutz Gruppe Neun (GSG9), a highly-trained mobile force for emergencies. A terrorist department began coordinating operations from Wiesbaden, where a police computer data-bank collated information on suspects. Successful attempts were made to infiltrate the groups and emergency laws came into force as police strength was increased. Such moves were greeted with deep suspicion on the left – understandably, given Germany's recent past – and radical propagandists denounced them as fascist measures.

But they did begin to take effect. In June 1972, alerted by an informer, Hanover police raided a safe house and arrested Ulrike Meinhof. Andreas Baader was also seized that summer after a dramatic shoot-out in a surburban Frankfurt garage where he and

Above: Border guards, provided with a list of Baader-Meinhof terrorists, carefully check the identity documents of a traveller. Increased border security and an increased police presence were the natural result of an upsurge in terrorism.

Below: Hanns-Martin Schleyer is photographed by his kidnappers for publicity purposes. Schleyer was kept hostage for some weeks but the West Germans' reluctance to accede to Red Army Fraction demands could only have one result; Schleyer was shot, his body discovered in the boot of a car near Mulhouse in eastern France.

Left: Gudrun Ensslin and Andreas Baader, who began the terrorist campaign that shook German society. Ensslin was the daughter of a Protestant Pastor, while Baader was an art-student who had dropped out. Their first acts of violence were the bombing of two department stores in Frankfurt in April 1968.

Holger Meins were surrounded. Within a week the arrest of Gudrun Ensslin followed. She was shopping in a Hamburg boutique when the assistant spotted a pistol in her jacket. Police grabbed her as she reached for the Browning automatic in her handbag.

The attitude towards arrested terrorists was now completely different from what it had been a few years earlier. A brand new high-security prison and courtroom was built at Stammheim in the suburbs of Stuttgart to house the three Baader-Meinhof leaders and 18 other members of the group. Some 600 armed police kept guard and an elaborate system of electronics provided almost fool-proof surveillance. Through the years of legal proceedings that followed, the Baader-Meinhof leaders were still able, by way of their lawyers, to be spokesmen for, and to some extent directors of, terrorist action.

The Second of June Movement, organised in cells under the leadership of Ralf Reinders, enthusiastically took over from the Red Army Fraction, copying Palestinian tactics by taking hostages. In February 1975 they kidnapped Peter Lorentz, the prominent Christian Democrat candidate, on the eve of Berlin city elections. Within 72 hours an alarmed government gave in to their demands for the release from

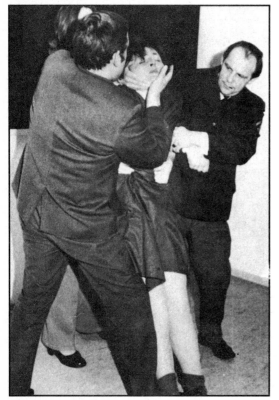

prison of five Baader-Meinhof terrorists. Two of them, Verena Becker and Ingrid Siepmann, were given ransom money of 20,000 deutschmarks each and an aircraft which, en route for Aden, capital of Marxist South Yemen, picked up the three other terrorists, Rolf Pohle, Rolf Heissler and Gabriele Kröcher-Tiedemann. Their reception in Aden proved that the Arab connection was still working.

Any hopes that the terrorists could be bought off with such concessions were soon dashed. Within two months, another attempt to free Baader-Meinhof prisoners by hostage-taking was staged. The perpetrators were known as the Holger Meins Commando, a squad connected to the Second of June Movement. They were named after Holger Meins, Baader's old comrade, who had died in a prison hunger strike in 1974.

A challenge to democracy

Now, in April 1975, the six-strong commando group burst into the West German embassy in Stockholm and took hostage the ambassador and his staff, issuing an ultimatum for the release of all Baader-Meinhof members held in prison. It was, in the words of West German Chancellor Helmut Schmidt, 'the most serious challenge in the 26-year history of our democracy.' This time the government refused to discuss terms, believing that to do so would simply release the hardcore prisoners to begin a new wave of violence. The Stockholm commando murdered two diplomats as a warning before blowing up the embassy with high explosives, killing two more embassy staff and injuring some of their own number. Despite the bloody ending, the government considered they had scored a point.

As things became more difficult for the terrorists in Germany their acts of vengeance spread to neighbouring countries. Just before Christmas 1975 Baader-Meinhof supporters played a notable part in the Vienna raid master-minded by Carlos, the notorious mercenary of terror, in which he took as hostage all 11 oil ministers attending the Opec meeting. Both Hans-Joachim Klein and his girl-friend, Gabriele Kröcher-Tiedemann, the woman released in February 1975 who had now returned from Aden, took part. Klein was wounded and later renounced political violence.

In May 1976 came the brutal end of Ulrike Meinhof, found hanged in her Stammheim prison cell. Her lawyers claimed that she had been killed by the authorities, but the official account of her death states that she committed suicide. Another setback for international terrorism came on 3 July, when a group of hijackers on board an Air France airliner at Entebbe airport were overwhelmed by an Israeli commando force. Two Red Army Fraction veterans involved in the hijacking, Wilfred Böse and Brigette Kuhlmann, were both shot dead.

Yet the climax of the terror campaign was still to come. Despite all the precautions taken, the terrorists struck again in April 1977, only just before the end of the Stammheim trial of members of the Baader-Meinhof gang. Red Army Fraction members ambushed and murdered Siegfried Buback, the federal chief prosecutor, in Karlsruhe. In the hit group this time was Varena Becker, liberated after the Lorentz kidnapping, who had returned from Aden.

Then, after life sentences had been passed on Baader, Ensslin and their colleague Jan-Carl Raspe in April, their comrades operational in Germany

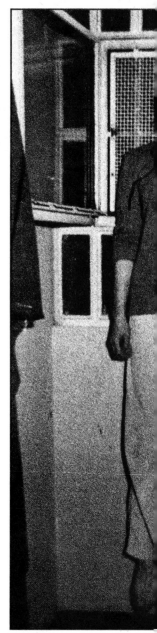

Left above: Defiant to the last, the only surviving terrorist from the Mogadishu hijacking, raises her blood-covered arm in salute to her dead comrades as she is stretchered away from the scene. Left: Ulrike Meinhof struggles with prison officials as they attempt to line her up for mugshots for her prison file. Above: The body of Gudrun Ensslin in the prison cell at Stammheim, May 1976. Right: Faces covered to conceal their identities, mourners attend the funeral of Ensslin, Baader and Raspe. There was a widespread suspicion that the three had been murdered, although international experts had certified that suicide was the cause of death.

embarked on a campaign against what they called the capitalist ruling class. In July their target was Dr Jürgen Ponto, an influential banker. They got past his bodyguard by using Susanne Albrecht, his goddaughter, who told him over the security intercom, 'It's me Susanne, let me in'. She and her two friends presented flowers and then shot him dead. At Dr Ponto's funeral, Hanns-Martin Schleyer, a director of Mercedes and head of the employers' federation, prophetically remarked: 'The next victim is almost certainly standing in this room now'.

His prediction was correct, and he himself was that victim. On 5 September, as he drove through Cologne with an escort car carrying three armed bodyguards, he was ambushed by a Red Army Fraction squad. They slaughtered guards and drivers and took him as a hostage. In skill and cunning the new generation of terrorists completely outmatched their rather amateurish predecessors. Not for several weeks did they publish pictures of the captured Dr Schleyer bearing their logo with demands for the release of 11 of their people, money and an airliner to take them to a safe haven in the Middle East. Although the West German government were under no illusions about what would happen if they refused to bargain, they were staunchly determined not to give in. Such was the public outcry and alarm about the terror war that for several weeks it seemed that normal life in West Germany had come to a standstill.

While the search for Schleyer still continued and tension mounted, news came on 13 October that a Lufthansa Boeing 737 flying from Majorca to Frankfurt had been hijacked. Mahmoud Zuhair Yousef Akache, the terrorist leader who held a gun at the head of Captain Jürgen Schumann, demanded a ransom of $18 million and the immediate release of Baader-Meinhof prisoners. The new crisis again proved the collusion between the Red Army Fraction and the Popular Front for the Liberation of Palestine (PFLP). As the airliner flew towards Rome to refuel, security men examined two identical sets of demands from the two organisations which had been written on the same typewriter.

Again the German government stood fast. As the wild flight around the Middle East continued, Col-onel Ulrich Wegener embarked a squad of his crack GSG9 anti-terrorist unit aboard another Boeing which headed for the Middle East. After a stop at Aden the hijacked plane made for Mogadishu. It was there that fate and GSG9 caught up with the terrorists.

After a session of hostage bargaining on the spot, the German squad was joined by Major Morrison and Sergeant Davis of the British SAS, and together they stormed the aircraft early on 18 October, hurling in stun grenades and then blasting the hijackers. Three terrorists were killed and one was wounded, but all the passengers escaped. It was a famous victory which produced a general feeling that at last something was being done to combat terrorism. But the Red Army Fraction soon took its revenge by murdering Hanns-Martin Schleyer. His body was discovered in the boot of a car near Mulhouse in eastern France.

The whole ghastly affair ended in a welter of blood and violent death as at the end of a Shakespearian tragedy. As soon as news of the Mogadishu affair reached the Stammheim prison, it appears that Andreas Baader shot himself in the head with a revolver smuggled in by his lawyers, while Jan-Carl Raspe shot himself in the mouth, and Baader's 'revolutionary bride', Gudrun Ensslin, hanged herself. Red Army Fraction survivors claimed that their leaders had been murdered on government orders. But meticulous post mortem examinations by international as well as German experts concluded that suicide was the cause of death.

There is no doubt that the year 1977 marked the high-water point of terrorism in West Germany. Although Siegfried Haag, an active lawyer and capable leader, managed to reorganise and regroup the shattered organisation it never again recovered the power to strike hard at will.

The security forces subsequently succeeded with growing confidence in breaking the Red Army Fraction and its successor groups. One by one the faces on the long-wanted notices which decorated every police post in the Federal Republic were struck off, as arrests were recorded. Yet even in the decade of the 1980s and despite the decline of the groups, West German security forces had to remain constantly on the alert.

Christopher Dobson and Ronald Payne

The Wrath of God

Israel's undercover war against the PLO

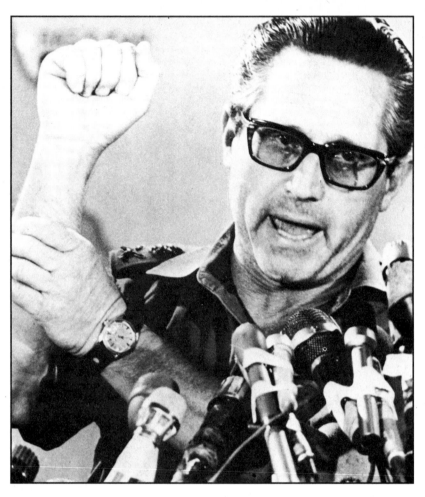

The underground war launched by Israel's Wrath of God hit teams against Arab terrorists in Europe is generally agreed to have started after the Munich Olympics massacre of Israeli athletes in September 1972. Certainly that is the time when the Israeli nation cried out for revenge and Yosef Burg, the minister of the interior, threatened: 'The hands of Israel will know what to do. Israel's blood is not for the taking.'

There was nothing new, however, about Israel exacting revenge for attacks on its own people. The established response to any Palestinian guerrilla raid on Israeli territory was a punitive action by Israel's armed forces against Palestinian camps or generally against those countries that gave the guerrillas refuge. In an extension of this principle, on 28 December 1968 Israeli commandos had landed by helicopter at Beirut international airport and blown up 13 Arab airliners in retaliation for a machine-gun and grenade attack on an El Al airliner at Athens airport, carried out by a Palestinian group based in Lebanon.

Earlier in 1972, before the Munich massacre, Israeli agents had already begun an assassination campaign against the Popular Front for the Liberation

of Palestine (PFLP). The head of the PFLP's terrorist operations, Wadi Haddad, was fortunate to survive when an Israeli hit squad fired a barrage of rockets into his Beirut apartment, and the PFLP's chief propagandist, Ghassan Kanafani, was killed when the Israelis booby-trapped his car (his 17-year-old niece was also killed in the explosion).

But these operations were confined to the Middle East. It was Munich which widened the war, with the Israelis determined to hunt down those responsible for the massacre and to destroy the infrastructure of the Palestinian terror groups in Europe.

Israeli Prime Minister Golda Meir gave this task to Major-General Aharon Yariv who was just ending his tour of duty as head of military intelligence. Yariv had started his military career as an officer in the Jewish Brigade raised by the British to fight the Germans in the Middle East in World War II. He had been involved in the espionage operations leading up to the Six-Day War in 1967 and in the series of commando raids carried out by Israeli special forces against Arab targets after the war.

Meir gave him the title of 'Special Assistant for Terrorist Affairs' and virtually unlimited power to destroy the Palestinian groups in Europe. He was able to call on Mossad, the Israeli secret service, for intelligence work and on the highly trained men of the Sayaret Matkal, the Israeli equivalent of the SAS, to carry out operations. He could also co-opt civilians with special aptitudes or knowledge of a certain country for specific tasks, and he could rely on the Israeli diplomatic network for back-up.

Armed with these formidable powers he went to work, but it was not until December 1972 that the

Major-General Aharon Yariv (above), an Israeli intelligence expert. Yariv was given virtually unlimited powers by the Israeli prime minister, Golda Meir (left), to destroy Palestinian terrorist groups in Europe. Within his network Yariv could rely on Mossad, the Sayaret Matkal, civilian specialists and the diplomatic corps in order to further his task.

Above right: Arab students in Paris burn an effigy of Golda Meir in protest at the murder of Mahmoud Hamshari, the PLO representative in the city, by the Israeli intelligence services. Right: Hussein Bashir, the leader of the Fatah organisation in Cyprus, is loaded into an ambulance after an Israeli bomb attack. He died shortly afterwards.

Wrath of God teams claimed their first victim. He was Wael Zwaiter, officially a clerk at Libya's embassy in Rome, but actually the representative of Fatah – Yassir Arafat's organisation. As he entered the lift leading to his apartment, he was shot 12 times by two men armed with .22 pistols, favourite weapons of the Israelis. His friends argue that he was a peaceful intellectual but the Israelis are positive that he was involved in the planning of a number of terrorist actions. He was certainly an apologist for the Munich massacre and had suggested that the Israelis had plotted to have the hostages killed so that they could gain political advantage from it. That alone was sufficient in Israel's eyes to condemn him to death.

The next man to die was Mahmoud Hamshari, the Palestine Liberation Organisation (PLO) representative in Paris. The Israelis staked out his apartment in Paris noting the time when his French wife, Marie Claude, took their daughter, Amina, to nursery school. One Israeli, posing as an Italian journalist, made contact with Hamshari on the pretext of interviewing him. While they were meeting at a cafe another member of the hit team took an impression of the lock of Hamshari's apartment door. The 'Italian' arranged a further meeting, and this time his colleague walked into the apartment and fitted an electronically-controlled bomb into Hamshari's telephone.

The next day the phone rang just after Mrs Hamshari and Amina had left. Hamshari answered it. A voice at the other end said: 'This is the Italian journalist who had a rendezvous with you. That really you, Monsieur Hamshari?' The Palestinian replied: 'Yes, this is Mahmoud Hamshari.' As soon as he said that, the telephone exploded. He lived long enough to tell the police what had happened and they were able to piece together the device which had killed him.

The Palestinians exacted their revenge in Madrid a month later, in January 1973, when Baruch Cohen, one of Israel's most experienced intelligence officers, was shot dead while waiting at a cafe on the Grand Via for an Arab contact. The Palestinians claimed he had taken part in the killing of both Zwaiter and Hamshari.

And so it went on. Hussein Bashir, leader of the Fatah organisation in Cyprus, was blown up by a bomb hidden under his mattress in the Olympic Hotel

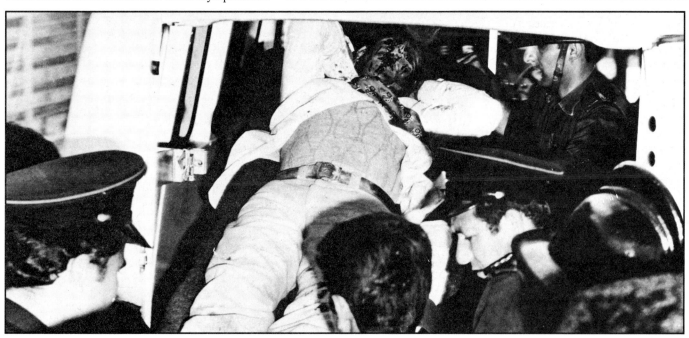

in Nicosia. Two months later Simha Gilzer, an Israeli veteran of the Irgun terrorist movement of the 1940s, was shot down on the steps of the Nicosia Palace Hotel, not far from where Bashir had been killed.

In June 1973 Mohammed Boudia, the leader of the PFLP's international terrorist network in Europe, was killed in Paris by a landmine filled with nuts and bolts that had been placed under his car seat. It was a coup for the Israelis since Boudia had been responsible for a number of terrorist attacks, but his death meant that his post was occupied by an even more dangerous figure – 'Carlos' (Ilich Ramirez Sanchez), the Venezuelan assassin.

Assassination or intelligence?

By this time there was considerable disquiet in the Israeli intelligence community about the war of assassination. For a number of Israeli agents, especially the younger members who had not suffered the traumas of the Holocaust, the campaign smacked too much of the very terrorism they wished to eradicate. They preferred to work through classic intelligence methods, infiltrating the Palestinian groups and passing on information about prospective Arab operations to the European countries concerned. So successful were they in this that the French and Italians – who had not then recognised the full dangers of international terrorism – complained that they were being swamped with information from the Israelis.

Those who doubted the wisdom of the campaign of assassination were not yet strong enough, however, to overcome the desire for revenge, even though the Wrath of God teams were running out of targets. To halt the killing, it took a disastrous mistake in the quest for the one marked man still at large in Europe. He was Ali Hassan Salameh, one of the leaders of Black September and the man the Israelis believed had planned the Munich operation. There were reports in July 1973 that he had been spotted in Norway and so a hit team was sent to Lillehammer. But it was a

low-grade team and they identified the wrong man, with the result that an innocent Moroccan waiter was filled with .22 bullets and died in the arms of his pregnant Norwegian wife. To make matters worse for the Israelis, several of the agents involved in the murder were arrested and jailed. The resulting scandal discredited the assassination campaign.

The Lillehammer debacle therefore became the last operation executed by the Wrath of God in Europe. But the Israelis were determined that one last action had to be carried out: Salameh had to die. They got him eventually with a car bomb in Beirut on 22 January 1979. Even that was not a clean operation, however, for the bomb also killed six innocent passers-by including a young British secretary. So the undercover war which had started with one massacre of innocents ended with another.

Christopher Dobson and Ronald Payne

In July 1973, Israeli intelligence operatives reported sightings in Norway of Ali Hassan Salameh (above, shown to the right of Yassir Arafat), who the Israelis believed masterminded the 1972 Munich Olympics massacre. Hit teams were sent to Lillehammer but an innocent civilian was killed. Members of the team were arrested (below left, one being led away by Norwegian police) and their ensuing trial (below, the courtroom under heavy guard) discredited the 'Wrath of God' as an instrument of Israeli policy.

Key Weapons
WESTERN SPGs

Although SPGs (self-propelled guns) were in use before 1939, World War II acted as a significant impetus in the development of this hybrid type of weapon, half artillery and half tank. Since 1945 a wide range of SPGs has come into service, becoming an integral part of all armoured formations.

Self-propelled guns can be divided into two fairly distinct categories. The first is the tank destroyer or assault gun which is, in effect, a cheap tank. Usually lacking a turret and having less armoured protection than the conventional tank, the tank destroyer nevertheless has a large high-velocity gun and its main function – like that of the main battle tank – is to knock out opposing tanks. Relying for survival on manoeuvrability and careful defensive positioning, the tank destroyer lacks both overall power and flexibility when compared to the main battle tank – admittedly more expensive to produce – and only a few armies deploy this kind of SPG.

Few doubts, if any, are attached to the importance of the second type of SPG, the self-propelled artillery piece: a gun or howitzer mounted on a caterpillar-tracked vehicle provided with some form of armoured protection. A considerable degree of variation exists within this categorisation. Some SPGs have turrets while others rely on the vehicle moving to traverse the gun; a number are equipped with elaborate automatic loading devices and the level of protection afforded the crew is far from uniform.

The main role of self-propelled artillery is, as its name suggests, to act as highly mobile artillery, able to keep up with and support armoured units. Towed artillery, in contrast, must largely keep to hard road surfaces and thereby lacks this cross-country mobility; and, in addition, it cannot be deployed on the battlefield with the same speed as the SPG and is without any real means of crew protection. This latter point is of growing importance when the possibility of NBC (nuclear, biological and chemical) warfare is an ever-present danger, and consequently the more advanced SPGs are fitted with NBC protection.

During World War II Britain relied upon improvised SPGs – an artillery gun directly mounted on a tank chassis – so that the 25-pounder on the M3/M4 chassis became the Sexton and the 17-pounder anti-tank gun mounted on the Valentine tank became the Archer. After the war Britain relied upon American imports and it was not until 1958 that work began on a British gun which entered service in 1964 as the FV433 Abbot.

The Abbot was developed to utilise components from the FV432 APC series, notably the chassis, and is armed with a turret-mounted 105mm providing a traverse of 360 degrees and a maximum elevation to over 70 degrees. The gun has a maximum range of 17,000m (18,600yds) and can fire high explosive, smoke, target indicating, illuminating and HESH (high-explosive squash-head) ammunition. Supplementary armament comprises a 7.62mm light machine gun for anti-aircraft protection and smoke dischargers. Weighing less than 17 tonnes, the Abbot is a lightweight SPG, capable of a top road speed of 48km/h (30mph), and is fitted with a flotation screen enabling it to cross water obstacles. Infra-red driving lights and an NBC system are fitted. Although the Abbot serves with the Royal Artillery in Britain and Germany, the 105mm gun is now considered to be too small a calibre and has been superseded by SPGs of larger calibres by the United States.

France produced a 105mm SP howitzer in the 1950s utilising the versatile AMX13 chassis, and this gun was supplemented by the larger 155mm Mk F3 in the early 1960s, similarly based around the AMX13. Although successfully exported to a number of Third World nations, both SPGs were relatively primitive weapons and in 1969 a new SPG was developed to replace them in French Army service.

Previous page: A US M110 self-propelled gun fires on Viet Cong positions at Fire Base Carol in South Vietnam. Above: The long-barrelled 155mm gun of the French GCT self-propelled gun is raised to maximum elevation.

Left: Britain's Abbot SPG was developed from the FV432 APC series and is armed with a 105mm gun. Right: The massive turret of the Italian Palmaria SPG houses a 155mm gun which can be fitted with either a manual or an automatic loading system. Below right: The West German Jagdpanzer Kanone features a 90mm anti-tank gun set in a sloping glacis plate. Bottom right: The Swedish VK-155's heavy and cumbersome automatic loading system is mounted directly above the turret.

The 155mm GCT is a heavy (42 tonnes loaded) and expensive weapon but has many advanced features. Mounted on an AMX30 tank chassis, the 155mm gun is enclosed in a turret providing a full 360-degree traverse. Maximum range with an HE projectile is 23,500m (25,700yds) and 30,000m (32,800yds) with a Brandt RAP (rocket-assisted projectile). An automatic launching system is employed which enables eight rounds a minute to be fired.

Following on from the success of her SP anti-tank guns during World War II, West Germany has produced a 90mm Jagdpanzer Kanone SP anti-tank gun. It has an effective battlefield range of 2000m (2200yds) and fires both HEAT (high-explosive anti-tank) and HESH ammunition, at a rate of 12 rounds per minute. The gun is set in a sloping glacis plate and an infra-red searchlight is mounted directly above the gun and moves in traverse and elevation with the gun. A total of 750 have been built for the West German Army and a further 80 ordered by Belgium which have been modernised to include an improved fire-control system incorporating a laser rangefinder.

Although the 155mm SP-70 is a joint West German/Italian/British venture, Germany is the project leader. The SPG's chassis is based on the Leopard 1 tank and the gun is a modification of the successful FH-70 towed howitzer, produced by these countries. The initial 12 prototypes were completed in 1976 and feature a high rate of fire with a maximum range of 30,000m (32,800yds). As with the FH-70 it can fire advanced Copperhead precision ammunition.

Italy already has a 155mm SPG, the OTO-Melara Palmaria which utilises the Italian OF-40 MBT chassis. The welded aluminium turret is positioned in the centre of the hull and the gun features either an automatic or manual loader.

The Swedish have produced their own SPG, the 155mm Bandkanon 1A or VK-155 which is a very heavy vehicle weighing some 53 tonnes and consequently suffering a penalty in mobility so that its maximum speed is only 28km/h (17mph). Sharing component parts with the S-Tank, the VK-155 entered service in 1963 and was an early example of an SPG having an automatic loading system. A magazine of 14 rounds is attached to the rear of the SPG's turret, providing it with a high rate of fire so that it can expend its entire magazine within a minute. The advantage of a high rate of fire for an SPG is that if it can loose off a barrage of shells at the enemy in a short space of time it can then move to a new position before

Top: Three US SPGs of the 1950s at the Aberdeen Proving Ground. From the left, they are a 155mm M44, a 155mm M53 and an 8in (203mm) M55. All three types have their rear spades dug in to absorb the recoil, and reveal the easy access to the firing compartment characteristic of American SPGs. Above: An early SPG, the US M7 Priest armed with a 105mm howitzer. Above right: A 155mm M40 'Long Tom' SPG being prepared for action by a British gun crew. Right: The 8in howitzer of the M55 in action.

its presence is detected.

The major manufacturer of self-propelled guns, both in numbers and types, has been the USA. During World War II, besides producing the small 105mm M7, America brought out the 155mm M40 'Long Tom' SPG which saw service in the closing stages of the war and was also used to considerable advantage in Korea. The 155mm M44 howitzer followed, based on the chassis of the M41 light tank which was also used on the 105mm M52 SPG. A larger calibre SPG

was also considered necessary and in 1952 the prototype M55 SP howitzer was developed which mounted a 203mm (8in) gun, capable of lobbing an HE projectile 16,800m (18,500yds).

These 'early generation' SPGs were replaced in the 1960s by a new range of models. The M107 and the M110 were designed to use a common chassis, the M107 mounting a long-barrelled 175mm gun, the M110 being armed with the 203mm gun. Both types were notable for not employing an armoured fighting

Above: A British Army M107 being prepared for action. The rear spade is well dug in and the 175mm shell is about to be loaded into the breech. Right: An M107 is fired in Vietnam, where it was used for long-range interdiction work.

Right: A line of M110A1s of the US Army. They can be distinguished from the M110 by their longer barrels and muzzle brakes. Below: An M110 at maximum recoil during a bombardment of enemy positions in Vietnam.

compartment, so that only the driver is provided with protection. The M107 came into service in 1963 and its gun had, at that time, the very long HE range of 32,700m (35,750yds) and while the M110 lacked this range it could fire heavier and a wider variety of shell types, including nuclear rounds. Both models are now being phased out of service in favour of the 203mm M110A1/A2 which has a greater range over the M110, being able to fire RAP rounds to a maximum distance of 29,000m (31,700yds).

The 155mm M109 has become the most important of America's SPGs; over 3000 have been built and since its introduction in 1962 it has been exported worldwide. The M109 has proved a highly successful design: its turbo-charged diesel engine provides range with reliability and its gun – housed in a 360-degree traversing turret – in the later M109A1 variant has a range of 18,000m (19,700yds). Besides conventional HE, illuminating and smoke rounds, the M109 can fire tactical nuclear and chemical warfare ammunition. The M109 was widely used in Vietnam by both the Army and the Marine Corps, its low weight of 23 tonnes providing a useful degree of cross-country mobility in Vietnamese conditions. Like other modern SPGs in Western service the M109 is able to fire the advanced Copperhead laser-guided projectile.

While SPGs are more expensive than conventional towed artillery their obvious benefits in mobility and protection guarantee them an increasingly important place within the West's artillery forces. SPGs of the type of the European SP-70 will set the trend for the future.

Above: A rear-view photograph of a US M109 SPG taken during a break on manoeuvres, with M16 smallarms neatly piled alongside. Of interest is the ammunition rack at the rear of the turret ready for re-loading. Left: The turret of an M109. In contrast to a tank an SPG requires easy access for both crew and equipment, hence the number of open panels and hatches that are shown here.

Above and right: The SP-70 self-propelled howitzer. The SP-70 is fitted with an automatic ammunition re-supply mechanism, attached to the rear of the turret. Once the SPG's own supply of shells is exhausted, a speedy re-supply system is highly important if the gun is to operate effectively. The SP-70 utilises the gun of the tri-national FH-70 and the chassis of the German Leopard I tank, an exceptional combination of gun and chassis.

Yom Kippur:

the preparations

The build-up to the 1973 Arab-Israeli War

In June 1967 the Israeli Defence Forces (IDF) had proved crushingly superior to the Arab armies, and during the most intense phase of the so-called 'War of Attrition' (1969-70) the IDF had maintained the upper hand against Arab air and ground forces. Rather to the Israelis' surprise, however, in neither of these cases had military victory been translated into diplomatic success. Nor did the increasing intervention, and concern, of the superpowers in the early 1970s lead to a settlement in the Middle East. The American peace initiative of 1970, known as the Rogers Plan, came to nothing despite enjoying Soviet support. Any agreement would have required at least a partial Israeli withdrawal, but the Israelis were intransigent over the status of the lands they had captured in 1967: in May 1971 Moshe Dayan, Israeli minister of defence, said, 'We want security, not just peace documents, and would prefer that Israel hold sensible, effective lines for her defence even if the Arabs refuse to regard them as permanent, rather than return to the 4 June (1967) borders.' The Arab states, in their turn, refused to make concessions, or to recognise Israel's right to exist. When Egypt's President Anwar el Sadat expelled the 20,000 Soviet military personnel stationed in his country in July 1972, it appeared that Israel's relative military position had been strengthened, even if Soviet arms supplies to Egypt continued.

By 1973, then, the Israelis were disillusioned with diplomacy, but they retained confidence in their own military strength as the basis of security. For this security, Israel relied on mobilising a much higher proportion of her population than did her neighbours. Thus in war Israel was not outnumbered nearly as badly as the vast disparity in population between

Israel and the Arab states would have suggested. The superior performance of the Israeli forces, especially the air force, was considered enough to compensate for whatever numerical inferiority remained. But Israel could not maintain its forces on a war footing for long without crippling its economy. In peacetime the Israelis maintained a small cadre of regular forces along its borders, with a large number of training and reserve units in the interior. The well-proven ability of their intelligence agencies encouraged the Israelis to believe that they would have at least 48 hours warning of an Arab attack, which would be enough to call back their reservists from civilian occupations, fill out their skeleton formations and deploy them to the forward area to meet the Arab attack. Mobilisation was a well-rehearsed procedure, and all reservists spent several weeks on duty each year, ensuring that their training was up-to-date.

In 1973 the active part of the Israeli Army numbered at least 75,000 men: 25,000 of these were regulars, 11,500 each in the army and air force and 2000 in the navy. About 50,000 conscripts were under training at any time and a varying number of reservists would also be on duty. Within the army 12 to 15 brigades would be operational, although these were usually not at full strength. On mobilisation the armed forces grew to 350,000 and rather more than 30 brigades could be deployed. They would be grouped into division-sized task forces or Ugdahs of which one was active in Sinai and another on the Golan in peacetime. The other Ugdahs were based on training establishments or other cadres and even their commanders could be reservists.

The army was equipped with an unusual variety of equipment, much of it bought from abroad and

Above: Batteries of SA-6 missiles (with SA-2s visible in the background) are paraded outside Cairo before being deployed into defensive positions to the west of the Suez Canal. The capabilities of the SA-6 had not been fully realised by the time the Yom Kippur War broke out and Israeli aircrews, used to dealing with the comparatively crude SA-2 and SA-3, were taken by surprise as their losses to SA-6 missiles mounted alarmingly. The Israelis' limited electronic counter-measures had little effect on the SA-6 fire-control radar which was simple yet devastatingly effective.

extensively modified in Israel. About half the tank fleet were Centurions from Britain; there were 600 M60s, or up-gunned M48s from America; about 250 T67s (Russian T54/55s captured in 1967) and around 250 Super Shermans (conversions of the American World War II tank). Self-propelled 155mm guns were the backbone of the artillery, either American M109s or the locally-produced Soltam (on a Sherman chassis). There were also captured Soviet pieces and some of the American long-range M107 175mm guns. Armoured personnel carriers were a mixture of World War II half-tracks and modern American M113s, with the usual sprinkling of captured Russian vehicles. The Israeli Air Force possessed about 550 combat aircraft, including 130 Phantoms, 170 Skyhawks and older Mirage jets. The navy possessed five submarines, 21 patrol boats, nine motor torpedo boats and 10 tank landing ships.

The frontier defences of Israel had mostly been constructed during the artillery and air battles of the War of Attrition. On the Golan plateau they consisted of a 5m (17 feet) deep anti-tank ditch and minefields running along the border with a series of defence positions sited on small volcanic hills, or *tels*. Each post was held by about a platoon of infantry and a platoon of three tanks. Their role was to watch the border and report the strength and direction of a Syrian crossing. Further back a large number of ramps had been built. The ramps were designed to give tanks long fields of fire and they were grouped to cover the natural routes through the difficult Golan terrain. When the war started there were three brigades, one infantry and two armoured, on the Golan.

The Suez defences had been called the Bar-Lev Line by the newspapers, but this gives a misleading impression of their strength. The first line of defence was the Canal itself, a formidable obstacle which the Israelis had improved by raising the embankment on

Above: Soviet-supplied T62 tanks of the Egyptian Army. The influx of Soviet weaponry after the 1967 debacle was virtually the only means by which Egypt could hope to maintain an effective fighting force to counter the IDF. Although not as sophisticated as its Western counterparts, the T62 proved itself a rugged fighting vehicle. The number of these tanks knocked out by Israeli armour was less a reflection of the T62's battle capability than of its misuse in the field.

their side. Along the Canal was a line of strongpoints and behind it the Israelis built a network of roads. At the start of the war a small brigade of reservists held the Bar-Lev forts, with an armoured division in immediate reserve.

The Arab armies were well aware of the general layout of the Israeli defences and they knew that the Israelis would try to counter-attack as quickly as possible and then rapidly carry the war onto Arab territory. They began planning very soon after the 1967 war and revised their plans continually over the years. The Egyptian staff identified three main problem areas. Firstly there was the Canal itself, secondly the need to achieve surprise and ensure that the Sinai defences were not fully manned and thirdly how to neutralise the superior Israeli air and tank forces so that the counter-attacks failed.

Gradually the Egyptians acquired the equipment needed to breach the Canal barrier. Much of their assault crossing equipment came from the Soviet

Above: The Egyptian chief of staff, General Saad el Din Shazli. Although he had raised objections to the proposed armoured breakout from the Egyptian bridgeheads in Sinai, political pressure forced his hand. His plans for the crossing of the Suez Canal, however, proved to be extremely successful.

Union or its allies; this material included PMP pontoon bridges, GSP and PT-S ferries. An Egyptian engineer officer had the brilliant idea of breaching the embankments by washing the sand away with high-pressure hoses rather than trying to break them down with bulldozers. The Egyptian Army practised canal crossings over and over again; some units rehearsed the operation over 300 times. At El Ballah, south of El Qantara, the Canal splits into two channels, one of which was completely in Egyptian hands and provided the perfect training area.

To deal with the Israeli counter-attacks the Egyptians decided to rely on Soviet-supplied anti-tank and anti-aircraft missiles. Under cover of the ceasefire agreement that ended the War of Attrition the Egyptians brought forward SA-2, SA-4 and SA-6 missile batteries, so that a considerable belt of Sinai was covered by their air defences. In addition the Egyptian forces were equipped with mobile low-level systems such as the ZSU-23-4 self-propelled anti-aircraft equipment and the SA-7 shoulder-fired anti-aircraft missile. These systems would be taken across the Canal at the earliest possible stage and quickly followed by the SA-6 missiles. The Egyptians did not try to match the Israelis in tank-to-tank fighting. Instead they provided their troops with light anti-tank weapons ranging from the RPG-7 rocket launcher, through various recoilless rifles and anti-tank guns to the AT-3 Sagger wire-guided missile. Armed with these they hoped that their infantry would be able to hold their bridgeheads and cause serious attrition to the Israeli tank force before their own armour even crossed the Canal.

The Syrian factor

Thus the Egyptians were planning a limited offensive strategy, combined with defensive tactics. However, a political complication was introduced in the last year of peace. President Sadat decided that Syrian cooperation was essential so that the Egyptians did not have to face Israel's full strength. The price of the alliance was a more ambitious plan which entailed a break-out from the bridgehead towards the Sinai passes. The danger of this plan was that it meant fighting a mobile battle on the Israelis' own ground and it was strongly opposed by General Saad el Din Shazli, the Egyptian chief of staff. The advantage of splitting the Israeli effort was considered to outweigh the risk, although Shazli was assured that the break-out plan was only window-dressing to satisfy the Syrians.

The Syrian plan for an attack on the Golan was not as sophisticated as the Egyptian concept for Sinai. It involved little more than massing large concentrations on certain axes, equipping the leading elements with gap-crossing and obstacle-clearing equipment and advancing in accordance with a rigidly-phased plan. The Syrians followed the Egyptians in relying on Soviet-supplied anti-aircraft systems to neutralise the Israeli Air Force but they made much less use of anti-tank systems. In particular they failed to appreciate how useful infantry armed with light anti-tank weapons could be in the broken Golan terrain.

The Syrians did follow the Egyptians in their search for surprise. Both armies realised that it was essential to capture their initial objectives before the Israelis completed their mobilisation. The Egyptians developed the most comprehensive system of deception measures. Over a period of several years they adopted

After the crushing defeat of 1967, President Anwar Sadat (right, taking the salute at a military parade in Cairo) was determined that his forces should inflict a similar humiliation upon the Israelis. To support the regular forces that would spearhead the Canal assault, Egypt also deployed a substantial reserve of civil defence volunteers (above, on parade).

Below: Egyptian troops ferry a T54 across a waterway on an exercise prior to the great assault. During the extensive preparations for the 1973 crossing, the Egyptian forces utilised their inland waterways to perfect river-crossing techniques.

a regular pattern of exercises and of mobilising and demobilising reserves. The Israelis noted these and at first reacted by alerting their forces. In December 1971 and 1972 they increased their front-line forces in response to Egyptian mobilisation but nothing happened. After December 1972 the Israelis were aware of no less than 20 occasions when Egypt called up and released reserves. In April 1973 the signs of an impending Egyptian attack were particularly obvious; troops moved up to the Canal, new gaps were opened on the Egyptian embankment, blood donors were called up. The Israeli director of military intelligence, Major-General Eli Zeira, did not believe that an attack was imminent but he was overruled by the chief of staff and Dayan. A partial Israeli mobilisation took place which was very expensive. This experience made the high command unwilling to risk another false alarm.

The Egyptians adopted a number of short-term deception measures as well. Twenty thousand troops were demobilised, officers were allowed to apply to go on pilgrimage to Mecca and Sadat let it be known that he was about to attend the United Nations in New York. Up until the last moments before the attack Egyptian troops on the Canal line maintained a show of non-aggressive behaviour, fishing, swimming and washing laundry. The Syrians exploited a dog-fight between Israeli and Syrian planes in September. They moved new forces up onto the Golan plateau, but deployed them into a defensive array, as though expecting Israeli retaliation. Just before the attack the Syrian divisions moved out of their defences into assembly areas for an attack.

The timing of the attack played its part in achieving surprise. It was to take place during Ramadan when the Israelis considered the Arabs were least likely to start a war. The date of the attack was fixed for 6 October, Yom Kippur, the Day of Atonement, the holiest day in the Jewish calendar, on which neither transport nor broadcasting would be operating.

Under cover of these deception plans the Egyptians deployed five infantry divisions, each reinforced with a tank brigade, along the Canal line. The Second Army commanded three divisions north of the Bitter Lakes, the Third Army two divisions to the south. Each army had a second echelon consisting of a tank and a mechanised division. In all the Egyptians had 285,000 men, 2000 tanks and 600 aircraft. The Syrians had three mechanised divisions, supported by 1000 guns along the border with Israel. Waiting to exploit their success were two tank divisions. In total 100,000 Syrian troops, 1500 tanks and 210 aircraft were ready.

There is no doubt that the Israelis were surprised by the Arab attack but it is important to be clear what is meant by surprise. Israeli military intelligence had not failed to detect signs that the Arabs were preparing an attack. The families of Soviet advisers were being evacuated, for example. New approaches to the Suez Canal were being prepared under the cover of darkness. One junior officer on the Sinai Command's intelligence staff did report that the Egyptian preparations were inconsistent with an exercise and that they were possibly cover for an attack. However, these indicators were not given their full weight and General Zeira continued to assess that the Arabs would not attack. This time the high command believed him.

Why did this intelligence failure occur? Traditional explanations of the problems of intelligence work concentrate on the problem of distinguishing the 'signal' (the true indicators of enemy intentions) from the 'noise' (the background of misleading or irrelevant information being received). Up to a point this is what happened in Israel in 1973 but it is not the complete explanation. The real problem was that the Israelis blinded themselves by a number of misconceptions. They were contemptuous of the Arab soldier and did not believe that the Arabs would dare to attack until their air forces could guarantee air superiority. In Israeli eyes the balance of power was totally in their favour and they failed to think themselves into the Arabs' minds. They also only considered the possibility that the Arabs would try to destroy Israel completely and neglected the possibility that the Arabs might be satisfied with just a limited victory after so many defeats. All these ideas were enshrined in the so-called 'Concept', a rigid theory of the way the Arabs would approach a war with Israel. Any evidence which did not fit the Concept was ignored or, if sufficiently ambiguous, re-interpreted to fit the preconception. Thus when the Arab attack began the Israelis were not merely surprised but also shocked because the Arabs were not behaving as expected. The effects of this shock were increased by the tactical set-backs of the early fighting, so that it took even longer for the IDF to pull itself together. **Michael Orr**

Right: An Israeli Centurion tank in a hull-down firing position overlooks the field of a possible Syrian advance on the Golan Heights. The Centurions of the Israeli Armoured Corps performed well during the Yom Kippur War. Far right: General David Elazar, the Israeli chief of staff. Below: Lying beside his 0.3in Browning machine gun, an Israeli soldier on the Golan Heights looks out towards Syria.

The Bar-Lev Line

The Bar-Lev Line

★ Israeli fortifications and observation posts

Port Fuad
Orkal
Budapest
MEDITERRANEAN SEA
Lahtzanit
Drora
Suez Canal
Ketuba
El Qantara
Milano
Mifreket
ISRAELI-OCCUPIED SINAI PENINSULA
Hizayon
Ismailiya
Purkan
Lake Timsah
Tasa
Artillery Road
Matzmed
Lakekan
Great Bitter Lake
Lateral Road
Botzer
Little Bitter Lake
Lituf
Gidi Pass
EGYPT
Mafzeah
Mitla Pass
Suez
Nissan
Quay
GULF OF SUEZ

During late 1968, the IDF began work on the construction of a fortified observation line along the Suez Canal. The line was named after the then Israeli chief of staff, General Bar-Lev (above). The fortified positions provided well-defended observers with a clear view across the Canal to the Egyptian side (top, an Israeli soldier looks out from a bunker).

The Israeli defences along the Suez Canal

In the winter of 1968, during a lull in cross-Canal hostilities between Israel and Egypt, the Israeli Defence Forces (IDF) began work on a fortified defence line – soon to be known as the Bar-Lev Line after the Israeli chief of staff, Chaim Bar-Lev – stretching from the Gulf of Suez along the eastern bank of the Suez Canal as far as the Mediterranean, a distance of almost 160km (100 miles). The line included 30 *moazim* (strongpoints), each designed for a garrison of platoon strength. A typical *moaz* consisted of four defensive positions, each with its own bunker, connected to a central command bunker which would also house living quarters and medical facilities. The bunkers were of concrete, approximately 1.5m (5ft) thick, and were reinforced with sections of rail from the disused Sinai railway. Camouflage was provided by a sand layer held in place by steel mesh which effectively protected the positions from rocket attacks. The strongpoints also included conventional defences against an infantry assault, being bounded by a trench, a sand embankment, barbed wire obstacles and minefields. The garrison was armed with normal infantry smallarms, nothing larger than heavy machine guns and mortars.

The strongholds were strategically placed to cover roads and communications junctions leading back into the Sinai and were sited to allow the garrisons control over their immediate sector of the Canal. In the event of an attack, the garrisons' task would be to supply data on the enemy, to maintain the first exchange of fire and to block the access roads. At the outbreak of the war, 16 of the strongholds were fully manned, four partially manned and the remainder were closed up or manned only by daylight observation teams.

This chain of strongholds and observation posts was supported by an extensive infrastructure. Two roads were built running along a north-south axis to the east of the Canal at distances from it of 10km and 30km (6 and 20 miles) respectively. The first, known as the Artillery Road, held *toazim* or gun positions and allowed self-propelled artillery batteries to move rapidly between fire points. The first echelon of tanks and half-tracks was also held on this line, ready to advance at speed and deploy onto special firing ramps built into the strongpoints and along the Canal bank between them. The second road link held armoured reserves and also enabled logistics units to prepare for any major counter-attack.

These two main north-south routes were linked by east-west roads and communications to the Bar-Lev Line were secured by underground cables and several radio networks. The communications facilities proved invaluable, for while the garrisons were quickly surrounded and isolated by the attacking Egyptian formations in October 1973, the defenders were able to pass information back to HQ for the management of the battle.

The Bar-Lev Line was completed in March 1969, and was of great service during the War of Attrition over the next 15 months. It proved of less value in October 1973, however, being of only minor inconvenience to the well-planned Egyptian attack. Although it has been argued that the construction of the Line led the Israelis into the trap of believing that static defences were the answer to security, the Bar-Lev Line was, in fact, more the victim of a general failure in Israeli intelligence, and the difficulties of applying a defensive plan that was, in any case, not immediately activated by the divisional commander (Major General Avraham Mandler) who was supposed to provide the armoured vehicles which would give the Line its heavy support. It was not the Bar-Lev Line which failed in 1973, but Israel's contingency planning. **Simon Innes**

Above: Untroubled by thoughts of war, a mortar team on the Bar-Lev Line find time to play a little backgammon. At the time of the Egyptian offensive in 1973, the Line was manned by a brigade of reservists.
Right: Breakfast in the mess. All the quarters along the line were well-protected against possible Egyptian rocket attacks.

Below: Egyptian troops move quickly through a deserted position on the Bar-Lev Line. Despite the intricate arrangement of bunkers and trenches, the Bar-Lev strongpoints did not provide a substantial obstacle to the Egyptian forces.

Crossing the Canal
The Egyptian attack, 6 October 1973

At 1400 hours on 6 October 1973 over 2000 Egyptian guns, supplemented by heavy mortars, Katyusha rocket launchers and Frog surface-to-surface missile batteries, opened fire on Israeli fortifications on the eastern bank of the Suez Canal, while tanks crawled onto previously prepared positions on the sand ramparts lining the western bank of the waterway to engage targets with direct, flat-trajectory gunfire. During the first minute 10,500 shells landed in and around the Israeli positions. Simultaneously, Egyptian jets streaked eastward in the first of 250 sorties against Israeli command and logistical centres, radar installations, Hawk surface-to-air missile sites and long-range artillery batteries. Under cover of the bombardment, the first Egyptian assault wave sprinted to the water's edge, dropped into their rubber assault boats and began paddling furiously across the Canal.

The Egyptian Army was anxious to redeem national honour which it believed had been lost during the Six-Day War and the Egyptian High Command was prepared for heavy casualties – up to 30,000 men in the opening offensives. Indeed, the need for personal sacrifice had been emphasised time and again during the long months of training. To minimise casualties the crossing points lay between the widely separated observation posts of the Bar-Lev Line, but the Israeli defenders still managed to lay down a substantial field of automatic fire causing some confusion and a few casualties. The majority of Egyptian troops, however, reached the far bank only six minutes after the guns had opened fire. Flexible assault ladders were dragged up the sand ramparts and the infantry units, accompanied by tank-killer teams and artillery observation parties, scrambled up these and began moving inland to establish a defensive front, 3km (2 miles) from the Canal, while specially trained commando units isolated and neutralised the Bar-Lev strongpoints.

Twelve minutes into the offensive, the second echelon companies of the assault battalions left the Egyptian bank, followed 12 minutes later by the battalion heavy-weapon teams, and then a complete ammunition resupply after 41 minutes. Approximately one hour after the initial offensive the remaining battalions of the assault brigades began crossing, followed an hour later by the leading elements of the second wave brigades. Within the space of three to four hours each infantry division had established a bridgehead up to 7km (4 miles) wide and work was well in hand on blasting gaps through the sand ramparts which would provide vehicle exits for the follow-up mechanised and armoured formations. To the north of the Great Bitter Lake high-pressure water hoses achieved this without difficulty, but to the south of this feature the composition of the ramparts was clay-based and the water produced an impassable mixture of mud and slurry, so an alternative method involving explosives and bulldozers was employed.

The Egyptian Army possessed large quantities of

Above: The Canal is successfully traversed by Soviet-supplied PMP pontoon bridgeing equipment and Egyptian troops prepare final adjustments before armour begins to roll across into Sinai. Above right: Jubilant Egyptian troops greet the arrival of senior officers. The huge banks that had been built along the Canal by the Israelis were breached using high-pressure water hoses. Above far right: A BTR-50 APC (left) and a PTS-M amphibious transporter (right) carry Egyptian troops and supplies across the Canal.

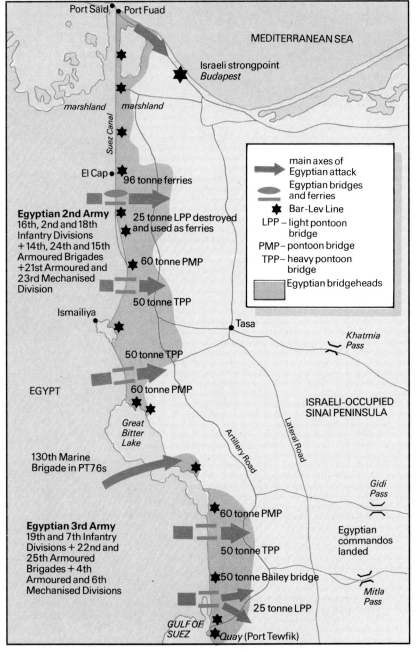

Port Said • • Port Fuad

MEDITERRANEAN SEA

Israeli strongpoint
Budapest

marshland   *marshland*

Suez Canal

El Cap •   • 96 tonne ferries

Egyptian 2nd Army
16th, 2nd and 18th
Infantry Divisions
+14th, 24th and 15th
Armoured Brigades
+21st Armoured and
23rd Mechanised
Division

25 tonne LPP destroyed
and used as ferries

60 tonne PMP

50 tonne TPP

Ismailiya •

main axes of
Egyptian attack

Egyptian bridges
and ferries

Bar-Lev Line

LPP – light pontoon
bridge

PMP – pontoon bridge

TPP – heavy pontoon
bridge

Egyptian bridgeheads

• Tasa

*Khatmia
Pass*

50 tonne TPP

60 tonne PMP

EGYPT

*Great
Bitter
Lake*

ISRAELI-OCCUPIED
SINAI PENINSULA

130th Marine
Brigade in PT76s

Artillery Road

Lateral Road

*Gidi
Pass*

60 tonne PMP

Egyptian 3rd Army
19th and 7th Infantry
Divisions + 22nd and
25th Armoured
Brigades + 4th
Armoured and 6th
Mechanised Divisions

50 tonne TPP

Egyptian
commandos
landed

50 tonne Bailey bridge

*Mitla
Pass*

25 tonne LPP

*GULF OF
SUEZ*

• Quay (Port Tewfik)

Soviet-supplied amphibious vehicles and bridging equipment, and while this work was in progress these were converging on specially prepared launching sites on the west bank. Included were 50-tonne motorised rafts each capable of ferrying four main battle tanks, or up to 10 lorries with four guns and trailers, or 16 jeeps; 96-tonne motorised rafts, with twice this capacity; and, most important of all, PMP pontoon bridging trains which could be assembled in about 30 minutes and which, being of sectional construction, could be repaired quickly if completed bridges were damaged. So thorough was the Egyptian planning that a dummy bridge had also been provided to absorb some of the anticipated counter-strikes by Israeli aircraft and artillery.

The result of this careful preparation was that between seven and 10 hours after the first assault wave had gone in, the infantry divisions' organic tank battalions were crossing the Canal to join their parent formations, followed an hour later by the divisional artillery and support elements.

On the southern front (from the Great Bitter Lake to the Gulf of Suez) the assault was made by Major-General Abd al Muneim Wassel's Third Army, spearheaded by the 19th and 7th Infantry Divisions, supplemented respectively by the 22nd and 25th Armoured Brigades which were crossing in their turn by the morning of 7 October. Moving forward to cross next were the 4th Armoured and 6th Mechanised Divisions. In the north (from the Great Bitter Lake to El Cap, whence the Canal ran northwards to Port Said through difficult marshland) the assault of Major-General Saad Mamoun's Second Army was led by the 16th, 2nd and 18th Infantry Divisions, now being joined respectively by the 14th, 24th and 15th Armoured Brigades, with the 21st Armoured and 23rd Mechanised Divisions to follow. Along the entire front, eight bridges were in operation and by the evening of the second day the five infantry divisions had consolidated and linked their bridgeheads, now about 5km (3 miles) deep, having been joined by approximately 1000 tanks.

Subsidiary operations, which coincided with the main offensive, included an advance eastwards along the coast road from Port Fuad by the 135th Infantry Brigade which would, with seaborne commando support, attempt to storm the Israeli strongpoint known as Budapest; and a crossing of the Great Bitter Lake in PT76 amphibious tanks by the 130th Marine Brigade. The latter failed in its primary object, which was to link up with Egyptian commandos who had been lifted by helicopter into the area of the Mitla and

Gidi passes. Fourteen of the commandos' helicopters had been shot down by the Israeli Air Force (IAF) and those units which managed to land intact were quickly neutralised or rounded up before they could close the passes to Israeli reinforcements approaching the front from the east.

In the overall context, however, General Ahmed Ismail Ali, the Egyptian minister of war, and his chief of staff, Major-General Saad el Din Shazli, could congratulate themselves on a meticulously planned and finely executed operation, for although the crossing of the Canal, a mere 180m (200 yards) wide, was not comparable with some of the river crossings undertaken during World War II, it was still a gigantic undertaking which had achieved complete success at a tiny fraction of the anticipated cost. It had been estimated that the crossing would absorb some 25-30,000 casualties, of whom one third would be killed; in the event, only 208 Egyptians died during the initial assault.

Divisions of command

Despite having worked together in harmony to secure their victory, Ismail and Shazli were men of very different temperament. Ismail favoured the step-by-step Russian approach to the problems which had confronted them, and this had clearly worked well. Shazli, who had managed to escape the 1967 debacle with his reputation actually enhanced, was altogether a more imaginative and thrusting commander, and as the war went on the views of the two would progressively diverge.

Shazli had believed that the Israeli response to the crossing, both on the ground and in the air, would be heavy and immediate. The assault had deliberately been launched on the broadest front possible so that the IDF would be uncertain of where to mount its initial counter-attacks. That these would come there was no possible doubt, but Shazli could hardly have foreseen that they would be so light, uncoordinated and easily dealt with. He had, for example, believed that the IAF would damage his bridges so often that insufficient armour would get into the bridgeheads to meet the counter-attacks, and had compensated for this by equipping each infantry division with no less than 470 anti-tank weapons, including 314 RPG-7s and 48 portable Sagger ATGWs. The flow of armour to the east bank had, in fact, continued with very few interruptions, so that both tanks and anti-tank weapons were now available to meet the threat.

The Israelis had, of course, been taken by surprise, but this was by no means total. By the early hours of 6 October the signs were that a major conflict was imminent, and at 0440 hours the IDF was alerted to full war status. At 0920 hours orders were issued for full mobilisation and a little later the plan for the defence of Sinai, codenamed *Shovach Yonim* (Pigeon Loft), was activated.

The General Officer Commanding the Israeli Southern Command was Major-General Shmuel Gonen, whose major reaction force was the 252nd Armoured Division, a regular formation of three armoured brigades commanded by Major-General Avraham Mandler, who had fought with distinction in both the Sinai and Golan battles of the Six-Day War. Nominally, Mandler's division could muster 280 tanks, but of these about 100 were strung out along the Canal, the intention being that they should move into the Bar-Lev strongpoints prior to an enemy

assault, although when the Egyptians attacked, only one strongpoint had been joined by its supporting armour. This dispersion, as Israeli historians have themselves pointed out, was a mistake comparable to that of the French High Command in its handling of armour during the campaign of 1940. Furthermore, the balance of Mandler's brigades were based approximately 100km (65 miles) east of the Canal, a distance too great for the rapid intervention required.

Other Israeli units based in Sinai included an infantry brigade holding positions in the marshlands at the northern end of the Canal, and 436 men of the Jerusalem Brigade who formed the garrisons of the 16 manned Bar-Lev strongpoints, the latter being

Above: One of the GSP tracked self-propelled ferries – this one captured by the Israeli Army – which proved invaluable to the Egyptian forces crossing the Canal. The ferry is capable of carrying tanks, which can use their main armament during a passage.

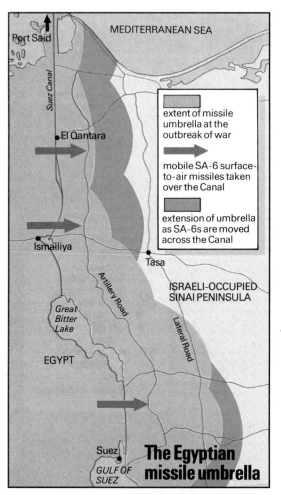

MEDITERRANEAN SEA

Port Said

Suez Canal

El Qantara

extent of missile umbrella at the outbreak of war

mobile SA-6 surface-to-air missiles taken over the Canal

extension of umbrella as SA-6s are moved across the Canal

Ismailiya

Tasa

ISRAELI-OCCUPIED SINAI PENINSULA

Artillery Road

Great Bitter Lake

Lateral Road

EGYPT

Suez

GULF OF SUEZ

The Egyptian missile umbrella

Below: Egyptian paratroopers go through final checks on their equipment before embarking on a low-altitude practice drop. Many paratroopers lost their lives in the Egyptian heliborne assault on the Mitla and Gidi passes.

reservists completing their annual training, many of whom were recently-arrived immigrants lacking military experience. Finally, following mobilisation, Gonen's command was to be augmented by two reserve armoured divisions, the 143rd under Major-General Ariel Sharon and the 162nd under Major General Avraham ('Bren') Adan, but these could obviously not be integrated into a major counter-attack plan until 8 October, although reserve units were thrown piecemeal into the fray as they reached the front.

From the outset, the IDF became a prisoner of its own tradition. Never since the formation of the Israeli Army had its members, and especially those who were wounded, been allowed to fall into enemy hands if rescue was humanly possible. Any call for help had to be answered promptly, even if it demanded heavy sacrifice. Thus, when the Bar-Lev strongpoints were surrounded and came under attack, their garrisons' repeated calls for relief and evacuation of the wounded exerted enormous pressure on Israeli officers to go directly to their aid.

From the Israeli viewpoint, therefore, the story of the first two days fighting in Sinai is one of small tank units, lacking infantry or adequate artillery support, attempting to break through to the strongpoints and suffering cruel losses from the Egyptians' integrated anti-tank defence and notably from the Sagger ATGWs. Many tanks, particularly on the northern sector, were also lost when they bogged down in

heavy going. By the evening of 7 October the IDF's tank losses had reached an appalling 170 for little return and Mandler's division had been reduced to a mere ghost of its former self. As for the strongpoints themselves, some, like Budapest, were relieved after hard fighting while the garrisons of others managed to break out with their wounded; some were overwhelmed and went down fighting; and some, like the Quay, which was built on the breakwater of Port Tewfik harbour, conducted an heroic defence, lasting days, before they surrendered.

Nor was the IAF able to influence the ground fighting. It flew a large number of missions against the Egyptian bridges and repeatedly damaged them all, but their sectional construction enabled them to be repaired very quickly. It also attacked Egyptian airfields and provided direct ground support but was unable to slow the enemy's rapid build-up.

During the evening of 7 October both Ismail and Shazli expressed themselves satisfied with the results of the fighting. Both knew, however, that the Israelis had now overcome their initial shock and that the two reserve armoured divisions allocated to Gonen's Southern Command had reached the front. It seemed certain that these would be employed in a fully coordinated counter-attack the following day. The orders issued to the Second and Third Armies, therefore, were to remain on the defensive and to consolidate their positions in anticipation of the counter-blow.   **Bryan Perrett**

The Sagger ATGW (below) inflicted heavy casualties on Israeli armour (bottom, a wrecked Sherman) which was thrusting forwards in an attempt to prevent Israelis manning the Bar-Lev Line being taken prisoner (right below, Israeli POWs).

Reservists and regulars

Mobilisation in the modern world

One of the most enduring of all military debates has been whether a voluntary system of enlistment or some form of conscription is likely to produce the more effective armed forces. Those armies recruited by voluntary means such as the British or that of the United States will be professional long-service armies but, almost by definition, they are likely to be far smaller than those raised by a system of short service conscription. Yet conscript armies, which are very much in the majority around the world, always require a regular cadre and their conscription system will almost certainly be selective in practice to enable the state to allocate adequate manpower to industry and agriculture. Both kinds of army will therefore be unlikely to believe that they have sufficient manpower to wage a major war without mobilising their reserves. The speed and effectiveness with which reserves can be mobilised is, necessarily, a major preoccupation of the high commands of all the world's armies.

Conscript armies will normally have proportionally more reserves available than volunteer armies. In the case of what might be termed defensive mobilisation, the actual army in being at the beginning of hostilities, as in the case of France in the 1930s or modern Israel, may represent what the former referred to as *couverture* – a covering force to win time for the defence while the full resources of the nation are mobilised in support. Thus in Israel after 1967 it was assumed that, in the future, the 11,500 regulars, 50,000 conscripts and those reservists undergoing their annual 33-day refresher training who together would compose the army in being, would need to hold an Arab attack for some 72 hours. After that period had elapsed the reserves would be fully mobilised and the army expanded to a strength of some 275,000 men and women.

Similarly, the Nato forces on the Central Front in Europe would be required to hold any Warsaw Pact offensive without reinforcement for at least 48 hours. In September 1980 Operation Crusader tested Britain's ability to reinforce the British I Corps within the stipulated time limit, the major reserve component being the part-time volunteers of the Territorial Army. The reserves were able to get into position, but only just and in favourable peacetime conditions. In such circumstances, much will depend upon sufficient warning time being given to begin the mobilisation process.

In the case of Nato, the US Department of Defense calculated in 1977 that a Warsaw Pact mobilisation would take at least 30 days and that Nato would, in consequence, have at least three weeks warning time, but it is now suggested that the Warsaw Pact forces could mobilise in as little as 72 hours. One of the major Israeli failures at the beginning of the Yom Kippur War in 1973 was to believe that there would always be sufficient warning time, the chief of staff, David Elazar, being particularly criticised for this misappreciation by the Agranat Commission of Inquiry after the war. The Israeli defence minister, Moshe Dayan, had ordered a low level of alert on 26 September after his visit to the Golan front, but the highest stage of alert was not ordered by Elazar until the morning of 4 October. Some but by no means all senior reservists were alerted on 5 October and Elazar later claimed that he would have mobilised then had sufficient information been available. In the event, precise warning of Arab intentions was not received until the early hours of 6 October when it was assumed that the attack would begin at 1800 hours. Five valuable hours were wasted while Elazar and Dayan argued over whether to mobilise or not. The prime minister, Golda Meir, finally ordered full mobilisation at 0925 hours, and the Cabinet was actually in session when news was brought of the Arab attack at 1355 hours.

The function of mobilisation is, of course, different

Above left: US student protests against the draft. The use of conscripts in Vietnam led to the most severe anti-conscription campaign that has taken place since 1945.

Below: Teenage volunteers in the Iranian Army. These young recruits, inspired by the ideals of Islamic fundamentalism, believe that death in a Holy War ensures automatic entry to Heaven.

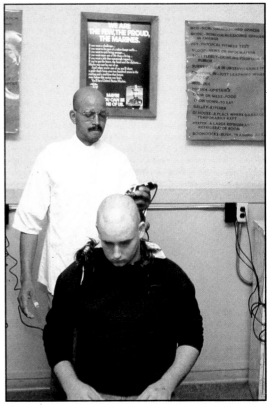

Above: A sergeant in the US Marines screams a command at a young teenager who has come on a three-week summer course in which the Marines show schoolchildren what the life of a member of the corps can be like. Above right: The first moments of the new life of a recruit in the US Marines. The creation of disciplined soldiers from raw civilian material is a long and often unnerving process.

where an offensive operation is contemplated, the classic example being the way in which major European armies of the late 19th and early 20th centuries conceived military victory in terms of achieving faster mobilisation and deployment than their opponents. In 1914 the Germans mobilised 1,400,000 men in just five days and some historians have characterised the contribution of the rigid mobilisation planning of the time as resulting in 'war by timetable'.

Mobilisation may not be easy where war is unexpected or where it has not been required for many years. Thus the mobilisation of the British and French forces for the Suez operation in 1956 was exceedingly slow. Precautionary measures were announced on 30 July, Nasser having nationalised the Suez Canal Company four days earlier. On 2 August a Royal Proclamation called up selected reservists in Britain. Men of the Regular Reserve, consisting of former regular soldiers, reported to their units to make them up to war establishment while men from the Army Emergency Reserve, consisting of specialist personnel not normally borne on army establishment in peacetime, reported to depots. The Territorial Army, into which most national servicemen passed at the end of their term of service, and the Army General Reserve, consisting of World War II 'temporary' soldiers still under the age of 45, were not required. Planning, however, did not begin in earnest until mid-August and the invasion task force did not sail from Malta and Cyprus until 31 October prior to the landings at Suez on 5 and 6 November 1956.

Suez is a good example of the kinds of problems that can arise in mobilising for war. Many errors were made in the process of calling up reserves; far too many reservists idled their time away in depots in Britain; others were clearly unfit or had little acquaintance with modern weapon developments. Astonishingly, the military authorities themselves appeared not to have kept abreast of developments

since reinforcement tank crews were called up in five-man crews when the Centurion only required a crew of four. The fading of specialised technical skills is, of course, likely to increase rather than decrease with the pace of current technological advances and the experience of Suez contrasted quite markedly with the major mobilisation test held in Britain in 1951 during the Korean War, in which some 250,000 wartime soldiers were recalled for 14 days and proved remarkably adept at fitting back well into military life. In 1951, however, weaponry had hardly changed in the six years since the end of World War II.

Mobilisation under pressure is bound to be hazardous and in 1973, ironically, the Israelis probably suffered from the unprecedented speed with which it was finally accomplished since the units that commandeered buses, trucks and even milk floats to reach the front were fed into the battle piecemeal. Similarly, the considerable achievement in despatching the British Task Force to the South Atlantic quickly in April 1982 (5000 tonnes of stores and equipment were loaded onto shipping in just 72 hours in order to allow the first elements of 3 Commando Brigade to sail on the SS *Canberra* on 9 April), was at the cost of considerable disorganisation in loading which had to be sorted out at the Ascension Island staging point.

The Falklands campaign is itself an example of the kind of mobilisation which can be achieved without actual recourse to calling up reserves, although the three Marine units of 3 Commando Brigade had to be recalled from Scotland, northwest England and from leave, and over 60 merchant ships had to be requisitioned, with their civilian crews in many cases. Similarly, the debate within Nato on the likely amount of warning time available before any Warsaw Pact offensive revolves around the extent to which the Soviet forces in Eastern Europe have developed a 'sudden attack' capability using only those resources which exist on the ground at present without

MOBILISATION

The Falklands saw the clash of two contrasting armies. The Argentinians (right, enthusiastic Argentinian volunteers at a recruiting office) had a conscript base, while the British Army (bottom, Welsh Guards embark for the South Atlantic) was a professional force. Neverthless, the British found the assembling of their force complex (below, stores are loaded).

reinforcement or appreciable mobilisation.

There is little doubt that the ability of the Soviets to attack from a 'standing start' has increased considerably since the late 1960s. Between 1968 and 1977, for example, the number of main battle tanks deployed in Eastern Europe increased by 31 per cent, the number of artillery pieces by 38 per cent, and the number of armoured personnel carriers by 79 per cent, while there were major increases in assault-bridging and field-engineering resources. Conventional military wisdom requires at least a 3:1 superiority for a successful offensive and, as they displayed in their attack on Japanese-held Manchuria in August 1945, the Soviets believe (as one authority has put it) that 'the cracking of nuts is what sledgehammers are clearly designed for.'

Ratios may in reality not mean very much and it is difficult, for example, to evaluate qualitative judgements, but in 1983 it was calculated that the Soviets and Warsaw Pact had nearer 2:1 than 3:1 real superiority in tanks, artillery and fixed wing combat aircraft on the Central Front while Nato had a superiority in anti-tank guided weapons and armed helicopters. This may suggest that the Soviets would not believe they had a sufficient superiority in the initial stages of an offensive launched with the forces in being in East Germany, Czechoslovakia and Poland, but it should be noted that Soviet doctrine lays great store on surprise negating unfavourable ratios and upon achieving local superiority of up to 10:1 on selected narrow axes of advance.

It should be borne in mind, finally, that in modern warfare mobilisation may not necessarily be for war at all. It can be a preventative measure, the Israelis mobilising in December 1971, December 1972 and May 1973 when a particular Arab threat was perceived. Similarly, as the last of those three Israeli mobilisations indicates, mobilisation may be used as a ploy by an opponent. It was the fact that Egypt had mobilised and then released her reservists on some 20 occasions between January and October 1973 and that nothing had occurred in May in particular that so misled Israeli intelligence. **Ian Beckett**

Key Weapons

RECOILLESS GUNS

When a conventional gun – whether a pistol or a howitzer – is fired, the weapon jumps backward with a force which is directly proportional to the energy expended in pushing the bullet or shell forward. This is caused by the explosion of the cartridge which exerts force in all directions: the sideways force is contained by the walls of the gun barrel, the forward force pushes the projectile, and the rearward force pushes on the weapon's breech and thus exerts the backward force – the recoil. Absorbing this recoil, in the case of the heavier types of weapon, is an expensive and complicated matter of applying hydraulic brakes to check the movement of the gun barrel and spring or gas recuperators to return it to its firing position in the mounting ready for the next shot. These recoil mechanisms are complex, expensive and heavy, and demand skilled attention for their maintenance and repair. If, therefore, it could be possible to make a gun which did not recoil then the cost and weight of this mechanism could be saved; moreover the gun mounting could be made much lighter since it would only have to support the weight of the barrel and not have to resist the recoil force.

Recoil systems first came into use in the late 19th century as guns began to become more powerful, and it was not until the early years of the 20th century that the advantages of a recoilless gun were first considered. The first innovator in this area of weapon design was an American, Commander Cleland Davis, who developed such a gun in 1914. Approaching the problem from basic principles he realised that a recoilless gun could be made by taking two identical guns and fixing them back to back. Firing them would thus mean that the recoil of each would cancel out the other's movement. Moving on from this he patented and developed a series of guns in which there was a central chamber and two barrels, pointing in opposite directions. The forward barrel was loaded with a conventional shell, the rearward barrel with a wad of grease and lead shot of the same weight as the shell. On firing the central cartridge, the shell was propelled forward to the target while the countershot went backwards and then disintegrated

due to air resistance and centrifugal force.

The idea was taken up in Germany in the 1930s in order to provide the Luftwaffe with a heavy-calibre weapon with which to attack warships. The Rheinmettal company developed a 35cm gun carried by a Dornier Do-217 bomber. The gun fired a 635kg (1400lb) armour-piercing shell and the recoil was balanced by the rearward ejection of a 635kg (1400lb) steel cartridge case. The weapon was perfected by 1939 but the Luftwaffe had lost interest and it was never used. This was a minor setback, however, as the Rheinmettal engineers had taken matters a step further and had developed a recoilless gun which did away with the countershot.

The German engineers took the concept of a recoilless weapon to its logical conclusion. If the same weight of shot is fired at the same velocity in both directions the result is recoillessness; but the same result can be achieved by having the countershot half the weight of the service shot and ejecting it at twice

Previous page: A British paratrooper prepares to put a shell into the empty breech of a WOMBAT recoilless gun. Above: The first practical battlefield recoilless gun, the German 75mm gun used to considerable effect by paratroops on Crete in 1941. Below: The portability of the recoilless gun can be appreciated in this photograph of Viet Cong troops in South Vietnam at the end of the Tet offensive. Opposite page: A US 75mm gun in Korea (top) and 57mm gun in action at Okinawa (centre) and a British 95mm gun in 1945 (below).

the velocity, or a quarter the weight and four times the velocity. Carrying on in this way one can reach a point where the weight of the countershot is minute and the velocity extremely high, and the weapon is still recoilless. The German weapon utilised this principle in the extreme so that a column of gas ejected at high velocity acted as the countershot. The gun was built with a hole in the breech block and a venturi – a restricted throat to accelerate the flow of gasses – in the hole. The cartridge case had its base pierced and plugged with a slab of plastic material. When the cartridge was fired this plastic remained whole for a fraction of a second, enough to allow the shell to begin moving up the barrel, after which it blew to pieces and released the high-pressure explosive gas through the rearward-facing venturi. In effect it was like having a rocket motor on the back of the gun pushing forward against the recoil.

Guns of this type in 75mm and 105mm calibre were secretly built and were unveiled by German paratroops in the battle for Crete in 1941. Their appearance led to experiments in Britain and the USA, and both countries had perfected recoilless guns before the war ended, though only the US Army managed to bring them into service. These differed from the German models principally in having cartridge cases with solid bases but which had their bodies perforated with holes. The propellant gas escaped through these holes into a chamber surrounding the gun, from which they were directed backwards through one or more venturis. Copies of the American 57mm and 75mm weapons are still in service with several countries, notably China and in South America.

After World War II the British scrapped their experimental recoilless guns and began a fresh programme of development which led, eventually, to the 120mm BAT (battalion anti-tank) gun in the middle 1950s. This reverted to the German system of using a blow-out plastic base to the cartridge but improved it by building the vitally important venturi throat into the cartridge case itself. When the venturi throat was situated in the body of the gun, it accelerated the escaping gasses, helping the recoilless effect, but the speed and heat tended to erode the throat so that after a few rounds had been fired the gun was no longer perfectly in balance and, indeed, would often begin to 'recoil' forwards. Placing the throat in the cartridge case meant that it was always of the correct size, since the case was only used once. The original BAT was a heavy weapon, weighing 1000kg (2200lb), but it was gradually refined, first into the MOBAT (765kg – 1680lb) which could be slung behind a jeep or Land Rover, and finally into the WOMBAT (295kg – 650lb). Besides a loss in weight, range was improved: while the BAT had an effective range of 500m (550yds), MOBAT's was 800m (880yds) and WOMBAT's 1200m (1300yds).

The Americans stuck to their perforated case system and issued first a 90mm and then a 105mm weapon. The 105mm gun turned out to be inaccurate and unreliable and was extensively redesigned; in order to distinguish the improved model the new gun was named the 106mm, and has since been taken into service by many armies throughout the world.

The principal role of the recoilless gun is that of an anti-tank weapon, though most have a secondary role as a general close-support weapon for the infantry. This came about because of the increasing size of conventional anti-tank guns designed to fire solid armour-piercing projectiles at high velocity. By 1945 these had gone beyond the size at which they were practical battlefield weapons; but at the same time improved methods of hollow-charge explosive attack on armour had appeared, methods which were independent of high velocity and therefore no longer demanded extremely powerful guns. What they did demand, though, was a large calibre so that the shell could carry a worthwhile charge of high explosive,

Recoilless gun operation (American Kromuskit system)

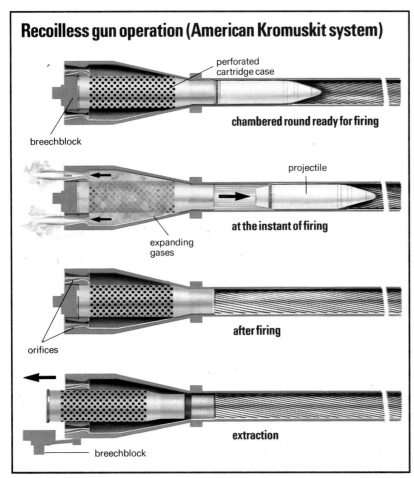

perforated cartridge case

breechblock

chambered round ready for firing

projectile

expanding gases

at the instant of firing

orifices

after firing

extraction

breechblock

Above: Troops of the Gordon Highlanders receive instruction on a MOBAT recoilless gun. The MOBAT features a Bren spotting rifle mounted above the main barrel. Above right: An FV 432 APC mounting a WOMBAT defends a river crossing during exercises in Germany.

and the recoilless gun was the obvious solution to this problem.

Another advantage of recoilless design was that it meant that if the weapon was light enough, there was no reason why it should not be fired from a man's shoulder, since there was no longer any recoil. The original German Panzerfaust of 1944 is often spoken of as a rocket, but it was in fact a small recoilless gun, and from this beginning has sprung a whole family of lightweight recoilless anti-tank weapons.

Opposite page: Early British recoilless guns were fairly ungainly weapons, eventually discarded in favour of the BAT series. The complex venturi system of the 3.7in gun can be seen (above) while the man-portable 3.45in model is demonstrated (below). Below: Some of the force of the backblast of a WOMBAT recoilless gun is indicated on this Salisbury Plain firing exercise.

Above: A shoulder-mounted Carl Gustav is loaded with a HEAT charge. Left: A tripod-mounted Carl Gustav alongside a complete round. Below: A US-made 106mm recoilless gun is fired by a detachment of the Swiss Army. Given Switzerland's mountainous terrain ease of movement is an especially important tactical requirement.

Above: A Swedish infantry man prepares to fire an M2 Carl Gustav. Above right: The Swedish Miniman short-range recoilless gun immediately after being fired.

Below: A soldier prepares to fire an Armbrust anti-tank weapon. The great advantage of the Armbrust over even lightweight recoilless guns is its 'enclosed' recoil which prevents the back blast from escaping into the open air where noise and flash can give away the firer's position.

One of the most effective is the Swedish 84mm Carl Gustav gun, used also by the armed forces of Nato and several other armies. This is exactly the same as the original German guns or the BAT, simply smaller and lighter so that it can be fired from the shoulder. The cartridge has a plastic blow-out base, venting through a venturi in the breech block, and the shell is a powerful shaped charge which can penetrate up to 400mm (16in) of armour plate at ranges up to 450m (490yds).

The recoilless principle has also been applied to disposable anti-tank weapons. The first disposable launchers were simply glass-fibre tubes with pre-packed rockets inside; the soldier placed it on his shoulder, fired the rocket, and then threw the tube away. But rockets, like recoilless guns, have one big tactical disadvantage: they emit a sheet of flame and a blast of hot gas and smoke from the rear when they fire, and this can reveal the firer's position for miles

around. Moveover if the weapon is fired in a confined space or in front of an obstacle, the hot jet will wash back and injure the firer. This effect is known as the 'firing signature'.

Conventional recoilless guns such as the British WOMBAT and the US 106mm suffer from a high 'firing signature' and so have been replaced by more advanced weapons which minimise this weakness. Of this newer type of recoilless gun, a good example is the West German Armbrust, a simple tube carrying a central propelling charge located between two piston-heads. In front of one piston is the projectile, a shaped charge anti-tank bomb, behind the other piston is a countershot, a tight package of plastic flakes. When the cartridge is fired, the two piston heads are blown violently down the launch tube: the front piston ejects the bomb and sends it to the target, while the rear piston ejects the plastic flakes which disperse and flutter to the ground, doing no damage should they hit anything. The piston heads, though, are trapped as they reach the end of the tube and locked into place, so preventing the explosive gasses or the noise of the explosion from reaching the open air. As a result there is no flame or smoke and the noise of the weapon firing is no more than that of a small-calibre pistol shot.

Once fired, the Armbrust is thrown away. It has a maximum effective range of around 300m (330yds), and the whole weapon weighs no more than 6kg (13lb). Since its appearance several other designs of countershot weapons have been developed, and these light disposable weapons represent the trend for the foreseeable future.

Armbrust recoilless launcher

projectile

ready for firing explosive charge columns of plastic flakes

at the instant of firing dispersing plastic flakes

projectile in flight **after firing**

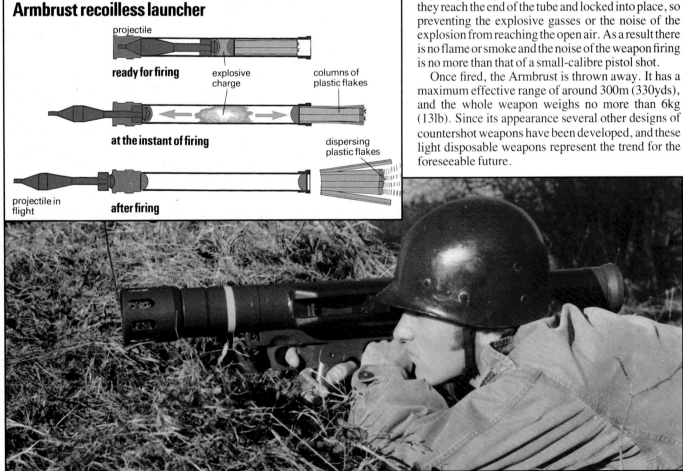

The valley of tears

Syrian assaults on the Golan, October 1973

Early in October 1973, Major-General Yitzhak Hofi, the General Officer Commanding (GOC) Israel's Northern Command, had become so seriously alarmed by troop movements on the Syrian side of the 1967 ceasefire line on the Golan Heights that he communicated his growing concern to General Moshe Dayan, the minister of defence. The Golan was garrisoned by a regular formation, the 188th (Barak) Armoured Brigade under Colonel Yitzhak Ben-Shoham, but Hofi believed the scale of the Syrian preparations was such as to dwarf any defensive measures a single brigade could provide along the 70km (45 mile) front. Dayan concurred and on 4 October released the 7th Armoured Brigade from GHQ reserve and ordered it to move north. This redeployment gave 7th Armoured, commanded by

Colonel Avigdor Ben-Gal, responsibility for the northern sector of the front from the shoulder of Mount Hermon to the line Bnot Ya'aqov bridge-Nafekh-Quneitra, while the Barak Brigade concentrated on the sector running south from this boundary line to the Jordanian frontier. The two brigades, which together could field a total of 170 Centurion and Patton tanks, were placed under the control of Major-General Rafael Eitan, whose divisional headquarters was situated at Nafekh.

The Golan possessed no natural features which would form a barrier to any Syrian attack, although the eastward tilt of the terrain did provide a gently sloping glacis beyond which Syrian movements were clearly visible. The main military obstacles to an offensive were provided by the minefields of both sides, which would have to be gapped, and a partly-flooded anti-tank ditch 5m (16 feet) deep which had been dug across the front of the Israeli positions. Behind the anti-tank ditch were 17 fortified observation posts, each garrisoned by about 20 men and a platoon of three tanks. The real strength of the Israeli Golan defence system lay in large numbers of carefully sited and ramped firing points which enabled the tanks to remain hull-down yet still engage in long-range gunnery duels.

The Syrian bombardment

On the Syrian side of the line the defensive perimeter was held by three infantry divisions, the 7th (which included a Moroccan contingent) under Brigadier-General Omar Abrash in the north, the 9th under Colonel Hassan Tourmkmani in the centre, and the 5th under Brigadier-General Ali Aslan in the south, each being organised along the lines of a Soviet mechanised formation, with its own organic armoured brigade. These would spearhead the Syrian attack while two armoured divisions, the 1st under Colonel Tewfiq Jehani and the 3rd under Brigadier-General Mustafa Sharba, would advance to exploit the breakthrough into Galilee. It was intended that this should take place on the southern sector of the front over the good tank country to be found north of Rafid, although part of the 3rd Armoured Division was detached to reinforce the 7th Infantry Division's assault in the north. Altogether, the Syrians had approximately 1500 tanks (against 170 Israeli tanks) deployed opposite the Golan, while 1000 artillery pieces were ranged against the Israelis' 60.

The attack was timed to coincide precisely with the Egyptian crossing of the Suez Canal and at 1400 hours on 6 October the Israeli positions were struck by a fierce artillery bombardment lasting 50 minutes, supplemented by air strikes. At that precise moment, the senior Israeli commanders were attending an orders group inside Eitan's headquarters at Nafekh, which itself came under air attack. None of the commanders were hurt and as they hurried to rejoin their units, their forward radio links confirmed that their deputies had already activated the contingency plans which had been prepared and that Centurions and Pattons were already crawling onto their ramps and engaging the dense columns of Syrian tanks and armoured personnel carriers (APCs) that were swarming across the ceasefire line.

The Israeli tank crews, trained to a high standard in long-range gunnery techniques, concentrated first on the gaps that had been made in the minefield, whittling down the enemy's strength. The Syrians, however, were as highly motivated as the Egyptians on the Sinai front and just as prepared to accept high casualties. Once through the minefields, they converged on the anti-tank ditch, knowing that the Israelis had turned all the probable crossing points into killing grounds. The Syrian MTU bridgelayers became specific targets until, one after another, they were knocked out, together with their escorting T55 and T62 tanks. One killing ground, that between Tel Hermonit and 'Booster' Hill, witnessed such carnage that the Israelis themselves called it the 'Valley of Tears'. Yet still the Syrians came on and such was their courage on this occasion that infantrymen with entrenching tools succeeded where the bridgelayers had failed, constructing causeways over the ditch despite intense fire.

For both sides the battle had now become a race against time. The Israelis knew that if they could not hold the Syrian attack until the Israeli Defence Forces' (IDF) reserve armoured divisions could mobilise and reach the front, northern Galilee would be swamped under a flood of Syrian armour; for their part the Syrians were aware that the thin screen of tanks confronting them was all that stood between them and victory, but also that by the following day this situation could change radically. As the afternoon wore on news was received that deeply depressed the Israelis and caused elation among the senior Syrian commanders – the Israeli stronghold on Mount Hermon had fallen to a helicopter assault by the Syrian 82nd Commando Battalion.

The battle fought by the 7th Armoured Brigade in the northern sector of the front was an epic. Its commander, Colonel Ben-Gal, struggled constantly to construct one reserve after another, throwing these

Previous page, above: A dead Syrian crewman lies beside his tank. Previous page, below: The remains of a Syrian convoy, hit by the IAF.

The Syrian attack on the Golan Heights
6 October 1973

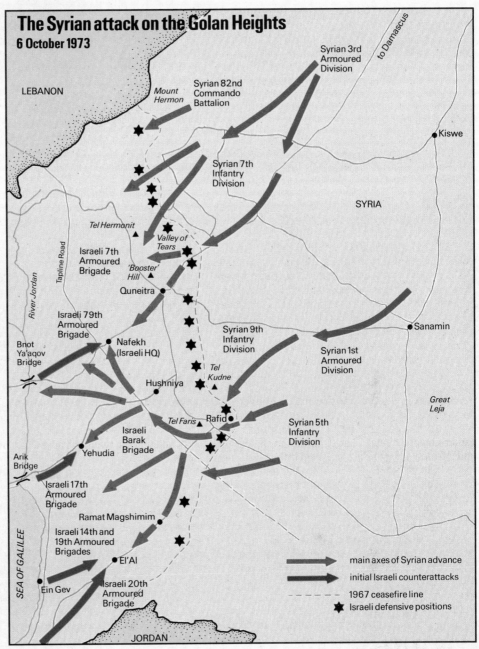

LEBANON

to Damascus

Mount Hermon

Syrian 82nd Commando Battalion

Syrian 3rd Armoured Division

Kiswe

Syrian 7th Infantry Division

SYRIA

Tel Hermonit

Valley of Tears

Israeli 7th Armoured Brigade

'Booster' Hill

Quneitra

Tapline Road

River Jordan

Israeli 79th Armoured Brigade

Nafekh (Israeli HQ)

Syrian 9th Infantry Division

Sanamin

Syrian 1st Armoured Division

Bnot Ya'aqov Bridge

Hushniya

Tel Kudne

Great Leja

Tel Faris

Rafid

Israeli Barak Brigade

Yehudia

Syrian 5th Infantry Division

Arik Bridge

Israeli 17th Armoured Brigade

Ramat Magshimim

SEA OF GALILEE

Israeli 14th and 19th Armoured Brigades

El'Al

Ein Gev

Israeli 20th Armoured Brigade

JORDAN

→ main axes of Syrian advance

→ initial Israeli counterattacks

– – – 1967 ceasefire line

★ Israeli defensive positions

Top: An Israeli machine-gun nest on Mount Hermon. Above: Defence Minister Moshe Dayan on a visit to Golan during October 1973.

Below: Centurions of the IDF swing into action during the fighting on the Golan. It was Israeli armour that blunted the Syrian spearheads.

in where they were needed most, but was hampered by having to send part of his strength to reinforce Ben-Shoham's Barak Brigade which, with only 57 tanks, was fighting off an estimated 600 Syrian tanks. Darkness brought little relief, for while the Syrians possessed infra-red night-fighting equipment for both driver and gunner the Israelis did not, and at times the range closed to only 300m (180 yards). The Israelis were forced to rely on the artillery's very limited supply of parachute illuminating shells, brief use of such xenon white-light projectors as had survived, and the local light provided by burning vehicles to identify their targets, simultaneously employing coloured flashers as recognition signals in the melée.

The morning of Sunday 7 October found 7th Armoured still holding its positions, but the Barak Brigade had been fought to destruction and 90 per cent of its officers were either dead or wounded. On the southern sector of the front the Syrian breakthrough was complete and the 1st Armoured Division was advancing along the Tapline Road (which ran beside an oil pipeline) towards Nafekh, which contained Ben-Shoham's headquarters as well as Eitan's. Bravely Ben-Shoham moved out with his few surviving tanks to inflict one final check on the enemy, his little group being wiped out in the process. The Syrian advance continued and one T55 actually broke into the headquarters before it was knocked out by the last tank of another ad hoc group which had so distinguished itself that its commander, Lieutenant Zwicka Gringold, was awarded Israel's highest decoration, the Order of Courage.

A suicidal stand

The Syrians also captured the village of Ramat Magshimim and, along the southern sector of the front generally, had reached a point at which they were only 10 minutes by road from the Bnot Ya'aqov Bridge. At this point, Syrian hesitation lost them the chance of success. Ben-Shoham's suicidal stand had gained just sufficient time for elements of two reserve armoured divisions to reach the front. By the evening of 7 October Major-General Dan Laner's reserve division was streaming across the Arik Bridge at the head of the Sea of Galilee and going straight into action against the Syrian 1st Armoured. Later that night the leading units of Major-General Moshe Peled's division moved up the El'Al road and began attacking the Syrian 5th Infantry Division.

Meanwhile, the Israeli Air Force (IAF) was doing its utmost to contain the Syrian assaults – at considerable cost in Israeli planes and pilots. Twenty-eight aircraft were lost in attacks during the first three days, and although the Syrian screen of SAM missiles was temporarily put out of action, it was soon working again and taking its toll of the Israeli aircraft. Nevertheless, in spite of heavy IAF losses, the ground-attack sorties were adding to the mounting casualty rates of the Syrian formations.

On the northern front, the 7th Armoured Brigade was still engaged in its murderous battle of attrition, which continued day and night until the afternoon of Tuesday 9 October. By then only seven tanks remained and as these were critically short of ammunition Colonel Ben-Gal felt that he had no alternative but to withdraw. The Syrians, scenting victory, surged forward past the now abandoned lines of ramps, but there now occurred one of those strange incidents upon which the results of battle turn.

When the war broke out Lieutenant-Colonel Naty Yossi was enjoying his honeymoon in the Himalayas. Somehow he had managed to reach Israel and from Lod airport had gone straight to the workshops behind the Golan front which were repairing battle-damaged tanks. Selecting the 13 fittest, he had rounded up crews, including some wounded volunteers, and headed for 7th Armoured Brigade's sector. He arrived just after Ben-Gal had begun his withdrawal, and the reinforcement, bringing the total of Centurions available to 20, proved just enough to blunt the Syrian spearhead.

Suddenly the Syrians, who despite their dreadful losses had fought with the same grim determination as the Israelis, seemed to lose heart; to the desperately tired and battle-weary men manning the T55s and T62s, Yossi's force looked very like the advance guard of a fresh and recently mobilised reserve armoured formation, and this finally broke their resolve. The Israeli fortified strong points, which had continued to hold out after they had been bypassed, reported a general Syrian withdrawal to the old ceasefire line. The 7th Armoured Brigade returned to the positions it had held unaided for so long, its utterly exhausted crews emerging from their hatches to survey the scene of devastation stretching away to the east. Over 500 tanks, APCs and other armoured fighting vehicles littered the landscape, providing mute evidence of the scale of the Syrian defeat.

Elsewhere on the Golan the fortunes of war had also turned against Syria. On Sunday 7 October the breakthrough achieved by Colonel Tewfiq Jehani's 1st Armoured Division had been hailed as a great victory in Damascus and although the divisional spearheads had been halted during the evening by the leading units of Laner's division, there seemed no reason to believe that an advance into Israel could not be continued the following morning, and to that end Jehani established a supply and administrative complex in the area of Hushniya.

When Monday dawned, however, it was not Jehani who dictated events but General Yitzhak Hofi, Israel's GOC Northern Command, who intended to isolate the Syrian penetration with converging attacks by Laner's and Peled's divisions. Nonetheless, there remained some tidying up to do and Laner despatched his 79th Armoured Brigade, under Colonel Uri Orr, along the road to Nafekh, where the Syrians had taken half the command complex in spite of determined resistance by Eitan and his headquarters personnel. Orr's tanks ran into those of Colonel Shafiq Fiyad's Syrian 91st Armoured Brigade and an encounter battle developed in which the Syrians were badly mauled and pushed away to the east and south. While Nafekh was being relieved, another of Laner's armoured brigades, the 17th, under Colonel Ran Sarig, advanced eastwards through Yehudia and, although less than 50 tanks strong, destroyed over 200 Syrian tanks in a series of actions which clearly demonstrated the Israelis' superior gunnery.

It was, however, the advance of Peled's 20th Armoured Brigade along the El'Al road towards Rafid that alerted Jehani to the danger posed to his force. By noon Peled's armour had reached Tel Faris, having overcome the most determined opposition, and was straddling Jehani's lines of communication. Most of the 1st Armoured Division was thus trapped inside a pocket and for the next 24 hours the Syrians struggled fiercely to break Peled's hold, while

concurrently, the northern sector witnessed the last attacks on the 7th Armoured Brigade in a desperate attempt to distract the Israelis' attention away from the climactic battles being fought around Hushniya. By now, however, the IAF was providing effective ground support and Peled's two remaining brigades, the 14th and 19th, had climbed the winding road from Ein Gev and were advancing eastwards across the plateau to relieve the pressure on the embattled 20th Armoured Brigade. The 19th Brigade beat off a counter-attack by the Syrian 40th Mechanised Brigade (part of the 1st Armoured Division) and the ring of steel tightened around the pocket. An attempt to break through from outside was made by the Syrian 3rd Armoured Division's 15th Mechanised Brigade, but was similarly defeated.

At dawn on Wednesday 10 October, Peled's three brigades advanced on Tel Kudne, where the Syrians' forward headquarters was located. The attack was halted with heavy loss and Hofi ordered Peled to remain on the defensive, so providing the anvil against which the pocket would be crushed by the hammer of Laner's division attacking from the north. Laner's advance was led by Orr's and Sarig's armoured brigades and by midday it was all over. Two Syrian brigades were wiped out and the Hushniya pocket had become a vast mechanical graveyard of smashed tanks, guns, APCs, lorries and stores. The remains of the routed Syrian Army streamed east behind the old ceasefire line and by evening no Syrian unit remained on territory which had formerly been held by the IDF.

The cost of battle

Five days of intense fighting had cost the Syrian Army 867 tanks, hundreds of guns and APCs, thousands of assorted vehicles and countless tonnes of abandoned equipment; its carefully prepared Soviet-style offensive had ended in a crushing defeat while the Egyptian Army, which had the more difficult task, had simultaneously scored a notable success. Reasons for this anomaly are not difficult to find.

First, of course, the Israelis were well aware of the impending attack on the Golan, and prepared accordingly. Secondly, the events in Sinai presented no immediate threat to Israel, but the Golan front possessed no depth at all and was therefore accorded priority by the Israeli General Staff. Finally, as Lieutenant-Colonel David Eshel, a founder member of the Israeli Armoured Corps who was present on the Golan front points out, there were markedly different command philosophies: 'In Sinai, instinctive reactions of small formations commanded by junior officers resulted in entanglement and an immediate fog of battle which did not clear for several days. On the Golan front, where the fighting was just as ferocious, if not more so, command remained generally in the hands of more seasoned commanders, who husbanded their forces within a much clearer overall combat picture. The fog of battle, even though dense, never obscured the priorities which were easier to define in the more restricted combat zone.'

On the night of 10 October, however, such questions remained for future consideration. The questions to which the Israeli formation commanders required answers were more pressing. Would the General Staff be content to halt on the old ceasefire line? Or would it order an advance into Syria, and if so with what objective? **Bryan Perrett**

Above: Israeli artillerymen man a US-supplied M110 self-propelled gun. It was concentrated fire onto the advanced Syrian units that destroyed much of the bridgelaying equipment with which the Syrians had hoped to cross the anti-tank ditch that was the first line of Israeli defence on Golan.

Left: The effects of bombardment on Syrian equipment. Below left: The high-water mark of Syrian advance – a knocked-out T55 just in front of the headquarters at Nafekh. Below: Israeli prisoners captured during the first wave of the Syrian assault.

Clearing the Golan

The Israeli counter-attack, October 1973

Left: Major-General David Elazar arrives at the Golan front accompanied by two aides. Elazar was eager to launch an offensive in the northern sector, in order to bring Damascus within artillery range and crush the Syrian Army before the IDF concentrated its efforts against the Egyptians in Sinai. Despite reservations from Moshe Dayan, Elazar's plan was adopted by the Israelis.

The decision to invade Syria was taken at a General Staff conference which began at 2200 hours on the night of Wednesday 10 October, being subsequently ratified by Israel's prime minister, Golda Meir. General Moshe Dayan, the minister of defence, had reservations about the decision, which he felt could well provoke direct Soviet intervention.

However, the chief of staff, Major-General David Elazar, believed that the Syrians' offensive capability should be destroyed as quickly as possible, particular-ly in view of reported troop movements from neigh-bouring Arab states into Syria, and that this could be achieved by a penetration 20km (12 miles) in depth, to form a defensible enclave from which Damascus itself could be brought under long range artillery fire. The effect of this, it was calculated, would neutralise Syria and enable the Israeli Defence Forces (IDF) to concentrate their efforts on the destruction of the Egyptian armies in Sinai. Elazar's view prevailed and detailed planning commenced at once.

Below: An Israeli armoured column pushes forward along the road to Damascus past the burning hull of a Syrian Soviet-made APC. Despite the arrival of Iraqi and Jordanian support, the Syrians could not throw back the IDF offensive.

Left: Captured by the Israelis, Syrian BM21 Soviet-made rocket batteries are turned against Syrian units. The BM21 is a 122mm multi-rocket system that can lay down massive high-explosive barrages. Each rocket has a maximum range of over 15,000m (16,500 yds). The rockets are vehicle-launched with 40 rounds per vehicle.

The offensive would begin with an advance by Major-General Rafael Eitan's division along the axis Tel Shams-Mazrat Beit Jan. This would protect the northern flank of the division's main thrust, which would be delivered by Major-General Dan Laner's division along the main Quneitra-Damascus highway. Along the southern sector of the front, Major-General Moshe Peled's division would, for the present, remain in position on the old ceasefire line and prevent interference by the still considerable Syrian forces present in the area. Eitan's start time was set at 1100 hours on 11 October, by which time the sun would no longer be shining directly into the Israeli gunsights; Laner was to move two hours later.

Eitan's advance would be led by Colonel Avigdor Ben-Gal's 7th Armoured Brigade which, since its epic four-day battle blunting the Syrian offensive on Golan, had been re-equipped with replacement tanks and joined by reserve armoured units and had absorbed the remnants of the Barak Brigade. This last, of which only three of the original company officers remained, was now commanded by the remarkable Lieutenant-Colonel Naty Yossi, whose timely arrival with a handful of repaired tanks had prevented a Syrian breakthrough on the northern sector only two days previously. Altogether, Ben-Gal could deploy four tank battalions, which he allocated evenly to the Mazrat Beit Jan and Tel Shams objectives.

Under cover of artillery and air strikes, the brigade broke through the Syrian minefield on both its axes and immediately found itself fighting its way through a prepared defence in depth in a landscape of rock-strewn wooded ridges which favoured the Syrians. This sector was held by two brigades, one of which was Moroccan, supported by a total of 75 tanks. A stiff resistance was initially encountered but the enemy were steadily ejected from one position after another by the Israelis' fire and movement tactics.

The northern wing of Ben-Gal's attack captured Hader crossroads during the afternoon. The following morning it beat off a counter-attack and then resumed its advance and took Mazrat Beit Jan after a fierce six-hour battle. The southern wing also made steady progress, capturing the village of Horfa on the first day. The Maatz crossroads were taken on Friday morning. At this point Ben-Gal ordered Yossi to take Tel Shams, a high rocky mound dominating the Damascus highway, without informing Eitan. This in itself was a mistake which emphasised the point that

Above left: Major-General Moshe Peled whose division was deployed to protect the right flank of the Israeli advance. Above: Major-General Dan Laner. Laner's division encountered the stiffest Syrian defences along the Damascus highway and despite heavy casualties, mounted a classic outflanking manoeuvre which placed his units in a position threatening Damascus. Laner, intensely fatigued, was eventually replaced by Peled.

Israelis on the move

'*Sunday Times* photographer Kelvin Brodie and I had joined the Israeli forces at first light on Thursday morning, as the counter-attack gained momentum. All through the previous night, endless convoys of tank transporters, half-tracks, ammunition lorries and artillery pieces were winding slowly up the tight curves of the main road to the Golan Heights. Looking up into the hills, we could see the flashes of heavy gunfire, followed a few seconds later by the crump of artillery explosions. We could also hear Israeli jets as they flew at low level above us without marking lights.

'It could only have been the Israeli army on the move – bread vans crammed with high-explosive shells; removal lorries full of rations and petrol cans; officers and other ranks driving themselves to the war in gleaming private cars. A major in full service dress except for his bright pink suede boots; an artillery sergeant sports a tee-shirt proclaiming '*Lets Go Mets*' – the fans' chant for a New York baseball team. In the back of a Dormobile, I saw a violin case; the owner, it turned out, had been playing in a symphony concert away from his home town. He had gone straight to his unit when his reserve unit was mobilised.

'When the tanks moved out, Brodie and I followed at a respectful distance. We were watching a Phantom sweeping in for a strike when puffs of white smoke rather like cotton wool, appeared in the bright blue sky. As the Phantom dived to attack the anti-aircraft positions, the white trail of a SAM missile appeared. There was a single bright flash, then the plane began tumbling almost lazily from the sky. Again, no parachute.

'While we were chatting with the tank crews, the Syrian guns began firing again. I had just begun to react, when a shell exploded 30 yards away, the blast tumbling me to the ground. Moments later, the Israeli tanks spotted Syrian T54s moving across the horizon and opened fire with their big 105mm guns, deafening Brodie and myself as we sprinted for cover. "I think it's time you left, my friends," an unruffled tank commander observed in perfect English. "It would be a shame to get hurt now."'

Nicholas Jacobson reported the 1973 war for the Sunday Times.

The Israeli counterattack on the Golan Heights

Israeli paras

Syrian and Moroccan forces

LEBANON

Mount Hermon

Syrian forces

to Damascus

Kiswe

Golani Brigade

Hader

Mazrat Beit Jan

Knaker

Israeli 7th Brigade

Horfa

▲ Tel Shams

Maatz

Khan Arnaba

Jaba

▲ Tel Shaar

Nasej

▲ Tel El-Alakieh

Israeli 17th, 79th and 19th Brigades

Quneitra

▲ Tel Maschara

▲ Tel Antar

Tapline Road

River Jordan

Nafekh

Syrian forces

Jordanian forces

Sanamin

Bnot Ya'aqov Bridge

Hushniya

▲ Tel Kudne

Iraqi forces

Great Leja

Rafid

Tel Faris ▲

SYRIA

Arik Bridge

Yehudia

SEA OF GALILEE

El'Al

Ein Gev

JORDAN

→ Israeli counterattacks to the ceasefire line 8-10 Oct 1973

→ Israeli advances 10-21 Oct 1973

--- 1967 ceasefire line

→ Arab forces

Above: A Syrian artillery shell explodes dangerously near to Israeli transport vehicles as they advance along the road to Damascus. The Syrians had mounted their strongest defences in this sector. Left: Israeli troops and armour halt their advance into Syria in order to rest and refuel. Below: An APC tows a knocked out tank away from the front for repair. Despite losses to Syrian ATGWs, the skilful deployment of armour and the speed with which damage was repaired allowed the IDF to maintain a strong field force superior to its Syrian counterpart.

since the Six-Day War the IDF had placed too much reliance on the tank alone, and had reduced the organic infantry and artillery elements of its armoured formations to a dangerously low level. The final assault on Tel Shams should have used infantry.

Nonetheless, Yossi complied with his orders. Leaving two companies to give covering fire, he led a third, 20 tanks strong, along a path which wound through the boulder-fields flanking the Syrian position, which he intended storming from the rear. Eight of his tanks got through, destroying 10 of the Syrians' which were taken unawares and engaged at close range. The Tel was now under artillery fire and Yossi detailed two of his vehicles to cover the attack of the remainder as they clawed their way towards the summit. His daring deserved to be rewarded with success, but at the critical moment concealed anti-tank guns opened fire, destroying four of the tanks and beating off the rest. Yossi was wounded and blown out of his turret, but that night a paratroop unit rescued him and his crews from under the Syrians' noses. Tel Shams remained in Syrian hands until the night of Saturday 13 October, when it was successfully stormed by the 31st Parachute Brigade.

To the south Laner's division, consisting of his own 17th and 79th Brigades as well as the 19th Brigade, which had been transferred from Peled's command, had encountered the toughest imaginable resistance as it advanced along the Damascus highway. This sector contained the Syrians' strongest defences and the leading Israeli brigade, Colonel Ran Sarig's 17th, was unable to penetrate beyond Khan Arnaba crossroads on 11 October. The column came under intense artillery and Sagger ATGW fire which disabled several tanks, while those behind were immobilised by mines when they took to the verges. Laner despatched the 19th Brigade south through Jaba with a view to bypassing the position, but at this point the Syrians mounted a counter-attack with infantry through the lava beds and succeeded in isolating those units which had reached Khan Arnaba.

As darkness fell Syrian RPG-7 anti-tank teams began claiming victims along the stalled column, again emphasising the terrible vulnerability of tanks lacking the protection of their own organic infantry. However, the division possessed a paratroop battalion and this was able to clean out the area in a night of heavy fighting.

The following morning Laner decided that he would still bypass Khan Arnaba in the wide right-flanking manoeuvre initiated the previous evening. The 19th Brigade captured Nasej and then, in company with the 17th, broke away to the east in a classic exploitation which ended just short of Knaker, leaving the 79th Brigade to follow after it had been replenished. All the indications were that the enemy had broken and was incapable of offering further serious resistance west of Damascus. The Syrian High Command gave way to panic, announcing that the fight would continue even after Damascus had fallen. One wretched brigade commander who had been forced to retreat was court-martialled, publicly stripped of his rank, and shot.

Syrian desperation

It seemed to President Hafez al Assad that while Syria was fighting for her life, Egypt was quite content to consolidate her initial gains in Sinai, and Cairo received a succession of frantic appeals to return to the offensive and so relieve the pressure on Assad's broken army. The Soviet Union, seriously alarmed by the Israeli offensive, was already attempting to make good Syria's losses and now threatened to intervene directly if Damascus was attacked.

The war on the northern front, however, was about to take a new direction. Laner had set up his divisional headquarters on Tel Shaar, which provided views right across the Syrian plain. That same afternoon, 12 October, a major armoured formation was spotted deploying for action some 10km (6 miles) to the south. At first it was thought to be Peled's division joining in the general advance, but Major-General

Above: Israeli-captured 130mm artillery, with adapted gun carriages, fires a salvo against Syrian positions. The Israeli aim was to bring their artillery within range of Damascus. Right: Amid a field of wrecked armour lies this Syrian SU100 medium SPG, a Soviet World War II design. Below: Carrying no more than weapons, ammunition and water, Israeli infantry scramble through the ruins of a Syrian village in pursuit of enemy units.

Above: An Israeli Jeep-mounted unit armed with recoilless guns. Units such as these provided support for the armoured advance, as they combined both mobile infantry and firepower. Below: A tank crew displays its jubilation at the defeat of the Syrians. The successful incursions into Syria and the subsequent containment of enemy counter-attacks broke Syrian morale and released valuable troops and aircraft for action on the Sinai front.

Yitzhak Hofi, the GOC Northern Command, assured Laner that Peled was still in position, although he had transferred another of Peled's brigades, the 20th, to Laner's command – this would be arriving shortly, but from an entirely different direction. That could only mean that the strange tanks were hostile. Laner promptly issued orders for the 17th and 19th Brigades to return from Knaker and take up positions facing south, orders which were at first received with total disbelief by commanders who were witnessing at first hand the disintegration of the Syrian Army.

The newcomers were the Iraqi 3rd Armoured Division, which consisted of two armoured brigades each with 130 tanks and a mechanised brigade with 50 tanks. The Iraqis had never fought an armoured battle before and this was very evident from the stiff manner in which their formations were handled. A probing attack, which indicated the direction their main thrust would take, was allowed to approach to within 275m (300 yards) of the 79th Brigade and then shot to pieces.

As dusk fell Laner deployed his four brigades in an 'open box' formation leaving a gap of 8km (5 miles) to the south between Tel Maschara and Nasej. As the night wore on the Iraqis were reported to be moving towards the trap but at 2100 hours they halted and for a while seemed suspicious. They were, however, only waiting for their second armoured brigade to catch up and at 0300 hours on 13 October they resumed their advance into the killing zone. The 19th Brigade, equipped with Shermans, opened fire at a range of only 180m (200 yards) and within minutes 80 Iraqi tanks were blazing fiercely; the remainder, harried by artillery, fled in disorder. The Israelis sustained no loss.

That could hardly be regarded as an end to the matter and Hofi ordered Eitan's division to take in more ground to its right, thus leaving Laner free to watch developments in the south. Eitan now had units of the crack Golani Infantry Brigade at his disposal and these, together with his paratroopers, conducted tactical defence during night time for the remainder of the war. Some of the equipment captured clearly indicated that Saudi Arabian troops had moved into the line.

Laner had identified the area known as the Great Leja as being the Iraqis' forming-up zone and on 13 October he pushed out the 19th Brigade to capture two hills which dominated this, Tel Antar and Tel El-Alakieh. On Tuesday 16 October the distant fluttering of red aerial pennants signalled the arrival of the Jordanian 40th Armoured Brigade, a formation which had fought well and gained the Israelis' respect during the Six-Day War. The Jordanians had no love for Syria, but equally they had none for Israel, and there was no doubt that they would fight. They advanced on Tel Maschara but were halted by the guns of the Israeli 17th Brigade and retired with the loss of 20 of their Centurions. Later in the day the Iraqis attacked Tel Antar and Tel El-Alakieh in a move which should have coincided with that of the Jordanians, but were held by the Israeli 19th and 20th Brigades and finally withdrew when attacked by the now disengaged 17th Brigade.

On 17 October Peled relieved Laner, who was now desperately tired, and resumed control of the 19th and 20th Brigades. From this point until the end of the war the Iraqis and Jordanians, joined briefly by the remnants of the Syrian 1st Armoured Division, mounted daily attacks on the southern flank of the Israeli enclave. These were not only punctual, starting every morning between 1000 and 1100 hours, but so uncoordinated that the Israelis experienced no difficulty in holding them. The most serious offensive against Israeli positions in the latter days of the war took place on 20 October and was repulsed with the loss of a further 60 Iraqi and 12 Jordanian tanks after a seven-hour battle.

The Syrian positions on Mount Hermon were attacked by Golani infantry and heliborne paratroops during the afternoon of 21 October. Fierce fighting raged throughout the night but by 1000 hours the following morning the vital peak was once more in Israeli hands. Syria's cup of bitterness was full. That evening, 22 October, both sides accepted the United Nations proposal for a ceasefire.

The war had cost Syria some 3500 dead, twice that number wounded and 1150 of her tanks. Iraq had lost almost 200 tanks and Jordan about 50. Israel's losses on the Golan front amounted to 772 killed and 2453 wounded; 250 Israeli tanks were knocked out, of which 150 were repairable. Under Hofi's calm direction the IDF had held the line in the most desperate circumstances and gone on to achieve a complete victory with none of the bitter recriminations and controversy which had accompanied operations in Sinai.

Bryan Perrett

Combat fatigue

Stress in modern war

Whatever nature a war may take, and despite the technologically advanced range of weapons that are now available, the actual fighting in any conflict is inevitably undertaken by a small number of fighting men. Their expertise and ability may well be the decisive factor in combat; and yet they almost always have to operate in conditions in which stresses of the most intense kind – both physical and mental – will make their task extremely difficult. Performing the simplest activities, such as reloading a rifle, can seem impossibly complex to an individual who has not slept for 36 hours and is in imminent danger of being killed.

The very basis of the military life – regimentation of the life of the individual, the establishment of rigid hierarchies, the attention paid to minute details of uniform, the seemingly endless and repetitive weapons drill – is, of course, designed to prepare the soldier for these moments of combat, in that he will be accustomed to behaving in an obedient and effective manner even under the stress of the battlefield. In addition, the psychological problems of stress have been more fully understood in the period since World War I and modern armies all incorporate 'stress tolerance exercises' into training programmes.

Nevertheless, training can only partially prepare troops for the particular stresses of combat. Clausewitz described the atmosphere of war as being composed of four factors: danger, physical effort, uncertainty and chance. It is the combination of these elements that is so debilitating, and the cumulative effect can be a marked deterioration in the performance of the individual soldier, the section, the platoon, or even large formations.

The background to stress on the battlefield is a combination of fatigue and lack of sleep. From the moment that soldiers engage in combat, tiredness of various kinds will gradually depress the efficiency of the soldier. Although every effort is usually made to ensure that each soldier is physically at his optimum, it is practically impossible to prepare a man so that he can disregard the loss of sleep, snatched meals, arduous physical activity and climatic extremes that commonly occur in combat.

A US GI who had served in Vietnam gave a graphic account of how tiredness diminished efficiency: 'I was constantly fatigued. The killing part is easy, but you're just fucking tired all the fucking time. Your strength is zapped out of your body. Waiting in a column going down a hill, you go to sleep leaning against a tree. Every day you're out on patrol. Go to this checkpoint, go to that checkpoint, go here, go

there. Day in, day out, day in, day out. You get into a mind-numbing routine and before long you're a fucking zombie.'

Loss of sleep is a common problem on the modern battlefield; gone are the days when armies disengaged at nightfall. Soldiers in forward positions have to be prepared for well-nigh constant action, and the development of night-fighting equipment has come on apace in the years since World War II. In its extremity, sleep deprivation can in itself lead to misperception of what is seen, the identification of false images, mistakes in identifying the passage of time, and the loss of control over thought processes, which tend to slow or to shift so that concentration is impossible.

These physical factors are, however, merely the background to the stresses of the modern battlefield. For the essential element that translates stress on the battlefield onto a different level from the kind of experience found in any other situation is the intensity of fear, accentuated by the destructive power of modern weapons. Fear is the body's natural reaction to danger; physically, the sensation is due to changes in the endocrine glands, blood circulation and nervous system that prepare the body for action or flight. It is characterised by such symptoms as a dry mouth, heightened awareness, and increased heartbeat.

These symptoms are ideal for preparing an individual to meet an immediate threat, but where the

The reactions to stress in battle can vary enormously. It can drain the individual of energy – above, a US serviceman in Vietnam, obviously affected by the strains of combat. In these circumstances the experience of NCOs is crucial in maintaining the fighting ability of a unit. Above right: Two NCOs of the Royal Highland Fusiliers in Northern Ireland demonstrate contrasting facets of the NCO's role. On the far right, a warrant officer, with baton and Sterling sub-machine gun, gives an example of unflinching determination in what is obviously a tense situation, while on the far left, another NCO gently helps away a young soldier who is unable to bear the strain any longer.

Active combat can be extremely debilitating for senior officers. Below left: Marshal Ky, vice-president of Vietnam, under strain in 1971. Commanders often work out unusual methods to reduce stress – below, Field Marshal Montgomery with his two dogs 'Rommel' and 'Hitler', outside his headquarters in Northern Europe in World War II. Montgomery created an atmosphere of isolated, almost domestic calm at his HQ in order to make command decisions unaffected by the confusion of battle.

tension is kept up for several hours, days or, in some cases, weeks, they can undermine a soldier's ability to function effectively. And whereas in the wars of previous ages safety was to be found a short distance away from the front line, or from the battlefield, 20th-century warfare has seen the battlefield extend to include large areas that may become vulnerable to artillery or air attack. So, for example, US troops in Vietnam came under a steady and debilitating series of mortar or sabotage attacks from the Viet Cong, even in the most heavily protected camps, while the Viet Cong in their turn would never know when the sudden clattering whirl of rotor blades would herald a surprise attack by US helicopter gunships.

The effects of fear, especially when combined with the physical stress associated with combat, rapidly result in the condition known as battle fatigue. The main symptom of this condition is that a soldier reacts to harmless events, such as the firing of friendly artillery or a small explosion in the distance, as if they represented a real threat to his person.

A GI in Vietnam recalled the effects of fear under intense combat conditions: 'Thank God the Vietnamese out there that night didn't speak English. They figured we were just crazy, running around in the dark shooting and hollering. Some of them started jumping out in front of us, throwing down their rifles, screaming *Chu Hoi* [I surrender]. Naturally, we were so scared, we were blowing them away anyway.'

The development of more complicated weaponry, and the higher skills that may be needed to operate such equipment, has meant that a particularly insidious and subtle form of stress in modern war is what military psychologists describe as 'skill fatigue'. This condition can be doubly dangerous in that the soldier may well be unaware of the extent to which his capacity to carry out complex, coordinated tasks has deteriorated. Skills that are more recently acquired are the ones that deteriorate the most rapidly; but on the other hand, the increasing pace of technological advance means that soldiers may well be required to use weapons systems on which they have had only a few months training.

Combat fatigue of various kinds is, then, an increasing problem for modern armies where the ordinary soldier is concerned; and it also has its effects all the way up the command structure. For although officers may not suffer the same physical stress as the men they command (or in the case of junior officers may be more able to withstand it) the pressures of responsibility in a fluid, potentially disastrous military situation can wreak havoc upon the personality. Both the Egyptian and Israeli armies experienced problems at the very top during the Yom Kippur War, caused by the kind of stress that the responsibilities of combat command brought in their train.

It was on the Egyptian side that the problems of tension at the top were worst. For when the Israeli defeat of the Egyptian armoured forces on 14 October

Army units come under greatest strain when their members become casualties, and the prompt treatment of wounded troops is one of the most important elements in maintaining morale. Above: The American Army in Vietnam made every effort to evacuate wounded soldiers as rapidly as possible, and here wounded casualties await helicopter transport back to base during combat just south of the DMZ. Right: The Israeli Army takes enormous pains to recover wounded personnel (here a tankman is pulled out of his Centurion during the Sinai battles of October 1973) and takes pride in the fact that very few dead Israelis are left for the enemy to recover.

exposed the West Bank of the Suez Canal to an Israeli offensive, General Saad Mamoun, commander of the Egyptian Second Army, had a heart attack, and had to be replaced at this critical juncture. The Israeli crossing of the Canal caused intense and acrimonious debate in Egypt: Chief of Staff Saad el Din Shazli insisted that troops must be withdrawn from Sinai to meet the threat, while President Anwar Sadat refused. Shazli was, according to some reports, in a state of extreme exhaustion and near collapse when

he was relieved of his post by Sadat on 20 October.

Stress is, then, a central factor in war, and affects an army from the bottom to the very top. Without an appreciation of the difficulties of acting under the physical and mental pressures that are unique to the battlefield it is impossible to understand military history. And it is clear that if an army can resist these stresses more effectively than can its opponent, it will be well on the road to victory.

Alexander McNair-Wilson

Key Weapons

AWACS

The origins of the AEW (airborne early warning) concept can be traced back to the work carried out by the US Navy during World War II. The great naval battles fought in the Pacific demonstrated the pre-eminence of the carrier-borne attack aircraft over the surface ship and the need to extend the range at which such strike forces could be detected. The immediate answer to the problem was radar and it was quickly realised that such equipment would be even more effective if it were possible to mount it in an aircraft which could fly ahead of the fleet and transmit its data back via a radio link. Such a flying 'radar picket' would enormously increase the range at which attacks could be detected and accordingly, Project Cadillac was instituted to develop just such a system.

Cadillac resulted in the TBM-3W Avenger and the B-1W Fortress. Both these Project Cadillac aircraft had a number of technical limitations not the least of which was the difficulty of distinguishing a target echo from the radio reflections generated by the sea when radar was used against low flying intruders.

Douglas and Lockheed produced the US Navy's second generation of AEW aircraft, both of which first flew in the late 1940s. The Douglas product, the AD-3W Skyraider, entered service during 1949 and developed versions remained on front-line service until 1967. A carrier-borne type, the AD-3W carried a pilot and two radar operators and was equipped with a version of the AN/APS-20 set. During 1950, this first model was superseded by the AD-4W which featured a number of airframe improvements.

Lockheed's Warning Star development of the Con-stellation airliner proved to be as long-lived as the AEW Skyraider. Conceived as a replacement for the B-1W, the prototype Warning Star first flew in June 1949 and entered service with the US Navy, under the designation WV-2, during 1954. Equipped with the ubiquitous AN/APS-20 radar in a belly radome com-bined with a dorsal mounted height-finding set, the WV-2 was a true airborne command post capable of using its radar information to direct the whole spec-trum of sea and airborne forces.

With a crew of between 20 and 30, the Warning Star remained in service until the late 1960s. The type's performance so impressed the US Air Force (USAF) that it ordered its own version in 1951 as the RC-121C. Entering service during 1953, RC-121s (later EC-121s) remained in front-line service until 1976 and played an important role in the Vietnam War. Arriving in Southeast Asia during 1965, the 552nd Airborne Warning and Control Wing's 'Con-nies' initially set up a radar barrier to detect south-bound sorties by the North Vietnamese Air Force. When these did not materialise, the Wing switched to being airborne command posts for the air battles generated by the Rolling Thunder and Linebacker bombing campaigns.

Aboard the US Navy's carriers the AEW Skyraid-ers were supplemented by the much larger Grumman E-1B Tracers in 1960. Based on the C-1A Trader airframe, the E-1B was equipped with the AN/APS-82 radar. Retaining elements of the earlier APS-20, the AN/APS-82 offered a detection range against aircraft of 80 to 90 nautical miles but still suffered from the problem of 'clutter' generated by unwanted echoes being reflected back from the sea. As with all the AEW radars developed up to this time, such unwanted returns could quite easily obscure a target like from a low flying aircraft, making its location

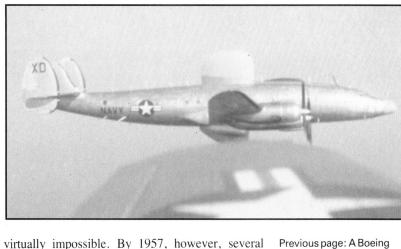

virtually impossible. By 1957, however, several technological breakthroughs suggested that the clut-ter problem was soluble and in 1959, General Electric was issued with a contract to develop the AN/APS-96 radar for future shipboard AEW use. This new set, amongst other things, incorporated an AMTI (air-borne moving target indicator) facility. This equip-ment filtered out all the permanent echoes from the radar screen and was able to differentiate between fast and slow moving objects.

AN/APS-96 was installed in the Grumman E-2 Hawkeye which entered service during 1965. To date, the Hawkeye has been produced in three distinct versions, the latest of which, the E-2C, is the US Navy's current carrier-borne AEW aircraft. The APS-96 radar has itself been the subject of develop-ment and in its APS-125 form, is matched to the current airframe. The main identification feature of the Hawkeye is its dorsal rotodome. Unlike all pre-vious scanner installations, the rotodome is an integ-ral structure containing fixed aerial elements which rotates as a whole.

At the same time as the Hawkeye's service intro-duction, the USAF was in the middle of its ORT (overland radar technology) programme. Convinced by the RC/EC-121 of the operational effectiveness of AEW aircraft in the defence of continental America, the ORT project was designed, as its name suggested, to develop the optimum AEW radar for use over land. Previously all the radars used in this field by the USAF had originally been designed for use over water and as such had certain limitations when used over land. By 1967, radars from Westinghouse and Hughes were

Previous page: A Boeing E-3 Sentry AWACS aircraft in flight. Based on the civilian 707 the E-3 is immediately recognisable because of its large fuselage-mounted rotodome. Above: One of the first early warning aircraft, the Lockheed EC-121 Warning Star, which with a range of 3380km (2100 miles) was an effective – if relatively simple – AEW platform.

Below: A Grumman E-1B Tracer AEW aircraft comes into land on the deck of the carrier USS *Essex* in 1968. The E-1B was the forerunner of the more advanced E-2 Hawkeye.

Grumman E-2C Hawkeye

Type Carrier-borne AEW aircraft
Dimensions Span 24.56m (80ft 7in); length 17.55m (57ft 7in); height 5.59m (18ft 4 in)
Weight Empty 17,241kg (38,009lb); maximum take-off 23,541kg (51,900lb)
Powerplant Two 3660kW (4910hp) Allison T56A-425 turboprops

Performance Maximum level speed 602km/h (374mph)
Endurance 6 hours
Ceiling 9390m (30,800ft)

Crew complement Flight crew of two plus three or four systems operators
Electronic equipment AN /APS-125 search radar, AN/ALR-59 passive detection system, AN/ARC-51 UHF radio, AN/ARC-158 UHF data link, AN/ARQ-34 HF radio/data link and AN/ASN-92 inertial navigation system

adjudged to be worthy of development and, in the same year, Boeing and McDonnell-Douglas were awarded contracts to develop airframes to carry the new radar. In the event, Boeing won the airframe competition with a development of its 707-320B airliner and Westinghouse that for the radar.

The new aircraft, known as AWACS (airborne warning and control system), first flew in 1972 and entered service with the USAF late in 1977 as the E-3 Sentry. Without doubt, the E-3 is the ultimate expression of the AEW concept, providing an ability to 'see' out to ranges of 370km (230 miles), five options in the way in which its radar can detect targets, extensive computer facilities to process the received data, an on-station endurance of six hours which can

Above: A Grumman E-2C Hawkeye displays its rotodome and its unusual four-finned tail. The rotodome mounts a General Electric AN/APS-96 surveillance radar and revolves through a fairing-mounted motor. Right: The cramped interior of an E-2C which houses the aircraft's four systems operators. Below: An E-2C Hawkeye photographed standing on an airfield in preparation for an AEW patrol.

be extended by in-flight refuelling, excellent working conditions for the operators and an extensive communications suite through which to pass information reliably and securely.

Indeed, far from being merely an adjunct to military operations, the effectiveness of the E-3 is such that it has become a tool of world diplomacy in its own right. The hostile Israeli response to its sale to Saudi Arabia reflects the fact that today's AEW types can materially affect regional balances of power and America has used the E-3 to political ends with a policy of deploying them in support of friendly nations in times of crisis, so that, for example, Saudi Arabian F-15 interceptors were able to shoot down Iranian F-4 Phantoms in June 1984 after being alerted by a US E-3 patrolling the Gulf.

Despite America's seeming monopoly in AEW aircraft, two other countries, Great Britain and the Soviet Union, have managed to produce such systems. The Royal Navy operated the Skyraider AEW1 during the 1950s and in 1958 Fairey flew an AEW variant of its Gannet anti-submarine aircraft which entered service with 849 Squadron in 1960. With a crew of three, the Gannet AEW3 carried the familiar APS-20 radar in a belly radome. Even after 15 years service, numerous modifications had kept this radar relatively effective and the sets installed in the Gannets could detect targets up to 320km (200 miles) away.

The Gannet AEW3 remained operational until the de-commissioning of HMS *Ark Royal* in 1978/9. The rundown of the Royal Navy's conventional carrier force had left many Gannets redundant long before this and 12 of their radars were installed in Avro Shackleton airframes to provide the Royal Air Force (RAF) with an interim AEW platform. The first Shackleton AEW2 flew in September 1971 and became operational with 8 Squadron, RAF Strike Command in 1972. Since that time, the type has undergone various modifications to make it more effective, but it was never intended to be anything more than a stop-gap until the arrival of a definitive type.

Such an aircraft appeared in the form of the British Aerospace Nimrod AEW3 which despite a much-delayed development programme, promises to be the

Above: The E-3A first flew in 1972, representing a successful combination of a Boeing 707 airframe and a powerful Westinghouse radar system. Left: Operators at work on the multi-purpose consoles of an E-3A; 13 specialists work within the E-3A's fuselage, able to process vast amounts of information and relay it on directly to friendly aircraft in the area.

Right: An E-3A Sentry deployed by Nato. Such aircraft were used to great effect in support of Israeli air operations over the Lebanon in 1982. Below: A side-view of an E-3A on public display at an air show, revealing the aircraft's rotodome and two of its Pratt & Whitney turbofans.

Boeing E-3A Sentry

Type AEW aircraft
Dimensions Span 44.42m (145ft 9in); length
46.61m (152ft 11in); height 12.60m (41ft 4in)
Weight Maximum take-off 147,400kg (325,000lb)
Powerplant Four 9526kg (21,000lb) Pratt &
Whitney TF331-100/100A turbofans

Performance Maximum speed 853km/h
(530mph); typical patrol speed 563km/h (350mph)
Endurance 6 hours
Ceiling Over 8850m (29,000ft)

Crew complement Four flight crew and 13 systems
operators
Electronic equipment Westinghouse AN/APY-1
search radar (frequency 3-4GHz), AN/APX-103
Mk10/12 IFF system, Tadil-A data link, Tadil-C data
link, AN/ARN-120 Omega navigation system and
HF, VHF and UHF radios

Below: The British
Aerospace Nimrod AEW3.
Based on the de Havilland
Comet the AEW3 has been
transformed into a less
than elegant aircraft,
'disfigured' by two
bulbous radomes at front
and rear (below inset). The
complexity of the Nimrod's
electronics makes it
comparable in function
and capability to the E-3A.
Bottom: An AEW3 flies
alongside a Shackleton
AEW2.

most effective system of its kind in the world. Based
on the Nimrod MR1 maritime reconnaissance aircraft, the AEW3 carries a very advanced Marconi
radar which is optimised for use against both aircraft
and shipping. Unlike its Russian and American counterparts, the Nimrod uses two scanners mounted in the
nose and tail rather than a rotodome. This is a uniquely
British configuration which it is claimed offers
superior radar performance.

The losses of the Falklands conflict highlighted the
importance of AEW cover for a naval force operating
at extreme range and prompted the Royal Navy to
re-enter the field with a conversion of the Westland
Sea King helicopter. In 1981, EMI had proposed such
an aircraft for use aboard the new Invincible-class
carriers but the idea was not taken up. As the losses in
the South Atlantic mounted, the necessity for an
AEW type became clearly obvious and the first AEW
Sea King was fitted aboard HMS *Illustrious* when she
left for the Falklands in August 1982. The AEW Sea
King is unique in this class of aeroplane as it is the only
helicopter to be so used. The radar installed is a
derivative of the EMI Searchwater maritime surveillance type and uses a scanner mounted in an inflatable
radome which is carried on the helicopter's starboard
side. Despite being produced in just 11 weeks, the
AEW Sea King appears to be a most workmanlike
solution with a radar performance described as having
'exceeded expectations'.

The Soviet Union's interest in AEW aircraft must
be a long-standing one when it is considered just what
an enormous land mass its air force has to defend. In
view of this, Western observers were not surprised
when such an aeroplane was identified in 1969. Based
on the Tu-114 airliner from the Tupolev bureau, the
Tu-126 Moss uses a radar known in the West as Flat
Jack, the antenna for which is housed in an 11m (36ft)
diameter rotodome carried above the rear fuselage.
American assessments of the Moss's capabilities
have been derisory, an estimate perhaps borne out by
a total production run of only 10 or 12 aircraft.

Four years after the discovery of the Tu-126,
American satellite reconnaissance revealed a second-
generation Soviet AEW type based on the Ilyushin
Il-76 Mainstay jet transport. Dubbed SUAWACS the

British Aerospace Nimrod AEW3

Type AEW aircraft
Dimensions Span 35.08m (115ft 1in); length
41.97m (137ft 8½in); height 10.67m (35ft)
Weight No figures yet released
Powerplant Four 5520kg (12,140lb) Rolls-Royce
RB168-20 Spey Mk 250 turbofans

Performance Maximum speed 926km/h
(575mph); typical patrol speed 370km/h (230mph)
Endurance 10-plus hours
Ceiling Approximately 12,800m (42,000ft)

Crew complement Flight crew comprising pilot,
co-pilot and engineer and tactical crew of one
communications officer and five systems operators
Electronic equipment Marconi pulse-Doppler
search radar (frequency 2-4GHz), ARI.18240/1 ESM
system, Jubilee Guardsman IFF interrogator, LF, HF
and UHF radios, VHF/UHF secure voice link, digital
data link and Smiths SFS.6 automatic flight control
system

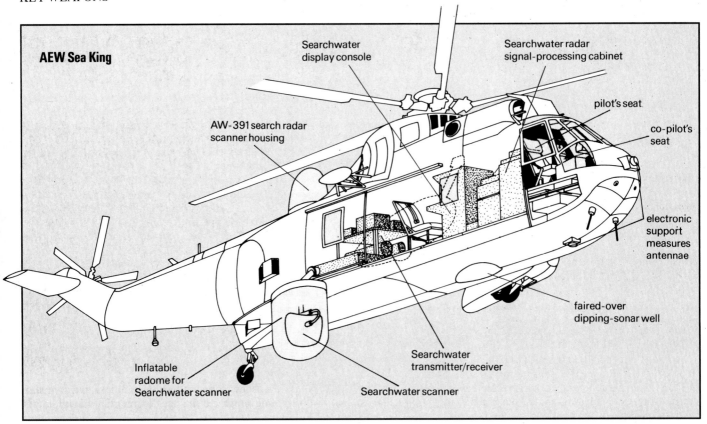

AEW Sea King

Searchwater display console

Searchwater radar signal-processing cabinet

AW-391 search radar scanner housing

pilot's seat

co-pilot's seat

electronic support measures antennae

faired-over dipping-sonar well

Searchwater transmitter/receiver

Inflatable radome for Searchwater scanner

Searchwater scanner

AEW Mainstay is regarded as a much more effective system than its predecessor with intelligence sources describing the radar used as being of a particularly advanced type.

Although the producers of AEW aircraft are small in number, the countries using them are rapidly increasing. One of the leaders in this export market is the Hawkeye with sales and firm orders currently standing at 20 aircraft. Although a carrier-based type, the E-2C with its APS-125 radar has proved to be equally effective over land. Customers include Japan, Israel, Egypt and Singapore.

An important factor in the Hawkeye's sales success is the fact that it has been used operationally both in Southeast Asia and the Middle East. Its most recent combat experience has been with the Israelis who used it extensively in the invasion of Lebanon in 1982. During this campaign, the Israeli Air Force's E-2s were used as airborne command posts to direct F-15 and F-16 fighters against Syrian MiGs trying to intercept friendly reconnaissance and strike forces.

Even more successful in sales terms is the E-3 Sentry with 18 supplied to a multinational Nato force, five ordered by Saudi Arabia and four by France. The Nato force grew out of the belief that an AEW capability was vital for the defence of western Europe but far too expensive to produce domestically. By 1974, the various partners were agreed that the E-3 made the most economic sense but it was to take another seven years of stormy debate (during which the UK withdrew from the programme and went ahead with the Nimrod) before a final agreement was reached to purchase 18 aircraft in 1981.

Airborne early warning has come a long way since its beginnings in the primitive TBM-3W of 1943. Whilst the capabilities of the radars and related equipment have been vastly improved, the basic concept of being able to detect an enemy attack in sufficient time to respond effectively has remained constant. What

has changed is AEW aircraft being a luxury available only to the richest and most advanced countries. In today's military terms, AEW is a necessity for the creation of any effective air defence system, a factor which is demonstrated by the ever increasing proliferation of these communication systems.

Tupolev Tu-126 Moss

Type AEW aircraft
Dimensions Span 51.20m (168ft); length 55.20m (181ft 1in); height 16.05m (52ft 8in)
Weight (Estimated) Empty 90,000kg (200,000lb); maximum take-off 170,000kg (374,785lb)
Powerplant Four 11,900kW (15,000hp) Kuznetsov NK-12MV turboprops

Performance Maximum level speed 850km/h (528mph); typical patrol speed 650km/h (404mph)
Endurance 18 hours
Ceiling Not known

Crew complement Reported as 12 including flight crew and systems operators
Electronic equipment Flat Jack search radar, SRO-2M IFF transponder, Sirena-3 radar warning receiver, RSBN-25 short-range navigation system, R-831 UHF radio, RSIU-5 VHF radio and ARL-5 data link

Above: The British Sea King AEW helicopter was developed as a flexible AEW aircraft, able to operate from small carriers like HMS *Illustrious*. Although of limited capability compared to conventional AEW aircraft, the Sea King is highly regarded by the Royal Navy, as it is able to identify aircraft at ranges far beyond that of a frigate or destroyer.

Below: The Soviet airborne early warning aircraft, the Tupolev Tu-126 Moss. Observed in the West for the first time in 1969 it is claimed that the Moss was deployed during the Indo-Pakistan War of 1971.

Drive to destruction

The defeat of the Israeli counter-attack in Sinai, October 1973

During the evening of 7 October a senior officers' conference took place at the Israeli Southern Command Headquarters. The purpose of the meeting was to develop plans for a counter-attack against the Egyptian positions the following day. Present were General David Elazar, the Israeli Defence Forces (IDF) chief of staff, Major-General Shmuel Gonen, the GOC Southern Command, Major-General Avraham Adan, the commander of the first reserve armoured division to arrive in Sinai, and Major-General Avraham Mandler, whose regular armoured division had been in continuous action for the previous 36 hours, since the Egyptian assaults across the Suez Canal on the afternoon of 6 October, and had lost more than half its tanks. The atmosphere was tense and the faces of the Israeli commanders revealed strain and fatigue. Elazar was additionally carrying the burden of the desperate battle being waged on the Golan, while Gonen and Mandler had spent the previous two days trying to cope with the unexpected scale of the Egyptian crossing of the canal. Adan had been up to the front that afternoon and seen for himself the chaotic conditions in which fighting was taking place. The conference should also have been attended by Major-General Ariel Sharon, whose reserve armoured division was also moving into Sinai, but in his absence Elazar decided to begin.

Lacking detailed intelligence, Gonen could only present a very general picture of the situation. He suggested that now the reserve armoured divisions had arrived, the Egyptians' own bridges should be seized and used to effect a crossing in force to the West Bank of the canal. This response was very much in the tradition of the IDF and received qualified approval from Adan and Mandler, who both felt, nonetheless, that with the resources presently available, such a course was slightly premature. Elazar, however, was of the opinion that immediate action was necessary to prevent a further deterioration of the situation. What he proposed, therefore, was a counter-attack by Adan's division along a north-south axis from El Qantara towards the Great Bitter Lake – an axis east of and parallel to the canal, as this would drive into the flank of the Egyptian Second Army's purported break-out. Because of the experience of the previous two days a 3km (2 mile) gap was to be left between the right flank of the advance and the coordinated Egyptian anti-tank defence lining the canal. While Adan's attack was in progress, Sharon's division would remain temporarily inactive opposite the Great Bitter

The immediate reaction of the Israeli High Command to the Egyptian invasion was to deploy armoured forces as quickly as possible into the battle area in order to contain the enemy. The fatal mistake of deploying armour without infantry support was soon realised when, despite the occasional success (top, an Israeli M51 knocks out Egyptian armour), Egyptian ATGW teams inflicted severe casualties against Israeli tanks (above, the wrecked hulls of an IDF M60 in the foreground and an M48 to the rear).

Lake. If Adan ran into difficulty, Sharon would reinforce him; if, on the other hand, Adan succeeded, Sharon would carry out a similar drive into the flank of the Egyptian Third Army. It was emphasised that the activation of Sharon's division in pursuit of either option must receive Elazar's personal approval. Mandler's division would remain on the defensive in the southern sector.

This, then, was the plan which had been adopted when Sharon himself arrived at the conference. He made a typically impatient, swashbuckling entrance, announcing that he had a plan of his own which not only included crossing the canal but also the relief of those Bar-Lev strongpoints that were still holding out. Elazar told him that a course of action had already been decided upon and, instructing him to discuss the details of the operation with Gonen, he left for his own headquarters. This was unfortunate, for Gonen actually possessed less seniority than either Adan or Sharon and clearly felt uncomfortable about imposing his authority. The result of this further discussion was that both reserve divisional commanders believed that they possessed more operational autonomy than was actually the case.

The plan itself was based upon a false premise,

although none of those attending the conference believed this to be so at the time. At this stage the Egyptians, despite the deployment of over 600 tanks on the east bank, had no intention of breaking out into Sinai and embarking on the sort of mobile war which favoured Israeli tactics. Instead, they were content to remain in the strictly limited, but easily defensible, objectives they had attained and to allow the IDF to batter itself to pieces against their anti-tank defences.

Adan held his own orders group at 0300 hours on 8 October and although he was quietly optimistic, the divisional situation was far from satisfactory. Only two of his armoured brigades were available for immediate deployment, Colonel Gabi Amir's 460th, which had been in action the previous day and now possessed only 50 tanks, and Colonel Natke Nir's 600th with 70 tanks, which was actually moving into the line. The third armoured brigade, the 217th commanded by Colonel Arieh Keren, was still advancing along the coast road from El Arish, while the division's mechanised infantry brigade, which included an organic Sherman battalion, had not yet left Israel. Only a very small proportion of the divisional artillery had arrived. Perhaps worst of all, Adan's reconnaissance unit had been detached and was now hunting the Egyptian commandos who had been inserted behind Israeli lines during the first hours of the war. Deprived of its services, Adan would have to feel his way forward without certain knowledge of where the enemy was. Finally, some aspects of the operational plan became blurred when Gonen issued amended orders with some ambiguous phrasing.

Nevertheless, by 0600 hours Adan had completed his deployment for the attack. Amir's brigade had as its objective the area opposite El Firdan, while Nir was to advance further south towards the area opposite Ismailiya. Keren's brigade, just arrived, would go straight into action and drive further south to the area of the Matzmed strongpoint. One tank battalion, under the control of Brigadier-General Kalman Magen, was held in reserve in order to guard the division's rear.

Above: The Egyptian defensive screen in Sinai made operations by the Israeli Air Force very hazardous – here, Egyptian infantry proudly display a piece of an Israeli Phantom shot down near the front line. Below: An Israeli M60 tank and two Greyhound half-track personnel carriers use dead ground, provided by a ridge, to conceal their presence from the enemy.

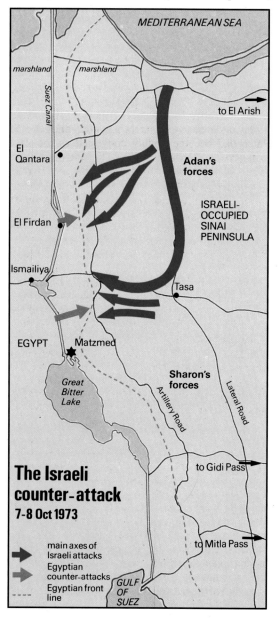

The Israeli counter-attack
7-8 Oct 1973

➡ main axes of Israeli attacks
➡ Egyptian counter-attacks
---- Egyptian front line

The attack began at 0800 hours amid scenes of chaos and confusion. A supporting air strike by the Israeli Air Force hit some of Nir's tanks, and when Adan's air controllers remonstrated they were told that, because of the Egyptian missile threat, all air activity was being coordinated by higher headquarters. Communications were also affected by Egyptian jamming, to such effect that at one point Adan lost contact with his brigades. Thirdly, the actual axis of advance passed to the east of the Egyptians, with the result that the division drove past Egyptian positions with little or no direct contact beyond artillery fire. This led to such unfounded optimism at Southern Command that at 1030 hours Gonen, with Elazar's approval, ordered Sharon's division to commence its advance southwards.

This Sharon was reluctant to do, for he was closer to the front and had just witnessed the entire operational concept collapse in the most dramatic fashion. Adan, realising that his line of advance lay too far to the east,

had swung his brigades hard right so that they were now approaching their objectives, not obliquely as intended, but head on. One after another the Israeli battalions drove into an inferno of artillery, tank and ATGW fire from both sides of the canal. The original plan had required Sharon to support Adan if he got into difficulty, but his objections to this latest order (to advance south) were ignored and at 1100 hours he began moving towards the southern sector. For his part Adan felt bitter about the decision, which left his left flank completely uncovered.

Thus, for the remainder of the day Adan's armoured brigades, lacking mechanised infantry or air support which could have dealt with the deadly ATGW defences, found themselves involved in a fruitless battle against the much stronger Egyptian deployment, sustaining serious loss. One of Amir's battalions had 19 of its 26 tanks destroyed within minutes and one of Nir's battalions lost 18 tanks in a similar period.

Fighting until sunset

At about 1400 hours Gonen realised the enormity of the mistake which had been made and recalled Sharon. The latter had a long way to travel and his leading units did not start entering the southern edge of the battle, thereby relieving some of the intense pressure which had built up against Keren's brigade, until well after 1700 hours. By then a fresh crisis had developed. At 1700 hours the Egyptian 2nd Infantry Division mounted a counter-attack with the 24th Armoured and 117th Mechanised Brigades, as did the Egyptian 16th Infantry Division with the 14th Armoured and 3rd Mechanised Brigades. These were simply intended to expand the Egyptian bridgehead, which had become unduly congested as the 21st Armoured and 23rd Mechanised Divisions continued to cross from the West Bank during the day. To the Israelis, however, they were heavy with strategic menace and Adan's battered units had the greatest difficulty in holding their ground, the last hour of daylight being a nightmare in which they fought with the full glare of the setting sun in their eyes.

As darkness fell, Adan disengaged. His division had lost 70 of its 170 tanks, but 20 of these were recovered during the night. The attack had failed because it had been hastily planned without adequate intelligence, because of poor staff work and because the resources available did not provide a satisfactory balance between arms. This does not detract from the fact that the Egyptians, who were frankly surprised at the ease with which the battalion-sized attacks had been contained, had conducted a brilliant defence throughout the day and had even been able to develop their own plans a little further, despite the considerable but still acceptable losses they had themselves incurred.

By the end of the day the Egyptians controlled an area of penetration up to 8km (5 miles) east of the canal waterline, including sections of the Artillery Road. In this the Egyptian forces had completed the first stage of their offensive, though not to the planned depth of 11km (7 miles). Conversely, the Israeli counter-attack, while a failure, did contribute towards containing the Egyptians. A breathing space had been gained during which the IDF commanders could attempt to set aside their differences, analyse the failure of their strategy and prepare a renewed and more effective offensive. **Bryan Perrett**

2.7kg (5.95lb) HEAT warhead — boost nozzles — wrap-round boost motor — rear nozzles — sustain motor — folding stabilising fins

range 300–3000m (330–3300yds)
time to maximum range 27 secs
armour penetration 400mm (15¾in)

target tank — missile is 'gathered' onto target and tracked by line of sight to impact — carrying-case lid used as launching ramp — monocular periscopic sight for use at ranges of over 1000m (1100yds) — operator guides missile with joystick control unit via fine wires attached to tail of missile

AT-3 Sagger anti-tank guided missile

The generals fall out

Dissension in the Israeli High Command

The Israeli commanders responsible for the conduct of the Yom Kippur War were men who had fought as company and battalion commanders during the War of Independence against their Arab neighbours in 1948-49, and had risen steadily in their profession as the Israeli Defence Forces (IDF) won their spectacular victories in 1956 and 1967. They were also strong-willed, outspoken personalities who had been brought up in the tradition that the Arabs could sustain 100 major defeats and still survive, but Israel could not survive one. Used to success arising directly from the exercise of their own initiative, they were not easy men to command in a battle which was going badly. It is in this light that the dissensions which arose between senior officers in the week following the Egyptian attack of 6 October must be examined.

If the sheer scale of the Egyptian canal crossing was a tremendous psychological blow, the failure of the IDF's response, and in particular that of the major counter-attack staged on 8 October, was an even greater one. Unused to defeat, senior officers looked for a scapegoat and soon Major-General Shmuel Gonen, the GOC Southern Command, found himself the centre of blame. In fact, Gonen had reported the Egyptian build-up to the High Command as it was taking place but, beyond increasing the general state of alert, he was not allowed to take further precautionary measures. It was, of course, quite true that in the recent past there had been numerous large-scale troop movements on the West Bank of the canal which had led to nothing, and since the Soviet Union was already suggesting openly that General Moshe Dayan's reinforcement of the Golan Front was the precursor of an Israeli attack, it was deemed impolitic to adjust the positions of major Israeli formations in Sinai for the present.

It was equally true that Gonen had failed to read the battle correctly as it developed during 6 and 7 October, but such criticism could be levelled at the Israeli General Staff as a whole, and in any event it would have been virtually impossible to penetrate the 'fog of war' which obscured what was taking place along the length of the canal.

Gonen enjoyed the complete support of Major-General Avraham Mandler, the commander of the one regular armoured division based in Sinai. (Mandler was killed on 13 October, his place being taken by Brigadier-General Kalman Magen.) The GOC Southern Command was, however, less fortunate in his relationships with the commanders of his two reserve armoured divisions, Major-General Avraham Adan and Major-General Ariel Sharon (who had himself been GOC Southern Command until July 1973), both of whom were technically senior to him and neither of whom had any great regard for his abilities or those of his staff.

Sharon, a former paratrooper, was a notably awkward and ungovernable subordinate who was determined to have his own way. During the 1956 war he had commanded the unit which had captured the Mitla Pass, but had then exceeded his orders and incurred needless casualties, coming dangerously close to a court martial. In 1967 he had commanded the division which successfully stormed the Abu Aweigila fortified complex, and he had entered the political arena shortly afterwards. Adan was a quieter but equally determined individual who believed that Gonen was 'out of touch with reality.' To make matters worse, neither Adan nor Sharon had any great liking for each other and friction between the two was inevitable.

After the failure of the counter-attack on 8 October there was a loss of confidence in Gonen. General David Elazar, the IDF's chief of staff, despatched General Chaim Bar-Lev to Southern Command as his

Above: While General Chaim Bar-Lev (left) recommended on two separate occasions that Major-General Ariel Sharon (centre) should be relieved of his command, General Moshe Dayan (right), Israel's defence minister, was reluctant to dismiss Sharon on the grounds that the removal of such a popular figure (with a considerable degree of political influence) might severely damage morale during the desperate battles of the Yom Kippur War.

Right: Stark reminder of a failed Israeli counter-attack – the wrecked hull of a Centurion lies half-buried in the sand. In the foreground are the helmets, bloody rags and skeletal remains of what was once a tank crew. It was the scale of the losses in the first few days of fighting that put such strain on the commanders of the IDF in Sinai.

between the Egyptian Second and Third Armies, a discovery of critical importance.

After the events of 8 October, Elazar decided that the IDF could not sustain the current rate of attrition in Sinai and Southern Command went onto the defensive. It was agreed that in future, attacks would be made with balanced forces in which tanks received the direct support of mechanised infantry and artillery. There was general agreement, too, that the Egyptians could only be beaten if the IDF effected a crossing in force to the West Bank of the canal.

Disputes and decisions

That did not mean that dissension among the Israelis' higher command echelon was at an end; if anything there were more disputes, although the extremely frank exchanges lacked the potentially destructive quality of the early days of the war. When the Israelis did mount their successful offensive on 15/16 October, Sharon bickered repeatedly with Bar-Lev about the way the crossing of the canal was to be achieved and even went so far as to propose tasks for some of Adan's units, but was overruled. He then became involved in a furious argument with Adan about whose division was to exploit the crossing, while Adan angrily pointed out that his own troops were having to complete tasks which should have been the responsibility of Sharon's division.

Ironically, perhaps, Adan had the last word: Elazar and Bar-Lev decided that it would be his division, followed by Magen's, which would spearhead the offensive across the canal, driving along the western shore of the Great Bitter Lake, while Sharon merely played a supporting role, holding the northern shoulder of the penetration. Sharon felt that he should be allowed to conduct a simultaneous drive against the rear of the Egyptian Second Army, and naturally chafed at this less attractive role. Nevertheless, the most insubordinate of the Israeli generals, and the one whose actions had led to three requests for his dismissal by the two separate commanders he served under, emerged with his reputation enhanced, and his political career in full bloom. **Bryan Perrett**

Above: General David Elazar (left), the Israeli chief of staff, sits with the GOC Southern Command, Major-General Shmuel Gonen (right) during a command meeting. An enquiry after the war criticised Gonen's handling of his forces in the early days of the war. Gonen was not replaced during the fighting, but General Chaim Bar-Lev (above right, arriving in Sinai) was sent to the front as Elazar's personal representative with authority over Gonen.

personal representative, with authority over Gonen. A lesser man would have found the position intolerable and resigned, but rather than add to public concern, Gonen agreed to remain as Bar-Lev's deputy, a task which he fulfilled efficiently for the remainder of the war. One of his last acts as GOC Southern Command was to recommend Elazar to relieve Sharon of his command; despite specific orders to the contrary, Sharon had persisted in mounting an attack of his own on 9 October. Bar-Lev was equally unprepared to put up with any nonsense and on 12 October he made the first of two similar recommendations that Sharon be dismissed. General Dayan, the minister of defence, refused to accept these on the grounds that Sharon had considerable political influence, was a popular figure, and that it would not be in the public interest if his departure were to reveal tensions among the generals. Moreover, he was an experienced divisional commander who produced results; during his unauthorised engagement on 9 October his reconnaissance unit had detected the vulnerable boundary

Waiting and watching

Major-General Avraham 'Bren' Adan commanded an armoured division in the Sinai in October 1973. Here he describes the tension of the night of 10 October, when Bar-Lev had just taken over as commander of the southern front, and the Israelis had still not formulated an effective answer to the Egyptian crossing of the canal.

"Bar-Lev opened the meeting by outlining the situation on the Syrian front, from where he had just come. The Syrians had been pushed back across the border. He told us that the IDF's main effort would continue to be in the north for the time being. We then reported on the situation in our divisions, followed by a discussion of what strategy we should adopt.

Sharon said that we had taken no initiative since the outbreak of the war. He suggested that we attack, with divisional force, through the empty zone opposite Bitter Lake, mop up the area toward the south, and push the enemy as far back south as we could as fast as we could. To me, this proposal seemed overly risky in our present condition. Sharon's division had only 170 tanks, I had about 160, Mandler around 140, and Magen had just 80 tanks. I said that the area being proposed for penetration seemed the right one, but that we should commit no more than one brigade there. Mandler put forward a more far-reaching idea: to mop up the area south of the lakes and then to continue by crossing the canal.

It was precisely Gonen and Ben-Ari who proposed the most realistic plans. Ben-Ari said we should not carry out an offensive operation at this time; rather, my division should be pulled back to reorganise, even if the Egyptians pushed us back as a result. Only after we had accumulated more strength could we carry out an attack in the sector proposed. Gonen noted that we only had about 600 tanks instead of the 1000 required for an all-out assault. Therefore a crossing attempt at this time would be dangerous and doomed to failure. His recommendation was that we preserve the tanks we had and build up to 1000 before launching an offensive; he would agree to Sharon's plan only if a ceasefire was about to be imposed.

Bar-Lev then summed up. It was his evaluation that the Egyptians would continue to attack, which would continue to wear down their forces. The attack ideas that had been proposed could not be implemented without prior planning and preparation. Bar-Lev said he attached importance to the capture of Port Fuad and Port Said. Such a move would have political ramifications because we would then hold a section of the canal, and it could be opened only with our consent. As to the operational plans, he charged Southern Command Intelligence, along with Sharon's intelligence staff – Sharon's division was now situated opposite Bitter Lake – with the task of collecting data toward a future crossing. Bar-Lev stated that we would not launch an attack in the immediate future. He then went on to speak of the tactical lessons we could learn from the war so far and of how we could improve our operational techniques in the defensive battle that would continue . . . .

The conference ended. I departed for my command post with the feeling that the worst of the crisis was behind us and with the hope that things would begin to get better.

Above: Deployed forward in the Sinai Desert, Israeli M2 half-tracks (modified by the IDF to incorporate anti-aircraft turrets) with camouflage netting slung from the hulls maintain a watch for incursions by Egyptian attack aircraft. The Israelis maintained a defensive position from 9 October, trying to work out methods of dealing with the Egyptian combination of weapons and to build up their strength for an assault across the canal.

It was midnight by the time I got back to my main command post at Kurkar, and my staff and brigade commanders were waiting for me – a bone-weary group. This was already the fifth straight night of action. I couldn't remember if or when I had slept or dozed – perhaps I had learned to live without sleep. Something was buzzing in my head, a constant irritating noise. It was something I was familiar with from previous wars; even when I did have the opportunity or time to get a little sleep, I was unable to doze off in this condition. Perhaps, I thought, it's possible to get along without sleep after all – but only on condition that things aren't dull. Dull it certainly was not. My mind was unceasingly active: What have I forgotten to do? What to do next? What to say? . . .

Suddenly we heard the close barking noise of heavy machine guns. It was the anti-aircraft battery deployed around the main command post firing like mad. Except for the duty officers, the war tent emptied in seconds flat. We burst out, scanning the night skies, but we saw nothing, not even Kelt missiles. Very bad, I thought; someone was edgy, opened fire, and others joined in. But when the firing stopped and the report came in, it emerged that helicopters had been spotted moving not far from us toward the northeast. It was thought that these were Egyptian helicopters seeking to land commandos to our rear. The radios were alive with activity. The reports coming in made it clear that none of our helicopters were airborne and that other helicopters had been spotted at various places. At once orders were issued, units were sent out to comb the area, and security measures around the bivouacs increased.

When we returned to the war room, the ensuing discussion on the past two days of fighting was interesting and fruitful. The brigade commanders had mostly recovered from the first shock of the Sagger missile panic. We now knew what to watch out for, from what directions, and at what ranges such attacks could be expected. Moreover, all units now had observers whose job it was to warn of incoming anti-tank missiles. They would call out, 'Missile from the left!' or 'Missile from the right!' – and the tanks would succeed in manoeuvring so as to avoid the missile. Everyone thought that whenever Zeldas [the Israeli name for the American M113 armoured personnel carrier] had been sent in ahead of the tanks the results were excellent, as the armoured personnel carriers had been able to deal with the Egyptian infantry that had moved into close range. We were used to the artillery barrages by now. We would close the hatches, shift position, and go on operating. As I listened to the reports, it crossed my mind that the division resembled someone initially ill with a high fever over whom everyone had been greatly concerned. Now, even though some fever remained, the crisis point had passed.

After we had analyzed battle techniques and the tactics of cooperation among tanks, armoured personnel carriers, and artillery I decided to redistribute our Zeldas amongst the armoured formations. We would be fighting with small tank battalions the next day, but now each battalion would have armoured infantry troops mounted on Zeldas grouped to protect its flanks. I then issued the order for the coming day of fighting. 99

Inset above: General Avraham 'Bren' Adan. Avraham Adan was born in Kfar Giladi and was brought up in Tel Aviv. He joined the Jewish armed force, the Palmach, when he was 17 and during the 1948 war commanded an infantry company, later transferring to the armoured corps. In 1973 he was serving as GOC Armoured Forces and was about to retire when war broke out and he was placed in command of a reserve armoured division. After a severe mauling in the initial stages of the war, his division spearheaded the Israeli offensive on the West Bank of the Suez Canal which cut off the Egyptian Third Army. After the war Adan was appointed representative of the IDF in the USA.

The struggle for aerial supremacy in the Yom Kippur War

The Israeli Air Force (IAF) was, in many ways, in a far stronger position on the eve of the Yom Kippur War in October 1973 than it had been in 1967. The territorial gains of the Six-Day War, particularly in Sinai, had created a useful buffer-zone between the Israeli homeland and the airbases of her principal antagonists, thus easing the major problem of her air defence, while an infusion of modern warplanes from the United States – notably the McDonnell Douglas F-4E Phantom and the Douglas A-4 Skyhawk – had served to maintain the IAF's qualitative advantage in equipment over the Arab air forces. Furthermore, the United States was to prove a stauncher ally of Israel than had France in 1967 and the IAF obtained a steady flow of spare parts and replacement aircraft in 1973. In addition, the small but fast-growing Israeli aircraft industry made significant contributions to the IAF's combat capabilities during the 1973 war. The IAF's greatest asset, however, was the superb quality of its aircrew.

On the other side, the Arab air forces had profited from the hard lessons of the 1967 war. Not only had the losses of the Egyptian and Syrian Air Forces been made good from Soviet stocks, but more modern warplanes had been supplied and in greater numbers. The strength of the Syrian Air Force had risen from some 142 combat aircraft in mid-1967 to 265 in October 1973. The Egyptian Air Force's overall increase in strength was less dramatic (from 450 up to 480 combat aircraft), but large numbers of Sukhoi Su-7 fighter-bombers had supplemented the elderly

MiG-17s in the ground-attack role and the early MiG-21Fs had given way to more powerful and better-armed versions of this fighter.

These Soviet fighters were less effective than the IAF's F-4 Phantoms and Mirage IIIs in individual combat, but the combined Arab fighter force outnumbered that of Israel by 130 fighters. Nor were these Arab aircraft again to be easily destroyed in a pre-emptive air strike, for they were now housed in hardened shelters and their airfields ringed with surface-to-air missiles (SAMs) and anti-aircraft (AA) guns. The Soviet Union not only supplied equipment to the Arab air forces, but also provided technicians and combat advisers. Indeed, in 1970-71 the air defence of Egypt had been in the hands of Soviet personnel, operating under the command of a general of the Soviet Air Defence Forces.

Soviet personnel were withdrawn from Egypt in the summer of 1972, but Soviet tactical doctrines greatly influenced the way in which the Arab forces fought during the Yom Kippur War. Most notably, the Egyptian and Syrian armies were to adopt the Soviet practice of relying on ground-based tactical air defence systems (SAMs and AA artillery) to protect their advancing armies from air attack.

For Israel, air power provided a first line of defence. Her conscript armies required time to mobilise and deploy, time that would be provided by the IAF's air defence umbrella, while enemy preparations were disrupted by offensive air action. Israel's most modern fighter in 1973, the F-4E Phantom, was well

Above: A Soviet-supplied SA-2 missile on its launch site deep in Egyptian territory, with its radar guidance station in the background.

Phantom

Above: Israel's most modern fighter deployed at the time of the Yom Kippur War: the F-4E Phantom. The IAF had about 140 Phantoms in action in 1973. Right: Watched by Israeli tank crews, a blazing Phantom plummets earthward after falling victim to Syrian anti-aircraft fire. Below: A blindfold Syrian pilot is led away by Israelis.

suited to this operational philosophy. It was a dual-role aircraft, having both air-to-air and ground-attack capabilities. Six IAF squadrons were equipped with about 140 F-4Es in 1973. They were primarily employed in the ground-attack role, although their medium-range Sparrow air-to-air missiles (AAMs) outranged anything in the Arab air forces' armoury and a well-handled F-4 was certainly capable of outperforming a MiG-21.

The IAF's primary air superiority and air defence fighter in 1973, as in 1967, was the Dassault Mirage IIICJ. Powered by a single 6000kg (13,200lb) thrust Atar 9C turbojet, the Mirage IIICJ reached a maximum speed of over Mach 2 and had a tactical radius (with no external fuel tanks carried) of 290km (180 miles). Israeli Mirages and Arab MiG-21s fought on equal terms as far as technical capabilities were concerned; the deciding factor was the tactical and flying skills of the pilots. By 1973 the IAF's Mirage inventory had fallen to some 50 of the 72 aircraft originally procured.

The third significant IAF warplane of the Yom Kippur War was the A-4 Skyhawk fighter-bomber. A simple and straightforward design, the Skyhawk combined a good flight performance with a heavy warload. In 1973, six IAF squadrons operated some 150 A-4s and the type bore the brunt of the close air support effort, with the F-4Es flying longer-range air strikes. Although the Skyhawk's defensive armament was limited to its built-in cannon, it was sufficiently manoeuvrable to outperform the MiG-21 in a dogfight.

The IAF's combat aircraft strength also included single squadrons of Dassault Super Mystère fighter-bombers and Sud Vautour long-range attack aircraft, while 38 models of the elderly Nord Noratlas were the mainstay of the transport force. The IAF's helicopter fleet comprised single squadrons of Sikorsky CH-53

Above: Dummy Egyptian SAM sites designed to draw Israeli fire. To counter the Arab screen of missiles and anti-aircraft artillery, the IAF was forced to adopt a variety of measures. Ultimate Israeli success was based on the winning of air superiority by such aircraft as the Mirage III (right, a Mirage in flight, and below right, a Mirage undergoing ground maintenance) in which the IAF pilots outfought the MiG-21s of their Syrian and Egyptian counterparts. (Left, a MiG-21 with afterburner on full and left centre, smoke streaming from a stricken MiG). This enabled the Israelis to retain control of their own airspace (left top, the remains of an Egyptian helicopter downed behind Israeli lines) and then launch a series of raids against targets within enemy territory (below, Syrian oil tanks ablaze after an IAF airstrike).

and Sud Super Frelon heavy-lift machines, plus 30 Bell UH-1s.

The most important aircraft type in the Syrian and Egyptian air forces' combat inventory was the Soviet-supplied MiG-21, a single-seat air superiority fighter with a secondary ground attack capability. Egypt had a total of 160 MiG-21s in service in October 1973, while Syria had about 100. The most modern version available to the Arab air forces was the MiG-21MF. The MiG-21's great advantages in air combat were its good manoeuvrability and relatively small size, which made it difficult to spot.

The Sukhoi Su-7 fighter-bomber required a wider range than a tactical fighter and was capable of covering some 1450km (900 miles) with two auxiliary fuel tanks but a small warload. Its low-level performance was excellent, however, and it was capable of a maximum speed of over Mach 1 at sea level. Egypt operated 130 Su-7s and Syria 45. They were popular with the pilots, because of their ability to evade interception at low altitude and their steadiness as weapons' aiming platforms. Also available to the Arabs was the vintage MiG-17, with a combat radius of 748km (465 miles); this plane was used extensively in the ground-attack role. There were 110 in Egyptian service but 120 with the Syrians. About 60 MiG-19s were also in Egyptian service but these, although both fast and manoeuvrable, could not carry a significant warload.

In general, the Arab air forces lacked a fighter-bomber which was capable of penetrating Israeli airspace to any depth. Consequently, they relied on Tupolev Tu-16 bombers armed with AS-5 Kelt stand-off missiles for such missions. The Egyptian Air Force had 18 Tupolev Tu-16s in service and during the course of the war launched 25 missiles against Israeli territory. As the Kelt is a relatively large, subsonic missile, it proved to be an easy target for the IAF air defences. Interceptors and SAMs accounted for 20 of them; the remaining five succeeded in destroying a supply depot in Sinai and (operating in a passive, radar-homing mode) two Israeli radars. The Syrians did not possess any bomber aircraft and their attempt to use FROG (free rocket over ground) artillery rockets for long-range bombardment of Israeli population centres was largely ineffective.

From the Arab viewpoint, the great success of the air war was the Soviet-supplied tactical air defence umbrella of SAMs and AA guns, which provided an effective cover over their advancing armies during the early days of the war. Thus not only did the Egyptian and Syrian armies achieve tactical surprise with their coordinated assaults across the Suez Canal and on the

Aircraft of the Yom Kippur air war

Israeli F-4E Phantom

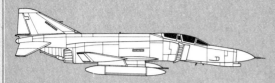

In 1973 the 140 F-4E Phantoms operated by the Israeli Air Force were deployed mainly in the long-range strike role while the task of close air support for ground troops was provided by the A-4 Skyhawk.

Type Twin-seat multi-role fighter/strike aircraft **Length** 19.20m (63ft) **Span** 11.68m (38ft 4in) **Maximum speed** Mach 2.17 or 2304km/h (1430mph) **Range** Radius with weapon load 840km (520 miles) **Armament** One 20mm cannon; four Sparrow, Sidewinder or Shafrir missiles; 7258kg (16,000lb) bomb load

Israeli Mirage IIICJ

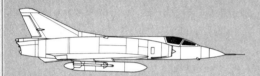

The Mirage IIICJ, although an equal in technical capability to the Arab MiG-21, scored far more successes in air combat where the flying skills and tactical training of the Israeli pilots proved the decisive factor.

Type Single-seat fighter/strike aircraft **Length** 15.03m (49ft 3in) **Span** 8.22m (27ft) **Maximum speed** Mach 2.1 or 2230km/h (1386mph) **Range** Combat radius 290km (180 miles) **Armament** Two 30mm cannon; two Sidewinder or Shafrir missiles; two 454kg (1000lb) bombs

Egyptian MiG-21MF

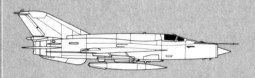

In 1973 the Egyptians relied mainly on their surface-to-air missile umbrella for air defence but as the Israelis overran areas west of the Suez Canal MiG-21s were deployed for combat air patrol, fighting some 18 major air battles in seven days.

Type Single-seat fighter/strike aircraft **Length** 15.76m (51ft 8½in) **Span** 7.15m (23ft 5½in) **Maximum speed** Mach 2.1 or 2230km/h (1386mph) **Range** Radius with weapon load 800km (500 miles) **Armament** One 23mm cannon; two ATOL missiles or four UV-16-57 rocket packs; 1500kg (3300lb) bomb load

Egyptian Su-7

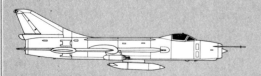

The Su-7 was very popular with Egyptian pilots, especially for high-speed combat at low-level, and losses to anti-aircraft fire and missiles during the war were surprisingly low.

Type Single-seat fighter-bomber **Length** 17.37m (57ft) **Span** 8.93m (29ft 3½in) **Maximum speed** Mach 1.6 or 1700km/h (1050mph) **Range** With external tanks 1450km (900 miles) **Armament** Two 30mm cannon; 2500kg (5500lb) bomb load – with external tanks 1000kg (2200lb) bomb load

---

Golan Heights, but they also blunted the IAF's initial counterstrokes and so denied the Israeli Army a full measure of air support. The weapons which provided this air cover were the SA-2 at medium altitudes, the SA-3 and SA-6 at low and medium altitudes and the hand-held SA-7 and the radar-directed ZSU-23-4 quadruple self-propelled AA gun at low level. The most effective SAM was the SA-6, the centrepiece of a fully-mobile system of three missiles on a tracked launcher vehicle which made use of continuous-wave radar guidance. The effectiveness of the Arab air defences depended not so much on the prowess of individual weapons, however, as on the effects of a deployment of large numbers of varying types of AA systems, posing threats from different types of missiles and guns.

Combatting AA defences

The IAF at first found it difficult to improvise counter-measures against these systems and aircraft losses were heavy (80 in the first week), while vital targets, such as the Egyptian bridges over the canal, remained in operation. IAF methods of combatting anti-aircraft defences included the use of terrain masking and evasive manoeuvring; simple use of flares to decoy infra-red guided SA-7s away from the aircraft's jet pipe; chaff (metalised strips released in a cloud to blot out radar returns); and finally, more sophisticated electronic counter-measures using jamming pods, or 'spoof' techniques to create false radar returns. One of the greatest problems faced by the IAF was its unfamiliarity with the SA-6. The Israeli electronic counter-measure (ECM) equipment was tailored to counter threats from the SA-2 and SA-3 but proved to be ineffective against the SA-6's 'Straight Flush' fire-control radar. One weakness of the SA-6, however, was its slow rate of elevation and depression; this could be exploited by carrying out a steep diving attack which the missile could not track. Yet, although Soviet air defence systems could be dealt with individually, the combined effect of several batteries was far more difficult to cope with.

In the early days of the war, the IAF concentrated its efforts against the Syrian forces threatening to break through on the Golan Heights, and was prepared to take heavy losses in what it saw as the crucial task of stopping an offensive that looked capable of reaching the northern plains of Israel. All observers of this grim struggle on Golan have stressed the fanatical bravery of the Israeli pilots.

On 7 October the IAF made a series of concentrated attacks against Syrian missile batteries and succeeded in neutralising them for 24 hours, yet at the end of this period the SAMs were back in operation and the IAF had lost 28 aircraft in obtaining this brief respite. Not until advanced ECM jamming equipment was supplied by the United States was the IAF able to deal effectively with the SA-6. Some idea of the intensity of the electromagnetic conflict may be gained by the fact that no fewer than 50,000 chaff packets were supplied to Israel by the United States in the course of the war. The supply of advanced ECM jamming equipment to Israel, together with the increasing expertise of IAF pilots in countering enemy air defence systems, combined to reduce considerably IAF losses in the latter part of the conflict. American AGM-45 Shrike anti-radiation missiles, which were able to home onto the emissions of the SAM guidance radars, also played an important part in reducing IAF losses, while by the latter stages of the war, the Israeli armoured thrust over the canal had succeeded in eliminating a number of missile sites and had opened a corridor through which IAF aircraft could safely penetrate into the Egyptian rear areas.

The hard-fought contest between Israeli fighter-bombers and the Arab SAMs has tended to overshadow other aspects of the air war. In contrast to the Six-Day War there were few successes gained against Arab aircraft on the ground. Despite heavy airfield defences and the protection provided to parked aircraft by hardened shelters, the IAF persevered in airfield attacks – notably against forward Egyptian airfields at Salihiyah, El Mansura and Tanta. The most vulnerable targets were the runways which were comparatively easy to crater with bombs, but were also equally easily repaired and returned to service by an enemy prepared for such attacks. Furthermore, as a fully-armed MiG-21MF can take off within a distance of some 760m (2500 feet), a typical 2450m (8000 feet) runway must be extensively cratered to render it totally unusable. On 11 October, for example, the IAF mounted attacks on all of the eight major Syrian Air Force airfields, but the results were negligible as only eight enemy aircraft were claimed as destroyed by Israel on both fronts and the Syrian Air Force was able to challenge the IAF in strength over the Golan Heights on the following day.

Close-range air battles

The great majority of the IAF's aircraft losses (approximately 100) were due to anti-aircraft fire or SAMs, whereas the IAF claimed that no fewer than 370 Arab aircraft had been shot down in air combat for the loss of only four of its own. The Israeli SAM armoury was modest in comparison with those of their enemies, comprising only some 50 Hawk missile batteries, primarily deployed in defence of Tel Aviv and the nuclear plant at Dimona. Some forward-based Hawk batteries went into action against the Egyptian Air Force in Sinai and claimed the destruction of more than 20 enemy aircraft. Yet it was the air-to-air missile that proved to be the most effective Israeli weapon of the air war, with a total of 200 'kills' over Arab fighters claimed for the AIM-9 Sidewinder and Shafrir. The air battles were generally fought at close range and little use seems to have been made by the IAF of the F-4's capability of engaging targets beyond visual range with its AIM-7 Sparrow AAMs. There are several reasons for this. Firstly, the IAF greatly prized the F-4's capabilities as a long-range strike aircraft and generally used the aircraft in this role. Secondly, engagements were usually fought between attack aircraft and their escorts and opposing air superiority fighters. In such confused melées there was little opportunity to use medium-range missiles and, unless positive identification was possible at long range, it was advisable to close to visual contact before engaging a target.

According to Egyptian sources, seven major air battles were fought over the Sinai front on the first six days of the war. One of these involved as many as 70 Egyptian Air Force aircraft. In the latter part of the conflict intense air battles were fought over those areas to the west of the Suez Canal which had been overrun by Israeli forces. Deprived of SAM cover, the Egyptian Air Force attempted to protect fighter-bomber missions by combat air patrols of MiG-21s. In seven days of fighting the IAF and Egyptian Air

Right: A flight of four A-4 Skyhawks adopts formation abreast after a successful bombing operation against Syrian targets. At the beginning of the Yom Kippur War the IAF deployed approximately 150 Skyhawks in six squadrons. Despite its limited air-to-air combat armament, the Skyhawk could outmanoeuvre the MiG-21 in a dogfight.

Force clashed in 18 major air battles and the Egyptians flew a total of 2500 combat sorties. Losses were heavy, with the IAF claiming 25 Egyptian aircraft shot down on 19 October, for example, with 11 victories claimed in a single air battle.

On the Syrian front, the IAF's close air support effort lessened after 13 October as the danger of an enemy breakthrough receded. The effort was switched to strategic targets such as oil storage sites, power stations and port installations within Syria. These attacks were mounted in reprisal for the launching of FROG rockets against Israel and consequently little attempt was made to avoid civilian casualties. This was in contrast to air strikes against Egypt, where purely military targets were attacked. In Damascus, the Syrian capital, over 100 civilians were killed or injured by Israeli bombing and other major Syrian towns came under attack.

Both sides in the conflict made considerable use of helicopters to carry out commando raids behind enemy lines. The Syrians opened hostilities on 6 October with a commando assault on Mount Hermon using Mil Mi-8s. This was the standard Soviet assault transport helicopter, which could carry up to 28 fully-equipped troops and was armed with a nose-mounted 12.7mm machine gun and four rocket pods each containing 16 57mm rounds. It can therefore provide a measure of fire support in the landing zone. Egypt, with a total force of about 120 Mi-8s and 12 heavy lift Mi-12 helicopters was able to use these forces on a more ambitious scale. About 100 Mi-8s carried teams of commandos across the Suez Canal on the evening of 6 October to operate against Israeli lines of communication and the vulnerable Sinai oilfields. After dropping the troops, the helicopters acted as close support aircraft and a number of machines were reported to have attacked strongpoints of the Bar-Lev Line with napalm. Although these raids achieved a limited degree of success, helicopter losses to enemy fire were heavy and as many as 50 Mi-8s were reported to have been lost.

The IAF's commando assault helicopters were the Sud Super Frelon with seating for 30 troops, eight of which were in service, and the Sikorsky CH-53D, which could carry 38 troops. Unlike the Mi-8, neither is fitted with armament. Israel carried out a number of heliborne commando operations inside Syria, operating against troop and supply convoys and lines of communication. The major Israeli helicopter assault operation of the war was a counter-attack on Mount Hermon carried out on 21 October. It was spearheaded by four assault helicopters, closely co-ordinated with an airborne drop, and followed up by a further 10 helicopters. Fighting to regain the strategic mountain top was fierce and it continued after the official ceasefire on 22 October.

There was no easy victory for the IAF during the Yom Kippur air war. Air superiority had to be won by the classic methods of fighter-versus-fighter combat over the battlefield and the rear areas. The IAF overcame the numerical superiority of the Egyptian and Syrian air forces with the superior skills of its pilots and the high performance of its aircraft, but needed technical assistance from the USA to neutralise the enemy air defence systems.

Anthony Robinson

Below: An Israeli Sikorsky CH-53D helicopter, capable of carrying 38 troops, airlifts sandbags to fortify IDF positions on Mount Hermon. Both Syria and Egypt used heliborne assaults during the Yom Kippur War. Israel's major heliborne operation was a counter-attack against Syrian defences on Mount Hermon on 21 October.

Key Weapons

WESTERN APCs

The Americans and the Germans made the most extensive use of APCs (armoured personnel carriers) during World War II, but both countries used half-track vehicles which had limited cross-country mobility compared with the full-tracked tanks with which they were designed to operate. The half-tracks also suffered the major disadvantage of having an open-top troop compartment which made the infantrymen very vulnerable to artillery and shell splinters. Towards the end of World War II the British and Canadians removed the turrets from tanks and successfully used them in a troop carrying role, some remaining in service well after the end of the war. These tank conversions also suffered from having an open-topped troop compartment – although they could operate with the tanks – and the troops they carried had to climb over the hull sides to enter and leave the vehicle.

The United States Army was the first to field a new fully-tracked APC, followed by the French and Germans in the 1950s and the British in the 1960s. Since then a number of other countries have entered the field. In many cases the APC has been sold overseas so helping to extend the production line and preserve jobs.

The major difference between the APC and the MICV (mechanised infantry combat vehicle) or IFV (infantry fighting vehicle) is that the first is designed to transport the infantry and its equipment from one part of the battlefield to another where they dismount and fight on foot, while in the case of the MICV the infantry will usually fight from within the vehicle. When first introduced most APCs had a pintle-mounted machine gun but experience in South Vietnam and elsewhere has shown that the gunner was very vulnerable and many countries have replaced the pintle-mounted weapons with a similarly armed turret. Most APCs have no capability to allow the infantry to fight from within the vehicle with any degree of safety, unless they expose the upper part of

Page 1583: Armed with 20mm M61A1 Vulcan cannons a line of US M113 armoured personnel carriers moves forward on exercises in Germany. Above left: An M113 rejoins the road after travelling cross-country. The ability of APCs to transport infantry over rough terrain while providing protection from smallarms is a crucial element in modern infantry tactical doctrine. Above: The M106A1 mortar carrier. Based on the M113 it carries 88 rounds of 107mm mortar ammunition, some of which can be observed racked behind the mortar.

Left centre: America's first fully tracked APC, the M75, seen here with a 0.5in machine gun. Left: The M59 was a considerably more advanced APC than the M75; troops could leave the vehicle with ease through a power-operated rear door.

their body through the roof hatches; and most APCs also have no observation devices in the troop compartment, so prior to dismounting the infantry have no clear idea of the terrain in which they are expected to fight.

Some APCs are fully amphibious needing little or no preparation, while others are only amphibious with some preparation or have no amphibious capability at all. This capability nevertheless only allows them to cross lakes or slow-flowing rivers; it does not mean that they can swim from landing craft offshore onto beaches. When most APCs were introduced they were not fitted with a NBC (nuclear, biological and chemical) warfare system to enable them to operate in a NBC contaminated area, but within Nato many vehicles have now fitted these systems. The original infra-red night vision equipment has now given way to passive night vision, which allows the vehicle to be driven in the dark without giving away its position to other infra-red sensors, as well as being able to dispense with standard white-light headlights which can be seen by an enemy for miles around.

In most cases the basic APC has also been used to form the basis of a complete family of vehicles that can support it on the battlefield: for example, mortar carrier, command, artillery observation/fire control, engineer support, ambulance and radar carrier to name but a few. Some are even used as weapons platforms, fitted with anti-aircraft or anti-tank systems.

While the MICV is a far more comprehensive combat vehicle than the APC, it is also much more complex and expensive. For example, in 1983 an American M2 Bradley MICV cost the American Army $1.4 million, while the M113A2 APC cost only $176,000.

Of all the nations producing APCs the most important has been the United States, producing an extensive range of vehicles. Following their early experience with half-tracked APCs the American Army

soon issued a requirement for a fully-tracked fully-enclosed vehicle and this eventually emerged as the M75 APC with just over 1700 being built between 1951 and 1954 by International Harvester. This was, however, a very large vehicle and had no amphibious capability so it was soon replaced in the US Army by the M59. Almost all of the M75s were then passed on to Belgium where they remain in service.

The M59 was designed by the FMC Corporation who first became involved in the design and production of armoured vehicles during World War II. Between 1954 and 1959 over 4000 M59s were built by the company for the US Army. The M59 was a major improvement over the M75 as not only was it fully amphibious but infantry could quickly leave the rear troop compartment through a power-operated ramp in the hull rear. Once the M59 was phased out of US Army service in the early 1960s it was passed on to other countries such as Brazil and Greece where it still remains in service.

The main drawback of the M59 was that it was a little on the heavy side for air transport and it had a short operating range. To meet a requirement for a lighter vehicle, prototypes of a new APC were built both in steel and aluminium and the latter was finally adopted for service as the M113 with prime contractor being FMC once again. First production vehicles were completed in 1960 and since then it has become the most widely used armoured vehicle in the world. By 1984 sales had been made to some 50 countries and over 80,000 vehicles had been built; licenced production has been undertaken in Italy and Belgium. The first model was powered by a petrol engine but in 1964 the M113 was replaced by the diesel-engined M113A1 which has a much improved operating range. The current production model is the M113A2 which has further automotive improvements and the fuel tanks mounted externally at the rear which not only saves space inside but reduces the fire risk.

There are more variants of the M113 family than any other armoured vehicle; these include 81mm and 107mm mortar carriers, an anti-tank vehicle with the TOW ATGW (anti-tank guided weapon), command vehicle (with higher roof), flamethrower, 20mm anti-aircraft vehicle, recovery and repair vehicles and a cargo carrier called the M548 which in turn is used for a variety of roles including Lance and Chaparral missile carriers.

The main drawback of the M113 is that there is no provision for the infantry to use their weapons from within the vehicle with any degree of safety. This has led FMC to develop the AIFV (armoured infantry fighting vehicle) which is mid-way between the M113 and the M2 Bradley. The AIFV has combined aluminium and steel armour and a turret-mounted 25mm cannon. In service with the Netherlands and Philippines, it has been ordered by the Belgian Army.

After the end of World War II the United Kingdom started a major development effort to produce a fully-tracked APC, although it was the six-wheeled Saracen that entered production first as this was urgently required for operations in Malaya. The FV432 series was produced by GKN Sankey with over 3000 vehicles being produced between 1963 and 1971. In many respects this is very similar to the American M113 except that it has a welded steel hull rather than a welded aluminium hull. There is no provision for the infantry to use their weapons from inside the vehicle with any degree of safety and when first introduced it was armed with a pintle-mounted 7.62mm machine gun. Many vehicles now have a fully enclosed 7.62mm machine-gun turret over the rear troop compartment which is a far more satisfactory arrangement. Some of the vehicles used by the Berlin Brigade have the complete two-man turret of the Fox armoured car armed with a 30mm Rarden cannon which is capable of destroying any Soviet MICV/APC as well as inflicting severe damage to the sides and rear of a main battle tank.

The chassis of the FV432 has been used for a wide range of specialised variants to meet not only the requirements of the infantry but other arms as well. These variants include a command vehicle with a tent that can be erected at the rear of the hull, 81mm mortar carrier, recovery vehicle, ambulance and cargo carrier. More specialised versions include the FV434 maintenance carrier that has a hydraulic crane for changing tank engines in the field, radar carrier (including the EMI Cymbeline mortar-locating radar), FV438 anti-tank vehicle with two Swingfire ATGWs and a variety of Royal Signals and Royal Engineers versions. Included in the latter is a variant that tows the bar minelayer while mounted on the roof is the Ranger anti-personnel mine dispensing system. The FV433 105mm Abbot self-propelling gun, used by the Royal Artillery and India is also based on the chassis of the FV432 APC.

The FV432 was offered on the world market but no sales were made as the American M113, which has similar characteristics, is so much cheaper. From the late 1980s the FV432 will be supplemented by the MCV-80, which is also being designed and built by GKN Sankey.

There is an APC version of the Alvis Scorpion family called the Spartan which is used by the British Army, Royal Air Force Regiment and the Belgian Army. This vehicle has a three-man crew – comman-

Britain has produced three fully-tracked APCs which provide a comprehensive series of infantry support vehicles. The FV432 (below) is the standard British Army APC and it has been supplemented by two Alvis produced vehicles, the Spartan (bottom left) which is part of the Scorpion family and the larger Stormer (bottom right). These APCs are being supplemented by the MCV-80 MICV (mechanised infantry combat vehicle).

der, gunner and driver – but carries only four infantrymen and so is a very limited APC. To meet the requirement for an APC with increased carrying capacity Alvis have developed the Stormer which was announced in 1980. The Stormer can can carry eight fully-equipped infantrymen in addition to its three-man crew and can be fitted with a wide range of weapon stations. Alvis supplied three Stormers for the American Light Armored Vehicle competition, fitted with a two-man power-operated turret armed with a 25mm Hughes chain gun and firing ports in the rear troop compartment, and more recently has supplied 25 vehicles to Malaysia, which also operates the Scorpion.

France was one of the first European countries to issue a requirement for a full tracked APC in the postwar period and after evaluating prototypes from several companies finally selected a model based on the AMX13 light tank chassis. This was originally called the TT CH for short, but is today known as the VCI (*véhicule de combat d'infanterie*). This was one of the first vehicles to have firing ports for the infantry, although it did lack any amphibious capability. When originally introduced it was armed with a pintle-mounted 7.62mm machine gun but most have now had this replaced by a turret armed with a similar weapon, although 20mm weapon stations can be installed if required. In addition to being used by France it has also been exported to Argentina, Belgium, Ecuador, Indonesia, Italy, Morocco, the Netherlands, Venezuela and the United Arab Emirates. In the French Army it is slowly being replaced by the AMX-10P MICV which, in addition to having a power-operated 20mm turret, is also fully amphibious.

For many years the Belgian Army has been equipped with the French AMX VCI and old American M75 APCs. After evaluating a number of tracked and wheeled vehicles the army selected both the American M113A2 and the AIFV in 1979. Rather than purchase the vehicles direct it was decided to make them under licence in Belgium. First production vehicles were completed in 1982 and production will continue to 1988. The Belgian company of ACEC has developed the Cobra armoured personnel carrier, which has an interesting range of armament comprising two 101mm rocket launchers, a 0.5in machine gun, two 7.62mm machine guns and two triple grenade launchers. An unusual feature of this vehicle is that it has an electric transmission.

To give Swedish infantry some experience of armoured personnel carriers Hägglund and Söner converted a number of light tanks into APCs and called them the Pbv 301. These were later replaced by the Pbv 302 designed by the same company. This vehicle entered production in 1965 and in many respects was ahead of the American M113 and British FV432 (introduced at about the same time) as it was fitted with a fully enclosed turret armed with a 20mm cannon. The driver is positioned at the front of the vehicle in the centre and the commander to the right. The latter has periscopes to give good all-round observation. Over the troop compartment roof are two hydraulically-operated roof hatches which allow the troops to fire their smallarms but with their heads and shoulders exposed. As there are so many lakes and rivers in Sweden the Pbv 302 is fully amphibious being propelled in the water by its tracks at a speed of 8km/h (5mph). The hull of the Pbv 302 is of double-

Top: The Italian modification of the M113 which provides firing ports for the infantry in the rear hull, becoming in effect an infantry combat vehicle. Above centre: The French APC, the VCI, based on the AMX13 chassis. Although it is being replaced by the AMX-10P MICV it has been an important export success. Above: The Swedish Pbv 302 with 20mm cannon and infantry firing position. Right: The improved Pbv 302 Mk2 which has stronger armour and an extra cupola.

Western Armoured Personnel Carriers

Vehicle	Crew	Weight	Ground Pressure	Speed (road)	Range (road)	Armament
Steyr 4K 7FA	2 + 8	14,800kg (32,634lb)	0.55kg/cm² (7.82lb/in²)	63.6km/h (39.2mph)	520km (323 miles)	one 12.7mm machine gun
Cobra	3 + 9	7500kg (16,537lb)	0.29kg/cm² (4.12lb/in²)	80km/h (50mph)	600km (373 miles)	one 12.7mm machine gun
AMX VCI	3 + 10	15,000kg (33,075lb)	0.70kg/cm² (9.95lb/in²)	65km/h (40.4mph)	400km (248 miles)	one 7.62mm/7.5mm machine gun
Pbv 302	2 + 10	13,500kg (29,767lb)	0.60kg/cm² (8.53lb/in²)	66km/h (41mph)	300km (186 miles)	one 20mm cannon two × 4 smoke grenade launchers
FV432	2 + 10	15,280kg (33,692lb)	0.78kg/cm² (11.09lb/in²)	52km/h (32mph)	480km (298 miles)	one 7.62mm machine gun two × 3 smoke dischargers
Stormer	3 + 8	10,700kg (23,593lb)	0.37kg/cm² (5.26lb/in²)	72km/h (45mph)	800km (497 miles)	one 7.62mm machine gun or 20/30mm cannon, 76/90mm gun, ATGW depending on role
M113A1	2 + 11	11,156kg (24,600lb)	0.55kg/cm² (7.82lb/in²)	68km/h (42mph)	480km (298 miles)	one 12.7mm machine gun

skinned construction which also provides protection against HEAT attack as well as additional buoyancy. The Pbv 302 has not been sold abroad owing to Sweden's strict policy against the export of arms. More recently the Pbv 302 Mk 2 has been developed with improved armour protection, Lyran target illumination launchers and an additional cupola.

The standard APC of the Swiss Army is the M113, although many of these have been modified to meet Switzerland's own requirements. To provide increased firepower some have also been fitted with the same 20mm cannon and turret as installed on the Swedish Pbv 302.

The first APC designed to meet the requirements of the reformed West German Army was the HS-30. This was based on a Swiss-designed chassis, powered by a Rolls-Royce petrol engine and armed with a turret-mounted 20mm cannon. It has now almost disappeared from service, having been replaced by the M113 and the Marder MICV.

In the 1960s Saurer-Werke built almost 500 fully-tracked armoured personnel carriers for the Austrian Army under the designation of the 4K series, some of which were fitted with pintle-mounted machine guns while others had a turret-mounted 20mm cannon. In 1970 the company was taken over by Steyr-Daimler-Puch and subsequently a more powerful version was built under the designation of the 4K 7FA and sales of this have already been made to Austria, Greece (where it is now made under licence), Morocco, Nigeria and Tunisia. More recently a model called the 4K 7FA-K Spz infantry fighting vehicle has been built with firing ports in the rear troop compartment. Variants include a mortar carrier, ambulance, command, anti-aircraft and a fire support vehicle with a 90mm gun.

Rather than design its own APC Italy made the sensible decision to build the M113 under licence. Prime contractor for this is OTO-Melara at La Spezia who also build tanks and a wide range of naval weapons. So far over 4000 vehicles have been built for the Italian Army and export and further develop-

ment has resulted in an infantry fighting vehicle which has firing ports in the rear troop compartment and a partly-closed weapon station.

Although mechanised infantry combat vehicles are being introduced in increasing numbers in many armies the basic armoured personnel carrier still fulfils its original mission of transporting troops into battle. Far more economical than the highly complex MICV, the armoured personnel carrier is able to carry out a wide range of support roles, and it will remain a battlefield vehicle for many years to come.

Below: The Steyr 4K 7FA which is armed with a turret-mounted 20mm cannon and is capable of holding eight infantrymen in the hull. Bottom: The Belgian Cobra, shown here without its rocket launchers. Its light weight of 7500kg (16,537lb) is an advantage in many respects but ensures only limited protection.

Clash of the Titans

The decisive tank battles in Sinai, 1973

Following the failure of the Israeli counter-attack against the Egyptians on 8 October 1973, neither side engaged in major operations for several days, but both concentrated on improving and consolidating their positions. On the following day, 9 October, Major-General Ariel Sharon, angry at the confused orders which had sent his division on a wild goose chase to the southern sector the previous day, deliberately exceeded his authority during a localised engagement and came close to being relieved of his command. One important consequence of his action, however, was that his reconnaissance unit discovered the boundary between the Second and Third Egyptian Armies. Sharon's unit was withdrawn the following morning as the Israeli Command did not wish to advertise the fact that it possessed such a sensitive piece of intelligence, for it was on this, the Deversoir sector, that the Israelis planned to cross the Canal themselves, in accordance with the strategic decision reached during the early days of the war that the Egyptians could only be defeated if the Israel Defence Forces (IDF) secured a bridgehead on the West Bank. Nonetheless, for the moment it was felt that no such operation was feasible until the still substantial elements of the Egyptian armoured and mechanised divisions remaining on the West Bank had crossed into Sinai.

In the meantime, Israeli commanders recovered their badly shaken nerve. Lieutenant-General Chaim Bar-Lev took over Southern Command while Major-General Shmuel Gonen remained as his deputy, and an immediate analysis was made of the mistakes which had resulted in such serious casualties during the first three days of the fighting. It was decided that the all-tank theories which had been adopted since the Six-Day War must be abandoned immediately in favour of balanced formations which would operate with full artillery support, including the use of smoke to conceal movements. Further, the ideal ratio of tanks to APCs would be adjusted from three-to-one to one-to-one whenever possible, as the storm of automatic weapon fire which could be generated, coupled with that of the artillery and the tanks themselves, would make it virtually impossible for the enemy's Sagger ATGW operators to guide their weapons efficiently. Simultaneously, the badly mauled armoured divisions recovered their strength and reinforcements began streaming into Sinai. Major-General Avraham Adan's division, which was the most exposed of the three, received a fourth armoured brigade commanded by Colonel Joel Gonen, the younger brother of the former GOC; this was equipped with 75 T55s captured during the Six-Day War and up-gunned to the Israeli 105mm standard. On 13 October the Israelis sustained the serious loss of a veteran divisional commander when Major-General Avraham Mandler, who had unwisely transmitted the position of his headquarters in an uncoded transmission, was killed minutes later by accurate Egyptian fire; his division was taken over by the experienced Brigadier-General Kalman Magen.

For their part the Egyptians were, in the main, content to remain in their positions, anticipating that the Israelis would continue to mount costly attacks. Neither the minister of war, General Ahmed Ismail Ali, nor his chief of staff, Major-General Saad el Din Shazli, wished to extend the conflict beyond the immediate confines of the bridgeheads since this would not only deny their divisions the cover of the dense surface-to-air missile (SAM) belt, but also expose them to the type of mobile warfare in which the Israelis were undoubtedly superior.

Stalemate in Sinai

Just how long the stalemate in Sinai might have lasted remains a matter for speculation. The next move arose not as a direct result of Egyptian or Israeli planning, but because of events which were taking place on the distant Golan Heights. Syria, facing total defeat, was broadcasting frantic appeals for Egypt to come to her aid and President Anwar Sadat, who was also commander-in-chief of the Egyptian armed forces, had no alternative but to order a general offensive along the front or be shamed before the entire Arab world.

Shazli embarked on the detailed planning with extreme reluctance. He disagreed with Ismail on a number of issues, but eventually a compromise was reached in which the Third Army would seize the Mitla and Gidi passes while the Second Army took Tasa; both armies would then swing inwards in a pincer movement to capture Bir Gifgafa, the major Israeli base in Sinai. Once this had fallen, the IDF would be compelled to withdraw towards its own frontier or perish. The plan was simple enough, but it was also predictable and would undoubtedly involve heavy fighting. Shazli, however, also added a third major thrust which suited his own concept of applying the indirect approach in mechanised warfare.

The target of this additional thrust was the Baluza Junction at the northern end of the line, where the coast road joined the principal lateral road running

Above: An Israeli Centurion tank on the advance. The Centurion, with its 105mm L7 gun and greater main armament depression providing it with a good hull-down position, had a distinct advantage over the Soviet-built T62 that was the main Egyptian tank. The Egyptian High Command was well aware of the Israeli strength in mobile warfare, and was extremely reluctant to move out of the well-defended bridgeheads across the Suez Canal that had been established soon after the opening of the war.

behind the Israeli front line. Since no other lateral route existed between Baluza and El Arish the loss of this would have most serious consequences for the IDF. Once the junction had been seized the Egyptians could either advance south into the Israeli rear areas, or east along the coast road to El Arish, or both. Luckily for the Israelis this element of the overall plan was much watered down in its final form, although it did include the insertion of helicopter commandos.

A conference to discuss the IDF's own plans for crossing the Canal was in progress when intelligence was received that virtually all of the remaining Egyptian armoured and mechanised formations had now crossed to the east bank and were clearly deploying for a general offensive. Such was the measure of the restored Israeli self-confidence that the news received general approval. It was decided that the IDF's crossing would be made directly after the enemy's attack had been contained and his armour written down. The scene was now set for the largest tank battle since World War II, with approximately 1500 Egyptian and 500 Israeli tanks facing each other along a 160km (100 mile) front.

After a postponement of 24 hours, Shazli's offensive began on 14 October. South of the Great Bitter Lake, Major-General Abd el Muneim Wassel's Third

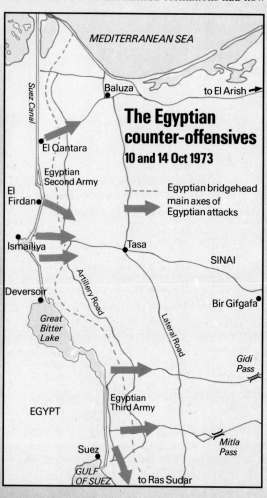

The Egyptian counter-offensives
10 and 14 Oct 1973

- - - Egyptian bridgehead
main axes of
Egyptian attacks

MEDITERRANEAN SEA

Suez Canal
Baluza
to El Arish →
El Qantara
Egyptian Second Army
El Firdan
Ismailiya
Tasa
SINAI
Deversoir
Great Bitter Lake
Artillery Road
Lateral Road
Bir Gifgafa
Gidi Pass
EGYPT
Egyptian Third Army
Mitla Pass
Suez
GULF OF SUEZ
to Ras Sudar

Above: Israeli Centurion tanks undergo resupply and field maintenance during a break in the Sinai fighting. The legendary invincibility of Israeli armour was quickly dispelled at the hands of Egyptian anti-tank defences. The tactics that the IDF initially adopted in Sinai (the use of almost unsupported tanks in attack) were a recipe for disaster in the face of the resolute Egyptian defence. Left: Observing an IAF strike against Egyptian positions. Below: Israeli half-tracks and lorries rush infantry to the front.

Army commenced its advance on the Mitla and Gidi passes at 0630 hours. Its principal thrust was directed at the Mitla Pass and was led by the 3rd Armoured Brigade of the 4th Armoured Division, followed by elements of the 6th Mechanised and 19th Infantry Divisions, the southern flank of the operation being covered by the 22nd Armoured Brigade. Wassel planned to break into the Israeli rear by driving up the Wadi Marbouk, which emerged near the lateral road and which he had been informed – incorrectly – was only lightly held. Opposing him was Magen's regular armoured division, which had suffered cruelly during the first two days of the war and wanted its revenge.

Informed of the Egyptians' progress by his mobile reconnaissance teams, Magen blocked the exit from the wadi with Colonel Dan Shomron's armoured brigade and a force of paratroops, and allowed Wassel's brigades to drive into the trap. The Egyptians were scourged with tank and artillery fire to which they could make no effective reply, but bravely continued to press on up the defile. More and more units were fed into the cauldron, adding to the congestion and confusion. A flank move by 22nd Armoured on the higher ground to the south was easily held by Magen and the Israeli Air Force (IAF) joined in the carnage. By early afternoon the Egyptians were in full retreat, leaving 90 of their tanks and a large number of APCs in a tangle of blazing wreckage which littered the floor of the wadi. Some way to the north a secondary thrust at the Gidi Pass, made by the T62s of the 25th Armoured Brigade and mechanised elements of the 7th Infantry Division, was quickly halted and then turned back after a long-range gunnery duel with another of Magen's brigades.

To the north of the Great Bitter Lake, Major-General Saad Mamoun's Second Army fared equally badly. The most southerly of Mamoun's thrusts was made along the general axis Ismailiya-Tasa by the 21st Armoured and 16th Infantry Divisions with a supporting barrage fired by 500 guns. They were met by two armoured brigades of Sharon's division, commanded respectively by Colonel Chaim Erez and Colonel Amnon Reshef. The Israeli tanks remained turret-down as their commanders watched the Egyptians advancing towards their positions on the rising ground. When the range had closed to a mere 1000m (600 yards) the Israelis edged forward to go hull-down along their ridges and opened fire simul-taneously. Great gaps were blown in the advancing ranks of armoured vehicles, and by 0800 hours the attack had clearly failed. The Egyptians rallied and came on again, making for Hamutal Hill and Hamadiya Junction, but this time their advance was uncoordinated and they sustained even more serious casualties as they struggled forward against Israeli fire. By noon the 21st Armoured Division had lost 110 tanks and the battle on the Ismailiya sector was at an end.

Egyptians under pressure

Meanwhile, the Second Army had simultaneously mounted a subsidiary thrust against Tassa from El Firdan. This, executed by the 24th Armoured Brigade of the 23rd Mechanised Division and the 2nd Infantry Division with part of the 15th Armoured Brigade covering the left flank, struck Colonel Joel Gonen's T55 brigade, which was deployed across Adan's divisional front. The brigade came under increasing pressure and Gonen was himself blown from his turret by a Sagger strike, but took over another tank immediately. Adan committed Colonel Ariel Keren's Centurion brigade to the battle and this stabilised the position while a mobile battlegroup under the division's second-in-command, Brigadier-General Dov Tamari, sealed off a small penetration which had been made. Significantly, on this sector mechanised infantry played a notable part in the defence, pinning down the enemy's Sagger teams. At midday the Egyptians abandoned their attempts to break through and withdrew, leaving 40 of their tanks behind.

At the northern end of the line the critical attack along the El Qantara-Baluza axis was carried out by the remainder of the 15th Armoured Brigade and the 18th Infantry Division. Here speed should have been the prime consideration yet, incredibly, the Egyptians chose to make a set-piece infantry-tank attack in the manner of World War II, with their T62s leading the advance at walking pace on either side of the road and the infantry following some distance behind. Ironically, it was on this very sector, commanded by Brigadier Yzhak Sasoon, that the Israelis were at their weakest, the main element of the defence being provided by Colonel Fedale's mechanised infantry brigade, which had been detached from Adan's division and contained an organic Sherman battalion. At 1000m (600 yards) the Shermans opened fire at what amounted to sitting targets and by 0845 hours

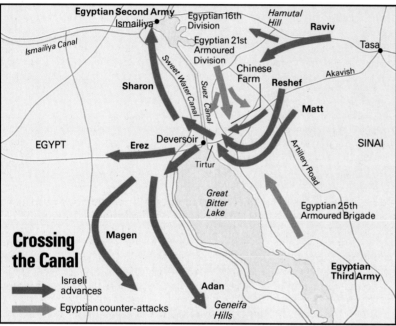

Crossing the Canal

Egyptian Second Army
Ismailiya
Ismailiya Canal
Egyptian 16th Division
Hamutal Hill
Raviv
Tasa
Egyptian 21st Armoured Division
Chinese Farm
Reshef
Akavish
Sharon
Sweet Water Canal
Suez Canal
Matt
EGYPT
Erez
Deversoir
Tirtur
SINAI
Artillery Road
Great Bitter Lake
Egyptian 25th Armoured Brigade
Magen
Egyptian Third Army
Adan
Geneifa Hills

→ Israeli advances
→ Egyptian counter-attacks

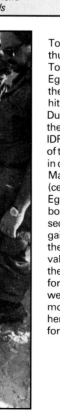

Top left: Israeli Centurions thunder toward the front. Top right: The turret of an Egyptian T62 lies beside the tank hull after a direct hit by an Israeli shell. During the fighting along the El Qantara-Baluza axis, IDF armour knocked out 34 of the Egyptians' 60 tanks in one engagement. Left: Major-General Adan (centre, standing) with an Egyptian POW who is bound and gagged for security. Intelligence gained from prisoners in the field was particularly valuable. Right: Vital to their pursuit of Egyptian formations across Sinai were these IDF tank-mounted bridgelayers, here about to bridge a gully for following armour.

the Egyptians had abandoned their attack, having lost 34 of their 60 tanks. The commandos who had been inserted by helicopter some way to the east were rounded up by mechanised infantry units. It was only after the war that the Israelis discovered the full extent of Shazli's original intentions regarding this area.

Altogether, the day's fighting had cost the Egyptians 264 tanks, a large number of APCs and 1000 casualties. The strain proved too much for Major-General Mamoun, who suffered a heart attack shortly after ordering the renewal of the assault on the Ismailiya sector; his place as GOC Second Army was taken by Major-General Abd el Munem Halil. With remarkable prescience, Shazli proposed withdrawing the two armoured divisions to the West Bank. Sadat, believing that this would result in loss of face, would not hear of it and when Shazli pressed the point he threatened to have him court-martialled.

The Israelis take the initiative

Some sources suggest that the Israelis lost as few as 10 tanks on 14 October. Whatever the figure, it was incredibly low given the scale of the fighting and, thanks to the revision in tactical method, the enemy's Saggers had scored very few kills. The initiative had now passed irrevocably to the IDF and, with the bulk of the Egyptian armour still pinned on the east bank, the Israelis promptly activated their own plan for crossing the Canal. This required Sharon's division to drive a corridor to the Canal in the Deversoir area where, in anticipation of such an event, a protected concentration area known as The Yard had been built in the years since 1967, as had a straight road code-named Tirtur along which the bridging train could be moved forward; a second and adjacent axis of approach to the Canal was code-named Akavish. A paratroop brigade would seize a bridgehead on the West Bank and tanks would be rafted across to support it. The bridge would then be launched and Adan's division would cross, swinging south to eliminate the SAM screen and to encircle the Egyptian Third Army. Simultaneously, holding attacks would be made along the front by Sasoon and Magen.

Operation Gazelle, as the Israeli canal crossing was known, began at last light on 15 October. Reshef's brigade, consisting of four tank and three mechanised infantry battalions, first moved towards the shore of the Great Bitter Lake, then swung north to penetrate the flank of the Second Egyptian Army. It struck the congested assembly area of the 16th Infantry Division, to which the 21st Armoured Division had also withdrawn following its defeat on 14 October. A furious close-quarter night action followed, centred on a group of buildings known as the Chinese Farm, which had large oriental script painted on its walls and had actually been a Japanese experimental agricultural station prior to the Six-Day War. This raged until dawn and Sharon was forced to feed more and more troops into the battle, including his own paratroopers. Both sides suffered heavily and by morning the landscape had become a wasteland of smashed and burning military equipment of every description, littered with the bodies of dead infantrymen.

A corridor had been established, however, and although this remained under fire, Colonel Danny Matt's paratroop brigade, which was to establish the bridgehead, had moved along it to enter The Yard, followed by the unifloat rafts and the tanks of Erez's armoured brigade which were to follow them across.

Matt's first wave crossed in their assault boats at 0135 hours on 16 October and by 0500 hours the brigade was across and moving out to consolidate a perimeter 5km (3 miles) wide and to secure crossings over the Sweet Water Canal. At 0643 hours the first of 28 tanks to enter the bridgehead was rafted across. As the morning wore on Erez broke out with 21 of these in a sweep which destroyed the nearest SAM sites. No further tanks would reach the West Bank for 37 hours.

Throughout 16 October Sharon's corridor came under continuous pressure from the Egyptian 21st Armoured Division and 14th Armoured Brigade. The greatest difficulty was experienced in bringing up the bridging equipment under fire. Both Tirtur and Akavish were at times closed by the Egyptian counter-attacks and Adan's division, which was moving forward to commence its own crossing, was forced to mount local operations to clear them. By evening the situation had improved somewhat but it was clear that there would be no further crossings that night, nor possibly the next. At Southern Command headquarters Defence Minister Moshe Dayan expressed doubt about the wisdom of continuing the operation, but Bar-Lev and Gonen insisted that it must be seen through to the end.

Matt's bridgehead was at first regarded by the Egyptian High Command as being of purely local significance, but as Erez continued to suppress SAM sites it began to assume growing importance. Shazli was for withdrawing the Third Army's 4th Armoured Division and 25th Armoured Brigade to the West Bank and using them to destroy the bridgehead, but he was overruled by Ismail who insisted that on the 17th the Israeli corridor would be pinched out by the converging attacks of the 21st Armoured Division from the north and the 25th Armoured Brigade from the south. Major-General Wassel, the Third Army's commander, reluctantly accepted the order, but commented privately to Shazli that in his opinion the 25th Brigade could be entrapped and wiped out during its approach march.

That is precisely what happened. When, next day, the brigade was reported moving north along the eastern shore of the Great Bitter Lake, Adan expertly disengaged his own armour and redeployed it in ambush positions along the flank of the enemy advance, simultaneously placing blocking forces which prevented escape. The result was a massacre in which the Egyptians lost 86 of their 96 T62s, all their APCs and their entire transport echelon. The Israelis had four tanks disabled when they ran onto a minefield during the pursuit of the survivors.

While this action was taking place, the Tirtur and Akavish routes had been finally cleared and the first of the Israeli bridges was being launched. Adan carried out an immediate replenishment and that night his division began crossing into Matt's bridgehead which, throughout the day, had successfully resisted determined attempts by Egyptian commandos and the 23rd Armoured Brigade to eliminate it.

Meanwhile Sharon's division continued its battle of attrition against the 21st Armoured and 16th Infantry Divisions. This cost it a quarter of its tanks but the Egyptian loss was far heavier and the latter's grip began to fail. Chinese Farm fell on 18 October, bringing the long and bloody struggle for the corridor to an end. That evening a second bridge was launched, followed next day by a third.

The whole tempo of the battle now quickened.

Feeding the war machine

On Tuesday 9 October 80 Soviet military transport planes, including Antonov An-12s and longer-ranged An-22s, and a further 20 Aeroflot commercial cargo planes set up shuttle services from Soviet bases in the Caucasus, the Ukraine and Southern Russia to Syria and Egypt, landing near Palmyra, Aleppo and Cairo. Military supplies flown in included Frog bombardment rockets, 30 SS-1 Scud missiles, SA-3 Goas, SA-6 Gainfuls, and smaller shoulder-fired SA-7 Grails. It is estimated that by the end of the war a total of 15,000 tonnes of Soviet war supplies were flown into Egypt and Syria in the course of 134 sorties.

The Soviet Union also supplied heavier equipment by sea. In the second week of the war T54, T55 and T62 tanks and MiG-21 fighters arrived at Alexandria, Tartus and Latakia by ship. At the end of the war Syria had more tanks than Britain and France combined.

The United States also supplied its client, Israel, with vast quantities of military equipment. On 13 October, the Israelis declared that the nation possessed war material for no more than four further days of warfare. Golda Meir telephoned an appeal to the US, asking for 75 aircraft (including 15 Phantoms), tanks, mobile artillery and missiles. High-priority items such as chaff and 'smart' bombs (to be used to hit the SAM sites and the Egyptian bridges over the Suez Canal), had already been secretly airlifted to Israel in 11 stripped-down El Al Boeing 747 airliners from as early as 9 October, along with limited quantities of anti-tank ammunition, and Sparrow air-to-air rockets. But from 13 October, a major US airlift got under way, and on 14 October President Nixon requested Congress to approve $202 billion of military aid to Israel. In 566 round trips of about 22,000km (14,000 miles) each, the US flew in some 22,345 tonnes of supplies in the 100-tonne payload Lockheed C-5 Galaxies and C-141 Star Lifter freighters, and these were supplemented by a further 5500 tonnes carried by El Al aircraft.

Many of the new American weapons, especially TOW anti-tank missiles, were needed in Sinai where the Israelis were expecting an Egyptian attack. M48 and M60 tanks together with CH-53 helicopters, 36 A-4 Skyhawks and 32 combat-ready F-4 Phantoms (which had been withdrawn from USAF fighter squadrons) were flown in.

The new Phantoms were fitted with the ECM equipment specifically designed to lock on to the guidance radars of the SA-2s and SA-3s. With the Phantoms also came a wide range of American 'smart' weapons – including Walleye television-guided bombs and laser-guided devices – together with Shrike anti-radar missiles to attack the SA-6 radars, and Sparrow and Sidewinder air-to-air missiles.

The enormously destructive nature of modern warfare had meant that the superpowers were now inevitably drawn to centre-stage in a purely regional conflict, having been forced to supply their clients with the material to prosecute the conflict. Their motives were to contain the spread of the war, but in fact they had fuelled the fighting and given the combatants hope of being able to continue the conflict.

Adan broke out of the bridgehead during the morning of 18 October, heading south on a two-brigade front to secure the Geneifa Hills and eliminate SAM sites. Bar-Lev decided to reinforce success and on 19 October Magen's division was pushed across to join the drive against the Third Army's rear, echeloned back to the west of Adan's troops. Part of Sharon's division also crossed and swung north to reach the outskirts of Ismailiya; Sharon would dearly have liked to develop a similar drive against the rear of the Second Army, but he was simultaneously required to clean up part of the east bank and for the remainder of the war his division provided a hard protective shoulder on both banks while operations in the south continued.

The full implications of the military situation were now starkly apparent to the Egyptian High Command. The threat to the Third Army was a grim reality; a similar threat to the Second Army was a distinct possibility; even the prospect of a drive on Cairo itself could not be ruled out. The fact was that most of the Egyptian Army still lay on the east bank and there were insufficient reserves remaining to cope with so many alternatives. Shazli had done his best, but he had been repeatedly opposed by a minister of war and a commander-in-chief who thought in political, rather than military, terms. He collapsed with nervous exhaustion and was replaced by General Abd el Ghani Gamasy.

Sadat was now desperate to achieve a ceasefire while Egyptian troops remained on the east bank of the Canal, still offering Egypt a strong bargaining point in the inevitable postwar negotiations. The superpowers were both now agreed on the desirability

Below: Pontoons are linked together to provide a bridge for the Israeli crossing of the Canal. The operation was code-named Gazelle and by early morning on 16 October a paratroop brigade, under Colonel Danny Matt, and 28 tanks had established a bridgehead on the West Bank.

In a desperate attempt to break the IDF corridor to the Canal, Egyptian armour advanced north along the east coast of the Great Bitter Lake. The Israelis ambushed them and knocked out 86 of their 96 tanks (above right, Egyptian casualties). The Israelis lost four machines (above, an M48 hits a mine).

of a ceasefire since US Secretary of State Henry Kissinger's visit to Moscow on 20 October. The Soviet Union therefore set the diplomatic machinery in motion at the United Nations, and on 22 October the relevant resolution was passed, to be implemented by 1852 hours that evening.

Meanwhile the Israelis also had their eyes fixed on the postwar diplomatic situation, and as moves towards a ceasefire had got underway, Adan and Magen had advanced south with all possible speed. Of ne-

cessity Wassel began transferring the 4th Armoured and 6th Mechanised Divisions back to the West Bank, but with the elimination of the SAM screen, the IAF completely dominated the air and soon severed his communications across the Canal. The Egyptians fought hard and threw everything they possessed into the battle, including Palestinian and Kuwaiti units, but were unable to halt the flood of Israeli armour. Shortly after noon on 22 October Wassel informed Ismail that his army had been cut off and faced complete destruction.

The final engagement

The ceasefire was observed on the Second Army sector, but the Israelis continued their advance in the south, while units of the Egyptian Third Army persevered in their attempts to break out. Adan and Magen shrugged off resistance, reaching Suez and Adabiah on the Gulf of Suez late on 23 October. Next day Adan attempted to penetrate Suez, but his units were ambushed in the streets and forced to fight their way out with the loss of 80 killed.

This was the last engagement of the war, because the continuing Israeli offensive and the desperate plight of the Egyptian Third Army were threatening to bring about a superpower confrontation. To avoid an intervention by Soviet forces, the United States put immense pressure on the Israelis to respect the ceasefire and permit the overland resupply of the Third Army. The Americans even threatened to supply the Third Army themselves, transferring their logistic machine from the Israelis to the Egyptians. By 25 October, the fighting had ceased, and the Israelis opened up a land corridor to the beleagured forces that they had cut off. The superpower confrontation now eased considerably.

On both sides the destruction of equipment had been immense, and both sides had suffered heavy loss of life – for Israel the toll in dead and injured was higher than in any of her previous wars, leaving few families untouched in some way. The IDF had found itself on the brink of defeat but had recovered and won a spectacular victory which left it in possession of 2500sq km (1000 square miles) on the West Bank of the Canal. The Egyptians, on the other hand, felt that they had regained their honour on 6 October, and still retained the gains made by the Second Army during the first days of the war. It was a reasonable compromise on which to commence the negotiations which not only led to Egypt recovering the Sinai, but also removed the long-standing threat to Israel's southern frontier.

Bryan Perrett

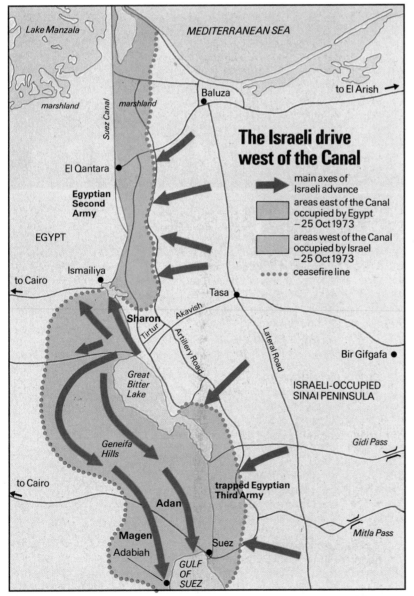

Lake Manzala

MEDITERRANEAN SEA

marshland

marshland

Suez Canal

Baluza

to El Arish

El Qantara

The Israeli drive west of the Canal

➡ main axes of Israeli advance

▨ areas east of the Canal occupied by Egypt – 25 Oct 1973

▨ areas west of the Canal occupied by Israel – 25 Oct 1973

•••• ceasefire line

Egyptian Second Army

EGYPT

Ismailiya

to Cairo

Tasa

Sharon

Akavish

Tirtur

Artillery Road

Lateral Road

Bir Gifgafa

Great Bitter Lake

ISRAELI-OCCUPIED SINAI PENINSULA

Gidi Pass

Geneifa Hills

to Cairo

trapped Egyptian Third Army

Adan

Magen

Adabiah

Suez

GULF OF SUEZ

Mitla Pass

Superpowers and the oil weapon

International repercussions of the Yom Kippur War

The outcome of the Yom Kippur War was as much determined by the attitudes and intervention of outside powers as by the forces in battle. Indeed, the Egyptian offensive had been chiefly conceived as a means of forcing the superpowers, the United States and the USSR, to take positive action to secure a satisfactory settlement in the region.

Ever since the 1967 Arab-Israeli War, the superpowers had expressed large areas of agreement over the Middle East conflict, based on their mutual acceptance of UN Resolution 242. But each superpower was also tempted to seek an extension of its influence in the region by increasing its support for its client – Israel in the case of the United States and Egypt in the case of the Soviet Union. By the end of the War of Attrition in 1970 the Americans were supplying their latest Phantom fighters to Israel and the Soviets had sent some 20,000 advisers and fighting men to Egypt.

The removal of Soviet influence in Egypt became a major objective of American policy, and this led Egypt's new president, Anwar Sadat, to make a bold bid for American support by asking all Soviet combat forces and most advisers to leave his country in July 1972. Instead of rewarding Sadat by pressuring the

Israelis into concessions, however, the Americans emphasised their support for Israel on the calculation that this would force the Egyptians even further into the Western camp. The calculation was mistaken: far from being offended at Sadat's expulsion of their men, the Soviet Union was quietly relieved, and in the winter of 1972 began supplying Sadat with more modern equipment than ever before. While their own men had been in Egypt the Russians had put pressure on Sadat to maintain peace, but now they washed their hands of responsibility for the situation, apart from occasional counsels of caution.

At this time the process of detente between the superpowers was in full swing. As part of this process in 1972 the United States and the Soviet Union had agreed on the Basic Principles of Great Power Behaviour, one of which was that each power should warn the other if it knew of any imminent danger to peace. The Americans were later to accuse the Russians of perfidiously breaking this accord, since they knew of the planned Arab offensive in advance but did not inform the United States. However, in the course of the conflict the mechanisms of detente on the whole functioned effectively, with both superpowers pursuing a possible advantage and yet cooperating to

Above: The oilfields of the Persian Gulf were vital to the economies of Western Europe and Japan. The decision of the oil-producing states of the Middle East to cut production on 17 October and the subsequent massive rises in oil prices altered world attitudes to the Arab-Israeli conflict – just as the Arabs had hoped.

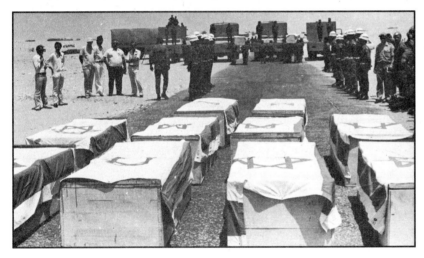

Top: Israeli chief of staff, Major-General David Elazar, at the press conference that followed the signing of the ceasefire agreement with Egypt. The Israelis had ostensibly accepted the UN Resolution 338 calling for a ceasefire on 22 October, but fighting continued on the following day. Most observers agree that the Israelis initiated this further round in an attempt to complete the isolation of the Egyptian Third Army; not until 25 October did all fighting cease. Above: Israeli dead await shipment back to Israel from Egyptian territory.

superpower auspices, to bring about a just settlement.

Soviet prestige was already undermined by the defeats inflicted upon her clients and it threatened to disappear altogether on 23 October when Israel, which had accepted Resolution 338 on the previous day, broke the ceasefire and reached the Gulf of Suez thus completely encircling the Egyptian Third Army. The Soviet Union was incensed by this action. She suspected that Israel now sought to crush Egypt altogether. The Soviet Union had persuaded the Syrians and Egyptians to accept the ceasefire. Now it appeared that the United States was unable to control Israel, and unless the Soviet Union took decisive action to protect Syria and Egypt, her entire position in the Middle East would collapse. When the Israelis rejected a further Security Council resolution calling upon them to withdraw to their 22 October positions, Moscow warned Washington of the imminence of Soviet intervention on the side of Egypt, and Soviet airborne troops and her large fleet in the Mediterranean were readied for this purpose. These moves were countered by an American declaration placing United States armed forces on a worldwide nuclear alert on 24-25 October.

Avoiding confrontation

This dramatic confrontation between the two superpowers was much less ominous than it seemed at the time. The American move effectively warned Moscow that the United States would not tolerate unilateral Soviet intervention in the Middle East. Kissinger had in fact already acted to restrain Israel, announcing that unless the Israelis opened a supply corridor across their lines to the beleaguered Third Army, the United States would be forced to airlift supplies direct to that army. This move was intended to stave off a threatened Soviet airlift and to decrease the chances of Soviet ground intervention to rescue the Egyptian troops. United States aircraft were transferred from the Israeli airlift to European bases in preparation for the projected Egyptian resupply role. This in turn resulted in a temporary cut-off of United States military supplies to Israel and re-emphasised Israel's total dependence on the United States. Israel duly pulled back her troops from the Canal and opened a land supply route to the Third Army.

American anxiety to end the conflict was not entirely due to her desire to limit Soviet influence in the Middle East or to the fear that the conflict might get out of hand. The actions of the non-involved Arab oil-producing states had an important restraining influence on United States policy during the war. For the first time during the long postwar history of Arab-Israeli conflict these states were able to act together to restrict the West's freedom of action in the Middle East. Both Western Europe and Japan were heavily dependent for their energy requirements on the availability of cheap supplies of oil from the Arab and North African oil-producing states. The United States had also begun to import considerable quantities of oil from these states by the 1970s and she was likely to need more in the future. However, the United States, could survive without Middle Eastern oil; Western Europe and Japan could not. The oil producers reasoned that restrictions on the supply of oil to America's allies would have a crippling effect on their economies, and the threat of further restrictions in the future would lead them to exert strong pressure on the United States to secure a Middle Eastern settlement

achieve a ceasefire and limitation of the war. In particular, both accepted the established principle that neither the Arabs nor the Israelis could be allowed to inflict an overwhelming defeat on the other side. Only when the Israelis threatened to ignore this principle did the risk of superpower confrontation seriously arise.

At the beginning of the war, the scope for a diplomatic initiative was limited. The United States was committed to the preservation of Israel's independence but this was never seriously threatened. When the Israelis passed to the offensive the Soviet Union was forced to mount a massive resupply operation to Egypt and Syria to replace the military equipment they had lost during the fighting. The United States provided a similar airlift of essential war supplies to Israel. With Israel now in a strong position, US Secretary of State Henry Kissinger felt the time was ripe to embark on an active effort to end the fighting. On 20 October he flew to Moscow and drafted with the Russians a ceasefire resolution which was adopted by the United Nations Security Council on 22 October as Resolution 338. This called for an immediate ceasefire in place, and negotiations between the respective parties in the Middle East, under against Israeli intransigence. To a large degree they succeeded in this aim and a serious rift opened over the Middle East between the United States on one side and her Nato allies and Japan on the other.

On 17 October the Arab oil states, led by the single largest producer, Saudi Arabia, which had grown increasingly impatient with United States Middle Eastern policies since the early 1970s, announced that they intended to cut oil production 'by a minimum of 5 per cent forthwith . . . and thereafter by a similar percentage each month . . . until such time as the total evacuation of Israeli forces from all Arab territories occupied during the June 1967 war is completed and the legitimate rights of the Palestinian people are restored, or until the production of every individual country reaches the point where its economy does not permit of any further reduction without detriment to its national or Arab obligations.' At the same time an embargo on oil exports was imposed on the United States and the pro-Israeli Netherlands, and other countries were threatened with a similar fate if they supported the Israeli cause. Furthermore, oil prices quadrupled during the Yom Kippur War. The immediate impact of the price rises and the production cut-backs was to cause panic in Western Europe and Japan and to lead the United States to institute contingency planning for possible armed intervention against the oil-producing states.

Oil on troubled waters

The Western Europeans (except the Netherlands) and Japan hastened to assure the Arab states of their pro-Arab credentials, urged the United States to force Israel to make peace and demonstrated their anti-Israeli bias by refusing to allow the United States to use European ports and airfields as staging posts for the resupply of Israel. In the period between the 1967 and 1973 wars, great differences had already opened up within the Western alliance on the subject of Israel. Now the oil weapon exaggerated this divide.

But Saudi Arabia and the other conservative Arab oil producers had in fact no desire to drive Western Europe into bankruptcy. The question of Israel apart, they were closely aligned with the West and hostile to Soviet influence. They soon accepted that Kissinger was genuinely trying to achieve a Middle Eastern settlement and that the peace process would be a lengthy one. Accordingly, increased supplies of oil to the West were authorised by the oil producers in February 1974, coupled with a warning that the supplies could be curtailed again if necessary. In March the embargo against the United States was lifted, followed by that against the Netherlands in May.

The point had been made and there is little doubt that, in many parts of the world, opinion which had hitherto been sympathetic to Israel, turned against her during and after the October war. The oil weapon was one factor; another was that the initial Arab military successes impressed many observers. World opinion also condemned Israel's refusal to abide by the terms of the ceasefire resolutions and her efforts to turn parts of the 1967 occupied territories into areas of permanent Jewish settlement. Such hostility increased Israel's sense of isolation and contributed to her loss of morale and her willingness to bargain.

Despite the oil embargo and the ensuing rift with her Nato partners, the United States was able to exploit the Yom Kippur War to enhance her position in the Middle East. Kissinger's subsequent 'shuttle diplomacy' between the capitals of Syria, Israel and Egypt resulted in an Egyptian-Israeli disengagement agreement in January 1974 and a similar Syrian-Israeli arrangement in May. Egyptian and Syrian willingness to negotiate an end to hostilities with Israel under American auspices resulted partly from their new-found confidence based on their initial victories during the war: the myth of Israel's military invincibility had been shattered. They realised that only the United States could control Israel, and felt that Kissinger was anxious to secure an even-handed settlement. Kissinger's step-by-step approach to the resolution of the immediate crisis led to the second Sinai disengagement agreement in 1975, and paved the way for further progress on this front in the future. Israel's compliance was secured by American threats to halt the supply of vital arms if she refused, coupled with promises of material support to enable Israel to maintain her military strength vis à vis her neighbours if she cooperated. The United States was also closely involved in the surveillance of the ceasefire, troop reductions and withdrawal agreements, sending 200 civilian personnel to man early-warning systems in the Sinai (a United Nations emergency force had been established there after the Yom Kippur War). Relations between the United States and Egypt improved after the war, with the United States assisting Egypt with aid and helping her to re-open the Suez Canal.

Conversely, the Soviet Union suffered a severe setback to her position in the Middle East. Her relations with Egypt deteriorated rapidly after 1973; Egypt complained bitterly about delays in the deliveries of Soviet arms and spare parts. In 1976 Egypt abrogated the Treaty of Friendship and Cooperation with the Soviet Union. While detente between the Soviet Union and the United States had been weakened, it was not destroyed; Kissinger subsequently accepted that the Soviet Union had generally behaved with restraint during the peace negotiations. He kept Moscow informed of the progress of the peace negotiations, although he refused to allow her to participate in the process. The Soviet Union could only wait on the sidelines in the hope that either a split in the Arab front or a further outbreak of fighting in the area would afford her the prospect of recovering her lost influence.
Michael Dockrill

Above: UN troops move into Sinai after the end of hostilities. Right: The ceasefire line within Egypt, seen from the Israeli side, as Israelis and Egyptian forces observe each other. In January 1974, a disengagement agreement was signed.

One of the most important results of the Yom Kippur War was the increase in importance of the United States in the politics of the Middle East. The accord between the Egyptians and the Soviet Union (left, Soviet President Podgorny, third from left, meets Anwar Sadat, fourth from left, before the war) began to disintegrate, while Henry Kissinger (right) undertook a whirl of 'shuttle diplomacy' that established US influence on a broader scale than ever before.

New perspectives

The military lessons of the Yom Kippur War

Even before the Yom Kippur War had ended, politicians, the press and strategic experts were trying to analyse the military lessons of the conflict. Many observers were impressed by new weapons, used for the first time in combat. They were quick to announce the obsolescence of older weapon systems, such as the tank or the manned aircraft. The opening of a new era in warfare was confidently proclaimed: an era in which the missile would revolutionise combat, as the long-bow or machine gun had in the past.

More than 10 years after the event it is clear that these predictions were less than accurate. The world's armed forces are still investing in new generations of tanks and aircraft, despite the appearance of missiles greatly superior to those available in 1973. Too many analyses were written too soon after the event, when detailed and accurate statistics were not available. Some commentators also neglected to take account of the tactical situations in which the weapons were used and generalised too widely from untypical incidents.

There is no doubt that the events of the first few days of the 1973 war and the shock defeat of the Israeli Defence Forces (IDF) had a disproportionate effect on the study of the war. Far too much has been made of Israeli losses at the start of the war. When IDF ground forces were caught unmobilised, the Israeli Air Force (IAF) was used to plug the gap by providing close air support to frontline units. This has long been recognised as the most dangerous sort of mission to fly and all air forces have tried to avoid risking expensive aircraft and pilots in this role. The IAF lost 30-40 per cent of its close-support aircraft in the first 72 hours. On the Golan, for example, the Israelis may have lost as many as 80 planes in the first four days. In return, however, the Syrian assault was broken, 50 per cent of the mobile surface-to-air (SAM) batteries were destroyed from the air and 200 Syrian planes were shot down.

Once the situation stabilised on the ground, the IAF was able to switch to a more normal pattern of sorties. Further aircraft could be allocated to suppressing ground fire, and targets away from the danger area of the frontline could be attacked. By the end of the war the balance had definitely swung in favour of aircraft.

Above: A satellite view of the Sinai Peninsula, from the south. The use of satellites took on a new importance during the Yom Kippur War, and the superpowers gave their clients valuable information – indeed the Soviet Union is said to have been able to tell the Egyptians that the Israelis had crossed the Suez Canal before the Egyptian High Command was aware of the crossing.

The average Israeli loss rate per sortie in the entire war was just over one per cent, compared to one and a half per cent in 1967 and about two per cent as the average rate in World War II. Even on hazardous ground attack missions the loss rate in the second half of the war was under two per cent, whereas it had been four per cent in 1967.

The effectiveness of the SAM batteries was considerably less than peacetime trials had predicted. Brezhnev is said to have told Sadat that the SA-6 had a kill rate of nearly 100 per cent in trials. Under battle conditions, however, 50-55 SA-6s were fired for every aircraft they destroyed. Figures for the shoulder-fired SA-7 were even worse. 4350 SA-7s were fired for a return of only two or three definite kills and 30 aircraft damaged. The most effective aircraft killer was the radar-controlled ZSU-23-4 tracked anti-aircraft gun which caused over 40 per cent of Israeli losses.

The war in the air

At the start of the Yom Kippur War the Israelis, with a limited range of electronic counter-measures (ECM) equipment did not have the facilities to neutralise the SA-6. Improved flares, chaff dispensers and new ECM pods supplied by the United States increased an aircraft's chances of survival, but the Arab air defence systems could still restrict the IAF's freedom of action, and therefore the army's effectiveness. Despite losing only slightly more than 100 aircraft, a larger number of Israeli planes were damaged and out of action for at least part of the war. To the SA-6's dozen or so kills should be added some credit for the effectiveness of the ZSU-23-4, because aircraft diving to avoid SA-6 missiles often came under ZSU-23-4 fire at lower levels. The cost to the Egyptians should also be noted. About 25 per cent of the Egyptian armed forces were involved in air defence over the SAMs and therefore not available for other combat roles.

Although the manned aircraft has survived and will continue to survive in the foreseeable future, a number of changes have followed the Yom Kippur War. More attention is being paid to defensive systems, such as infra-red radiation shielding and advanced ECM, although these tend to down-grade aircraft performance. Similarly there is also considerable interest in the new 'smart' bombs which would maximise the effectiveness of attacking aircraft. Some of these were used by the Israelis towards the end of the war. They included Shrike radar-homing missiles and the electro-optically guided Maverick bomb.

As with the air war, so the fighting on land pro-

duced change, but not a revolution. Much was made of such incidents as the destruction of the Israeli 190th Brigade. This formation blundered head-first into an ambush, ignoring all warnings, and was massacred, not just by anti-tank guided weapons (ATGW) but by tank guns and conventional artillery. The Israeli Army had drawn the wrong lessons from the 1967 war and developed a tactical doctrine which relied too much on the tank and ignored the necessity for the combined deployment of infantry and artillery as well. No other army would have suffered so heavily and by the end of the war the Israelis themselves were using their tanks more skilfully, combining them with the other arms.

ATGWs did cause about 25 per cent of Israeli tank casualties, but overall the tank remained the most effective tank killer. The Soviet-supplied Sagger missile failed to operate properly about once in every three firings and less than 25 per cent of missiles fired hit their target. The short-range RPG-7 performed well, particularly at night, when infantry could stalk tanks with this light weapon. The smallness of the RPG-7's warhead, however, meant that most tanks hit were damaged rather than destroyed.

The British L7 105mm gun was the standard armament for Israeli tanks, and its HESH and APDS rounds performed very well against Soviet-supplied tanks. The Soviet 115mm smooth-bore tank gun was very accurate out to about 1500m (5000 feet) but less effective overall. Among the lessons learnt by tank designers and incorporated in modern tank designs were the need for a low profile, increased protection for internal ammunition storage and the replacement of current hydraulic fluids with less flammable liquid.

The Yom Kippur War undoubtedly demonstrated that properly trained and equipped infantry have an improved ability to hold defensive positions against an armoured attack. In order to achieve more than local success, however, it was clear that defending armies were just as reliant on a proper mix of all arms as the attackers. The tank has not yet become the 1980s equivalent of the horse in the 1930s. New designs are being introduced, and the appearance of enhanced protective plating, such as the British 'Chobham' armour, has helped to reduce the effectiveness of the chemical energy warheads used on missiles. More attention is being paid to short-range suppressive fire to neutralise missile operators, using either machine guns or systems such as the Russian AGS-17 automatic grenade-launcher. Smokescreens can also be used in this role.

Several other aspects of weapons technology which were comparatively neglected at the time of the

Below: A balanced IDF unit moves forward, with half-tracks carrying supporting infantry and keeping close to the tanks. The first days of the Yom Kippur War exposed the danger to tanks of advancing without infantry close to hand. Below right: Israeli armour passes a captured SA-3 site. In spite of some extravagant claims, it was the variety of anti-aircraft weaponry employed by the Arabs – rather than the efficiency of any one particular weapons system – that proved so effective during the war.

Yom Kippur War are now receiving more attention. Satellites were used by both superpowers to monitor the progress of the war and the Soviet Union is said to have used satellite photography to prove to the Egyptians that the Israelis had actually crossed to the West Bank of the Suez Canal. Satellite reconnaissance has become even more important since the war.

Electronic counter-measures have already been mentioned but the whole field of electronic warfare is rapidly expanding. The Egyptians were very successful in jamming Israeli battlefield communications and may also have gathered useful intelligence from monitoring Israeli radio nets – the Egyptian fire that killed General Mandler is assumed to have been

the result of an intercepted radio message that gave the position of his HQ. Helicopters received a mixed press during the war but their loss rate was less than that of fixed-wing aircraft. They were mostly used for transport rather than ground-attack and were therefore less exposed to enemy fire. At sea the Israelis demonstrated their new fleet of missile-armed patrol boats and soon gained the upper hand over the Arab navies' older Soviet-built craft.

In all, it is clear that the events of October 1973 did not completely alter the face of battle, but that they added new ingredients to the mix of weapons whose combination is the key to success on the modern battlefield. **Michael Orr**

In spite of claims to the contrary, the Yom Kippur War did not render the fighter-bomber obsolete. Such aircraft were still devastating close-support weapons, especially when they caught an enemy force in the open (like the MiG-17 attacking ground targets above). The major Israeli ground-attack aircraft was the F-4 Phantom (below) which played an essential role in the Israeli victory.

Key Weapons

GRENADES

Although the rifle has been (and remains) the infantryman's basic weapon, the soldier needs to supplement the rifle with additional firepower and the grenade is one of the simplest and most effective ways of doing this. Arguably, next to the rifle the grenade is the infantryman's most useful weapon. Grenades have a long history dating back to the 17th century when special units were formed as grenade throwers, being termed grenadiers. The modern grenade came into being during World War I when the need for a simple hand-thrown bomb achieved a new importance in short-range trench warfare.

While the Germans produced the famous Steilhandgranate or stick grenade in 1915, of more lasting importance was the British 'Mills Bomb' which as the No.36 became the prototype for the modern grenade. The No.36 consisted of an egg-shaped cast-iron body filled with high explosive, set off by a delayed firing system. This combination of case, filling and fuze are the three essential elements of the grenade, although they will vary according to the type and function of the grenade.

A number of different materials can be used for the case including cast iron, sheet metal, plastic or even cardboard. Grenades can be filled with high explosive – TNT or simple gunpowder – in an anti-personnel or anti-armour role or with chemical compositions for the purposes of smoke, illumination or signalling. There are two types of fuzing system. The first employs a pyrotechnic (or burning) delay element which after being activated by a striker will burn down to a detonator which in turn sets off the filler. The period of delay can vary between two and seven seconds. The second is the impact type (common in rifle grenades) in which the grenade explodes when it hits any hard surface. As a safety measure the impact grenade requires the force of being launched or thrown into the air to arm itself.

To operate the delayed-action grenade the thrower holds it in his throwing hand and removes the safety pin with his other hand. The grenade is then thrown in the desired direction; once released from the hand, the absence of the safety pin allows the safety lever to fly off which in turn allows a spring-mounted striker to shoot forward and hit the fuze initiator, thus setting off the short delay prior to detonation.

The best-known class of grenade is the fragmentation (or defensive) grenade. The British Mills Bomb was an early example, followed by the similarly-designed American Mk2 and the Soviet F-1. All three grenades feature cast-iron cases with distinctive deep serrations, both horizontally and vertically. The idea of the fragmentation grenade is for the high explosive charge to shatter the casing into a number of jagged fragments that fly out from the blast point in all

Previous page: Pinned down by enemy machine-gun fire, US Marines in Vietnam bombard a communist position with grenades before making their final assault. Above: An early version of the modern grenade in action with French troops in the trenches of the Somme. Right: The fragmentation provided by a British No.36 'Mills Bomb'. Below left: The Soviet RGD-33 stick grenade fitted with a serrated fragmentation sleeve. Below right: Priming a batch of No.36s.

directions. While the range of such a grenade varies between 10 and 20m (11 and 22yds), isolated fragments can be thrown out to considerably greater distances so that the grenade thrower must be protected from the blast. Thus while the US Mk2 grenade can be hurled about 30m (33yds) at maximum by the average soldier, chunks of metal have been blasted up to 200m (220yds) on detonation.

The externally serrated case of the Mills Bomb type of grenade was subsequently found to be less than completely effective, as it did not fragment along the lines of the serrations but rather broke up at random. It has been improved upon by grenades which are serrated or notched on the interior, and fragment along the serration lines. By this method the fragmentation is far more uniformly even and the range and lethality of the blast can be controlled. Larger but fewer serrations produce fewer but larger fragments which carry further due to their greater momentum but at the same time have a less dense distribution pattern. Smaller serrations consequently produce smaller fragments which lack momentum and range but ensure that the target receives a dense distribution pattern. The manufacture of interior-serrated cast-iron bodies was found to be an expensive process and it was simplified by inserting a pre-notched wire coil behind a thin sheet-metal case. On explosion the metal case is vaporised allowing the wire fragments to fly outwards.

Besides the fragmentation grenade, the other important type is the blast or offensive grenade which is used in situations where a fragmentation grenade could endanger the thrower. During a rapid advance, for example, the soldier is not faced by the dangers of loose fragments flying through the air if a localised blast grenade is used. The blast grenade usually has a larger high-explosive charge than the fragmentation

Right: A pair of US Mk2 'Pineapple' grenades. Externally-serrated grenades like the Mk2 do not break up evenly on detonation and have been replaced in US service with lighter more efficient models such as the M26 (below right). The M26 utilises an internal pre-notched wire coil for fragmentation and has an improved throwing range and casualty radius.
Below: Grenades captured from Arab forces by the Israelis. The line to the left of the picture are Soviet F-1s, similar to the Mk2 and No.36, but fitted with the UZRG fuze protruding from the top.

British No. 36M fragmentation grenade

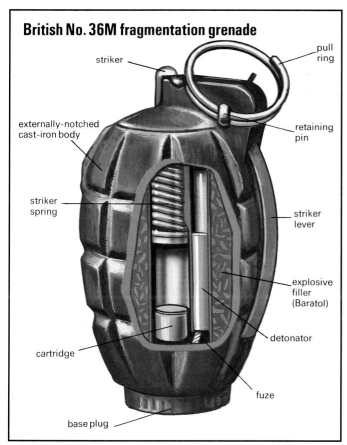

striker · pull ring · externally-notched cast-iron body · retaining pin · striker spring · striker lever · explosive filler (Baratol) · detonator · cartridge · fuze · base plug

US M26 fragmentation grenade

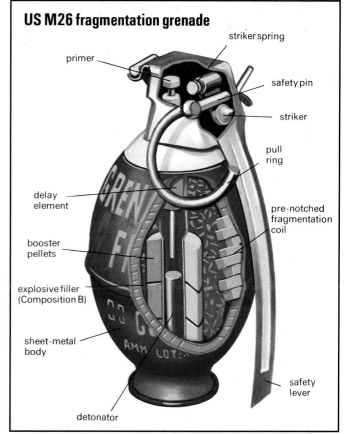

striker spring · primer · safety pin · striker · pull ring · delay element · pre-notched fragmentation coil · booster pellets · explosive filler (Composition B) · sheet-metal body · safety lever · detonator

grenade and relies for its effect on the shock wave of the blast which if it does not kill the enemy at least leaves him stunned and dazed for a sufficiently long period. The blast of offensive grenades is considerably increased in enclosed spaces and so they are highly effective when detonated inside vehicles and when used in house-to-house street fighting.

Offensive grenades are manufactured in a number of ways but most are cylindrical in shape and utilise the same fuze and striker system as a fragmentation grenade. The cylinder is a thin casing and is either made of sheet metal or cardboard. A representative example of the offensive grenade is the US Mk3 which weighs 440 grams (15.6oz) and contains 225 grams (8oz) of TNT as its explosive charge, providing a lethal radius of around 2m (6ft).

A number of grenades have been developed which combine the properties of fragmentation and blast grenades. In its basic form the grenade is a simple blast type but it can be quickly converted to a fragmentation grenade by slipping on either a pre-notched coiled steel sleeve or a plastic case containing tiny steel balls. The West German DM-51 is one of the more advanced of this type of grenade, consisting of a simple plastic body with fuze and a plastic fragmentation sleeve containing 3800 hardened steel balls. The DM-51 weighs 453 grams (16oz) and can be hurled to a distance of between 30 and 40m (33 and 44yds). The blast of the grenade is highly efficient and, with its fragmentation sleeve on, it has a casualty radius of around 10m (11yds).

Although grenades do not really make effective anti-tank weapons a few anti-armour types remain in existence and can be lethal against thin-skinned vehicles such as armoured personnel carriers. Most anti-

Right: Two types of modern grenade. In the foreground are four US Mk3 offensive grenades, designed to knock out enemy personnel at close range, while to their left are three Belgian PRB-8s, fitted with pre-notched fragmentation sleeves for defensive use. Below: The West German DM-51 offensive/defensive grenade which features a removable fragmentation sleeve. Bottom: A white phosphorous grenade on test with the US Army during World War II.

West German DM-51 offensive/defensive grenade

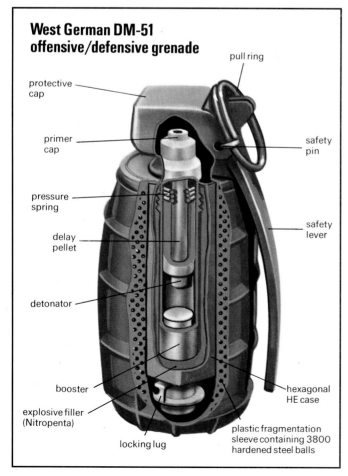

protective cap
pull ring
primer cap
safety pin
pressure spring
delay pellet
safety lever
detonator
booster
explosive filler (Nitropenta)
locking lug
hexagonal HE case
plastic fragmentation sleeve containing 3800 hardened steel balls

armour grenades are rifle- or projector-launched but the Soviet Union manufactures a number of hand-thrown types. The RPG-43 is a heavy stick grenade type holding a shaped-charge of 595 grams (21oz). The grenade can be thrown 20m (22yds) and in favourable circumstances it can penetrate 75mm (3in) of armour plate. The RPG-6 is similar in design and operation to the RPG-43 but is able to pierce 100mm (4in) of armour plate. Although these two models are still in use around the world they have been replaced in Soviet service by the more effective RKG-3. Like its predecessors it is by no means a light and handy weapon, weighing 1050 grams (37oz) and measuring 37cm (14.5in), but it can penetrate up to 200mm (8in) of armour plate.

Above: An Austrian ARGES HdGr 72 plastic/steel-ball offensive grenade. Right: The Soviet RKG-3 anti-tank grenade. Below: South African troops blast a foxhole.

Smoke grenades are used for either screening or signalling purposes and, like blast grenades, are usually cylindrical in shape. White smoke is used for screening purposes while coloured smoke – blue, green, red and yellow – is used for signalling. A related type is the incendiary grenade which provides heat of sufficient intensity to destroy buildings and equipment of many types. Packed with a thermite mixture which burns at temperatures over 2200°C (3992°F), it is able to melt even steel plate, and as it produces its own oxygen it is hard to extinguish.

Riot control or gas grenades have become an important weapon in the armoury of paramilitary forces and because of their non-lethality are useful in situations of civil disorder. Containing a lachrymatory (tear-producing) chemical agent, gas grenades produce eye and skin irritation, nausea and inhibition of respiration for a limited period after exposure.

While basic design and operation of grenades has remained broadly unchanged since World War I during the post-World War II period small but important refinements to grenade design have been made which make them far lighter and somewhat more powerful than their predecessors. And these modern developments ensure that the grenade will remain a key tactical weapon on the modern battlefield.

Right top: An Argentinian Marine Commando equipped with US M33 series 'Baseball' grenades. While the 'Baseball' has the same fragmentation radius and throwing range as the M26, tests have shown that it can be thrown far more accurately. Right centre: A British L2 anti-personnel grenade with rifle discharger. The L2 is now the standard British grenade, replacing the No.36, and was originally intended to be fired from a rifle as well as being hand thrown. The rifle-launch facility has now been phased out. Right bottom: A hand grenade used as a makeshift trip-wire booby trap on a jungle trail in Vietnam. Left top: The US M7A3 CS gas riot control grenade. Left centre: The US M14 incendiary grenade. This grenade should be placed directly on the target rather than being thrown and will produce an intense heat for up to 45 seconds. Left bottom: The US M18 smoke grenade.

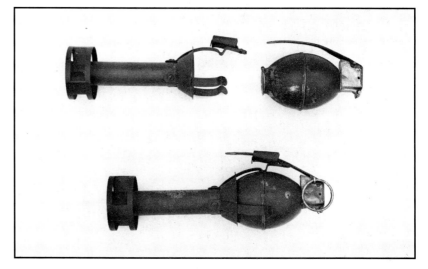

A

N

O

T